Instructor's Resource Manual with Test Bank

I Never Knew I Had a Choice
Explorations in Personal Growth

NINTH EDITION

Gerald Corey
California State University, Fullerton

Marianne Schneider Corey
Consultant

Prepared by

Gerald Corey
California State University, Fullerton

Marianne Schneider Corey
Consultant

BROOKS/COLE
CENGAGE Learning

Australia • Brazil • Japan • Korea • Mexico • Singapore • Spain • United Kingdom • United States

BROOKS/COLE
CENGAGE Learning

ISBN-13: 978-0-495-60328-3
ISBN-10: 0-495-60328-7

Brooks/Cole
10 Davis Drive
Belmont, CA 94002-3098
USA

Cengage Learning is a leading provider of customized learning solutions with office locations around the globe, including Singapore, the United Kingdom, Australia, Mexico, Brazil, and Japan. Locate your local office at: **www.cengage.com/international**

Cengage Learning products are represented in Canada by Nelson Education, Ltd.

To learn more about Brooks/Cole, visit **www.cengage.com/brookscole**

Purchase any of our products at your local college store or at our preferred online store **www.ichapters.com**

Printed in the United States of America
1 2 3 4 5 6 7 8 12 11 10 09

CONTENTS

PREFACE

In this *Instructor's Resource Manual for I Never Knew I Had a Choice: Explorations in Personal Growth,* 9th Edition, we present many ideas and suggestions for the content and structure of your course and share experiences and problems we have encountered in our teaching of personal-growth courses and in leading therapeutic groups. We offer chapter outlines, objectives, questions, defined key terms, exercises, activities, guidelines, and evaluation procedures with the expectation that you'll choose the ones that fit your goals and teaching style. In our textbook, we challenge readers to reflect on the choices and options available to them. In this resource manual, our goal is to share with you an abundance of ideas and allow you to incorporate those that suit you.

This updated and expanded *Instructor's Resource Manual* accompanies this ninth edition of *I Never Knew I Had a Choice.* It includes about 30 to 50 test items, both multiple-choice and essay, for every chapter; a student study guide covering all chapters; suggested reading; questions for thought and discussion; numerous activities and exercises for classroom participation; guidelines for using the book and teaching the course; examples of various formats of personal-growth classes; guidelines for maximizing personal learning and for reviewing and integrating the course; PowerPoint presentation slides; additional Website resources; and a student evaluation instrument to assess the impact of the course on readers.

Before we completed the final drafts for the first and third editions of *I Never Knew I Had a Choice*, Brooks/Cole arranged for a weekend seminar with the book's reviewers—instructors who were actually teaching courses in the psychology of personal growth. During these two seminars, we learned that we each approached this kind of course in different ways. Our stimulating exchange of ideas gave us new avenues to explore in our teaching; in this manual, we share some of those ideas and approaches with you. If you are like most instructors who teach personally oriented courses, you enjoy your course and are probably open to experimenting with new ideas and approaches from semester to semester. Many who teach such courses say they are challenged to review their own lives in the process of teaching and interacting personally with their students. The course can be truly exciting, and the content never has to get stale. We hope this manual provides you with a variety of ideas to consider. Many instructors have indicated that the study and discussion questions, suggested activities and exercises, and multiple-choice test items are useful as a timesaving resource.

Writing and revising the many editions of *I Never Knew I Had a Choice* has been an evolutionary process. We continue to get much of our material from the personal-growth workshops and courses that we co-lead. Our work as practitioners continues to reinforce our beliefs about some of the universal life struggles of the human condition. These are the topics we have addressed in *I Never Knew I Had a Choice*. This manual has been updated to reflect the changes made in the latest edition. In Parts 1 through 5, we provide guidelines for using *I Never Knew I Had a Choice*, suggestions for teaching the course, illustrations of ways that one of us (Jerry Corey) has structured and organized his personal-awareness courses, and guidelines for conducting experiential courses. Part 6 contains a variety of resources for each of the 14 chapters such as: chapter outlines, objectives, discussion questions, defined key terms, multiple-choice test items, and suggested activities and exercises that can be done both during class and for out-of-class assignments. Part 7 provides specific guidelines to help students review the course in a personal way and to integrate and apply what they have learned to their everyday lives, once the course ends. Part 8 offers ideas on ways to evaluate the personal-growth course, especially by tapping student feedback as a source to improve the course. Part 9 consists of five on-line quiz items for each chapter. Part 10 gives a detailed listing, chapter by chapter, of Website resources that you or your student may want to consult. Part 11 consists of a list of 123 Power Point slides that highlight key themes and concepts from each of the chapters in the book.

We want to express our appreciation to **Allison Bowie,** Assistant Editor, who worked closely with us on this supplementary product. We would like to also offer a special acknowledgement to **Dr. Michelle Muratori**, Johns Hopkins University, for her work on the revision of the Power Point Slides, and her contributions on other parts of this manual in addition to revising test items and creating new test items found in this manual.

If you'd like to contact us with questions or comments on the book, manual, or your course, the best way is by e-mail at: cordileone@aol.com ---- Best of luck in teaching your course!

Gerald Corey
Marianne Schneider Corey

Chapter 1 Invitation to Personal Learning and Growth

Ideas for Instruction	Videos	Media Resources for Instructors
Instructor's Resource Manual: See Parts 1-5 for ideas about designing and beginning your course. Part 6 — Supplementary Questions, Test Items, Exercises and Activities Part 9 — Online Quiz Items	**Brooks/Cole Annual "Clips for Coursework"** Video for the Helping Professions, 2005	**Web Site:** http://cengage.com/counseling/corey Access online resources for you and your students.
		Microsoft® PowerPoint®: Available for download at the Web Site http://counseling.wadsworth.com/corey06

Chapter 2 Reviewing Your Childhood and Adolescence

Ideas for Instruction	Videos	Media Resources for Instructors
Instructor's Resource Manual: Part 6 — Supplementary Questions, Test Items, Exercises and Activities Part 9 — Online Quiz Items	**Brooks/Cole Annual "Clips for Coursework"** Video for the Helping Professions, 2005	**Web Site:** http://cengage.com/counseling/corey Access online resources for you and your students.
		Microsoft® PowerPoint®: Available for download at the Web Site http://cengage.com/counseling/corey

Chapter 3 Adulthood and Autonomy

Ideas for Instruction	Videos	Media Resources for Instructors
Instructor's Resource Manual: Part 6 — Supplementary Questions, Test Items, Exercises and Activities Part 9 — Online Quiz Items	**Brooks/Cole Annual "Clips for Coursework"** Video for the Helping Professions, 2005	**Web Site:** http://cengage.com/counseling/corey Access online resources for you and your students.
		Microsoft® PowerPoint®: Available for download at the Web Site http://cengage.com/counseling/corey

Chapter 4 Your Body and Wellness

Ideas for Instruction	Videos	Media Resources for Instructors
Instructor's Resource Manual: Part 6 — Supplementary Questions, Test Items, Exercises and Activities Part 9 — Online Quiz Items	**CNN® Today Video:** Helping Professions, Volume II	**Web Site:** http://cengage.com/counseling/corey Access online resources for you and your students.
	Brooks/Cole Annual "Clips for Coursework" Video for the Helping Professions, 2006 (Coming summer 2005)	**Microsoft® PowerPoint®:** Available for download at the Web Site http://cengage.com/counseling/corey

Chapter 5 Managing Stress

Ideas for Instruction	Videos	Media Resources for Instructors
Instructor's Resource Manual: Part 6 — Supplementary Questions, Test Items, Exercises and Activities Part 9 — Online Quiz Items	**Brooks/Cole Annual "Clips for Coursework"** Video for the Helping Professions, 2005	**Web Site:** http://cengage.com/counseling/corey Access online resources for you and your students.
		Microsoft® PowerPoint®: Available for download at the Web Site http://cengage.com/counseling/corey

Chapter 6 Love

Ideas for Instruction	Videos	Media Resources for Instructors
Instructor's Resource Manual: Part 6 — Supplementary Questions, Test Items, Exercises and Activities Part 9 — Online Quiz Items	**Brooks/Cole Annual "Clips for Coursework"** Video for the Helping Professions, 2005	**Web Site:** http://cengage.com/counseling/corey Access online resources for you and your students.
		Microsoft® PowerPoint®: Available for download at the Web Site http://cengage.com/counseling/corey

Chapter 7 Relationships

Ideas for Instruction	Videos	Media Resources for Instructors
Instructor's Resource Manual: Part 6 — Supplementary Questions, Test Items, Exercises and Activities Part 9 — Online Quiz Items	**Brooks/Cole Annual "Clips for Coursework"** Video for the Helping Professions, 2005	**Web Site:** http://cengage.com/counseling/corey Access online resources for you and your students.
		Microsoft® PowerPoint®: Available for download at the Web Site http://cengage.com/counseling/corey

Chapter 8 Becoming the Woman or Man You Want to Be

Ideas for Instruction	Videos	Media Resources for Instructors
Instructor's Resource Manual: Part 6 — Supplementary Questions, Test Items, Exercises and Activities Part 9 — Online Quiz Items	**Brooks/Cole Annual "Clips for Coursework"** Video for the Helping Professions, 2005	**Web Site:** http://cengage.com/counseling/corey Access online resources for you and your students.
		Microsoft® PowerPoint®: Slides 46-50. Available for download at the Web Site http://cengage.com/counseling/corey

Chapter 9 Sexuality

Ideas for Instruction	Videos	Media Resources for Instructors
Instructor's Resource Manual: Part 6 — Supplementary Questions, Test Items, Exercises and Activities Part 9 — Online Quiz Items	**Brooks/Cole Annual "Clips for Coursework"** Video for the Helping Professions, 2005	**Web Site:** http://cengage.com/counseling/corey Access online resources for you and your students.
		Microsoft® PowerPoint®: Available for download at the Web Site http://cengage.com/counseling/corey

Chapter 10 Work and Recreation

Ideas for Instruction	Videos	Media Resources for Instructors
Instructor's Resource Manual: Part 6 — Supplementary Questions, Test Items, Exercises and Activities Part 9 — Online Quiz Items		**Web Site:** http://cengage.com/counseling/corey Access online resources for you and your students.
		Microsoft® PowerPoint®: Available for download at the Web Site http://cengage.com/counseling/corey

Chapter 11 Loneliness and Solitude

Ideas for Instruction	Videos	Media Resources for Instructors
Instructor's Resource Manual: Part 6 — Supplementary Questions, Test Items, Exercises and Activities Part 9 — Online Quiz Items	**Brooks/Cole Annual "Clips for Coursework"** Video for the Helping Professions, 2005	**Web Site:** http://cengage.com/counseling/corey Access online resources for you and your students.
		Microsoft® PowerPoint®: Available for download at the Web Site http://cengage.com/counseling/corey

Chapter 12 Death and Loss

Ideas for Instruction	Videos	Media Resources for Instructors
Instructor's Resource Manual: Part 6 — Supplementary Questions, Test Items, Exercises and Activities Part 9 — Online Quiz Items	**Brooks/Cole Annual "Clips for Coursework"** Video for the Helping Professions, 2005	**Web Site:** http://cengage.com/counseling/corey Access online resources for you and your students.
		Microsoft® PowerPoint®: Available for download at the Web Site http://cengage.com/counseling/corey

Chapter 13 Meaning and Values

Ideas for Instruction	Videos	Media Resources for Instructors
Instructor's Resource Manual: Part 6 — Supplementary Questions, Test Items, Exercises and Activities (Ch.13) Part 9 — Online Quiz Items	**Brooks/Cole Annual "Clips for Coursework"** Video for the Helping Professions, 2005	**Web Site:** http://cengage.com/counseling/corey Access online resources for you and your students.
		Microsoft® PowerPoint®: Available for download at the Web Site http://cengage.com/counseling/corey

Chapter 14 Pathways to Personal Growth

Ideas for Instruction	Videos	Media Resources for Instructors
Instructor's Resource Manual: Part 6 — Supplementary Questions, Test Items, Exercises and Activities Part 7 — Guidelines for the Wrap-Up and Integration of the Course Part 8 — Evaluation o f the Personal-Growth Course Part 9 — Online Quiz Items	**Brooks/Cole Annual "Clips for Coursework"** Video for the Helping Professions, 2005	**Web Site:** http://cengage.com/counseling/corey Access online resources for you and your students.
		Microsoft® PowerPoint®: Available for download at the Web Site http://cengage.com/counseling/corey

PART 1

An Overview of *I Never Knew I Had a Choice*

I Never Knew I Had a Choice is intended for college students of any age and for all others who wish to expand their self-awareness and explore the choices available to them in significant areas of their lives. It is also used by counselors in private practice settings and in public and private mental health organizations for workshops and groups. The topics discussed include choosing a personal style of learning; reviewing childhood and adolescence and the effects of these experiences on current behavior and choices; meeting the challenges of adulthood and autonomy; maintaining a healthy body and wellness; managing stress; appreciating the significance of love, intimate relationships, gender roles, and sexuality; work and recreation; dealing creatively with loneliness and solitude; understanding and accepting death and loss; choosing one's values and meaning in life; and pathways to growth.

A PERSONAL PERSPECTIVE

This is a personal book because we encourage readers to examine the choices they have made and how these choices affect their present level of satisfaction. (It is also a personal book in another sense, inasmuch as we describe our own concerns, struggles, decisions, and values with regard to many of the issues we raise.) The book is designed to be a personal workbook as well as a classroom text. Each chapter begins with a self-inventory **(Where Am I Now?)** that gives readers the chance to focus on their present beliefs and attitudes. Within the chapters, sections called "Take Time to Reflect" offer an opportunity to pause and reflect on the issues raised. Additional activities and exercises **(Where Can I Go From Here?)** are suggested at the end of each chapter for use in the classroom or outside of class. We wish to stress that this is an unfinished book; readers are encouraged to become co-authors by writing about their personal reactions in the book and in their journals.

CHAPTER OVERVIEWS AND CHANGE IN THE NINTH EDITION

Although the themes underlying this edition of the book are basically the same as previous editions, whenever possible we have updated material to reflect current thinking. The introductory chapter addresses the importance of self-exploration and invites students to consider the value in learning about oneself, others, and personal growth. Social concerns must balance self-interests, however, and we maintain that self-fulfillment can occur only if individuals have a sense of social consciousness. To improve the book and to keep current with developments in the field, we have added new topics, expanded and revised current topics, abbreviated the discussion of certain topics, and updated the references. Below is an overview of this book, along with what is new or revised in this 9th edition.

Chapter 1 (Invitation to Personal Learning and Growth) presents different models of personal growth. There is some revision of choices leading to change and new material on what constitutes happiness. Also added is a discussion of positive psychology, an emerging trend in the field. We have added sections on three women who have made significant contributions to the field of humanistic psychology through their therapeutic modalities: (1) Natalie Rogers, developer of person-centered expressive arts therapy; (2) Zerka T. Moreno, co-developer of psychodrama; and (3) Virginia Satir, pioneer in experiential family therapy. We have updated the discussion of multiple intelligences and learning styles.

Chapter 2 (Reviewing Your Childhood and Adolescence) contains an expanded discussion of the role of early childhood experiences on later personality development. This chapter continues to feature Erikson's psychosocial model and the self-in-context theories as they deal with development throughout the life span. There is a new discussion of the effects of parenting styles on children's social and intellectual competence. There is an extensively revised and more comprehensive discussion of the challenges faced by adolescents.

In Chapter 3 (Adulthood and Autonomy) we continue the discussion of the life-span perspective by focusing on the psychosocial theory and the self-in-context perspective. This chapter has been streamlined to highlight choices we can make at each of the phases of life and the unique challenges facing the individual at each stage. There is more complete coverage on learning how to identify our self-talk and critically evaluating our self-defeating thinking.

Chapter 4 (Your Body and Wellness) has an updated section on wellness and life choices. There is new material on the topics of sleep, exercise, eating, and spirituality. We have streamlined most of the topics and have given more attention to inviting readers to examine their lifestyle and examine choices that will enhance their health.

Chapter 5 (Managing Stress) examines the impact of stress on the body, causes of stress, ineffective and constructive reactions to stress, and stress and the healthy personality. There are revised sections on the topics of reliance in coping with stress, burnout, and addictions to alcohol and drugs. New to this edition is a section on trauma and posttraumatic stress disorders (PTSD). There is revised and increased coverage of incest, date rape, and sexual harassment (which has been moved from the chapter on sexuality). Other topics of discussion that have been revised include time management, meditation, mindfulness, deep relaxation, yoga, and massage therapy.

Chapter 6 (Love) deals with the many facets of love, the meaning of love, and our fears of loving and being loved. There is an expanded discussion of the ingredients in a long-term love relationship.

Chapter 7 (Relationships) contains guidelines for meaningful interpersonal relationships, including friendships, couple relationships (including gay and lesbian relationships), and family relationships. The section on gay and lesbian relationships has been updated.

Chapter 8 (Becoming the Woman or Man You Want To Be) contains some new resources to update the discussion of male roles, female roles, women in the world of work, and challenging traditional gender roles. There is new material on gender-role transcendence and striving for a gender-free society. There is a new section on the value of group therapy with men.

Chapter 9 (Sexuality) contains revised material on topics such as boundaries in sexuality, sexual abstinence as an option, sexual values and behavior, sexual responsibility, communication and sexuality, and the HIV/AIDS crisis and its effects on sexual behavior along with practical guidelines to reduce the risks of infection. The chapter has been streamlined and revised to emphasize more of the positive aspects of sexuality.

Chapter 10 (Work and Recreation) contains a revised section on creating meaning in work. There is expanded and revised coverage of retirement, a new discussion on life after work, and a revised discussion of the role of recreation in our lives.

Chapter 11 (Loneliness and Solitude) discusses the creative dimensions of solitude, along with increased coverage on the different kinds of loneliness we face. There is a fuller discussion of existential loneliness and the meaning this has on making life choices. Expanded treatment is also given to a revised section on shyness.

Chapter 12 (Death and Loss) contains an expanded discussion of the fear of death, the interdependence of life and death, and various models for understanding the process of death and dying. Increased and updated coverage has been given to topics of the importance of grieving our losses, the value of grief support groups, and cultural variations in the mourning process. There is a new section on the relational model of death and grieving, which challenges some conventional ways of viewing grief.

Chapter 13 (Meaning and Values) addresses the meaning of life, and in this edition there is more discussion on the relationship between facing death and finding meaning. There is a revised section on religion/spirituality and how this can be a source of unity or division. New coverage is given to the spiritual foundations of the Twelve Step program. The section on embracing diversity has been augmented and extensively revised. There is a new section on the global warming crisis and the choices individuals can make in protecting and preserving our planet.

Chapter 14 (Pathways to Personal Growth) encourages students to think about where they will choose to go from here. Readers are reminded that their journey toward personal growth is only beginning. The section on counseling as a pathway for growth has been expanded. This chapter offers a variety of avenues for growth that readers may wish to pursue now and in the future.

PROMISES OF *I NEVER KNEW I HAD A CHOICE*

Fundamentally, our approach in *I Never Knew I Had a Choice* is humanistic and personal; that is, we stress the healthy and effective personality and the common struggles most of us experience in becoming autonomous. We especially emphasize accepting personal responsibility for the choices we make and consciously deciding whether and how we want to change our lives.

Although our own approach can be broadly characterized as humanistic and existential, our aim has been to challenge readers to recognize and assess their own choices, beliefs, and values rather than to convert them to a particular point of view. Our basic premise is that a commitment to self-exploration can create new potentials for choice. Many of the college students and counseling clients with whom we work are relatively well-functioning people who desire more from life and who want to recognize and remove blocks to their personal creativity and freedom. It is for people like these that we've written this book.

In talking about the contents of this book with both students and instructors, we have found that students select a personal growth course because of their interest in discovering more about themselves and their relationships with others. Most of them are looking for a practical course, one that deals with real issues in everyday living and that will provide an impetus for their own personal growth. Accordingly, we have focused on helping readers recognize blocks to their creative and productive energies, find ways of removing these obstructions, and make conscious choices to modify their attitudes and behaviors.

WHO ARE THE READERS OF *I NEVER KNEW I HAD A* CHOICE?

The experiences of those who have read and used the earlier editions of *I Never Knew I Had a Choice* reveal that the themes explored have application to a diversity of ages and backgrounds. Readers who have taken the time to write us about their reactions say that the book encouraged them to take an honest look at their lives and challenge themselves to make certain changes. Many readers who have used this book for a college course have told us that they have shared it with friends and relatives.

I Never Knew I Had a Choice was developed for a variety of self-exploration courses. A few of the courses where *Choice* is used as the main textbook includes: Introduction to Counseling, Therapeutic Group, Psychology of Personal Growth, Personal Development, Personal Growth and Development, Personality and Adjustment, Introduction to Human Behavior, Life Processes, Personal and Interpersonal Effectiveness, Character and Conflict, Values of the Helping Professions, Human Potential Seminar, Psychology of Personal Well-Being and Adjustment, and Applied Psychology. *Choice* has also been adopted in courses ranging from the psychology of personal growth on the undergraduate level to graduate courses for training teachers and counselors. It is also used in group counseling courses as a catalyst for small-group interaction and for workshops in training group leaders. Courses that make use of an interactive approach will find *Choice* a useful tool for discussion.

We've written this book to facilitate interaction—between student and instructor, among the students within a class, between students and significant people in their lives, between the reader and us as authors—but most important of all, our aim is to provide the reader with an avenue for reflection. Readers are encouraged to look at the direction of their lives to see if they like where they are heading. Our experience has been that active, open, and personal participation in these courses can lead to expanded self-awareness and greater autonomy in living.

USING CLASS DISCISSION AND SMALL GROUPS

At its best, the text can be the catalyst for an interactive class and can serve as a basis for collaborative learning. As a class, the students might have some voice in choosing topics within chapters they would most like to explore in depth.

Many students may seem reluctant to speaking up for a number of reasons. They may be conditioned to sit and listen. They may be intimidated by expressing their thoughts in class. For this and other reasons we favor creating small groups in which students can interact amongst themselves. This is often an effective preparation for their interacting with you or with the class as a whole.

Small-group discussion activities --- of which there are many in the text and more in this manual --- give students opportunities to participate in class discussions.

SOME ETHICAL CONCERNS

Ensure confidentiality. A course that takes a personal, interactive approach to learning raises certain *ethical concerns,* for the content is not strictly cognitive. If students are expected to discuss their personal struggles, special precautions are needed to protect the welfare of the students. For example, we think it is ethically imperative to orient and prepare students enrolling in personal-growth courses. Part of this preparation involves discussing the meaning of confidentiality and stressing how important it is to respect whatever is shared in the small groups or the class as a whole. Students should know both their rights and responsibilities if they are expected to become actively involved in the learning process. It is impractical to screen and select students who want to enroll in personal-growth courses, but we can certainly build safeguards into the course so that they do not feel violated.

Withhold judgment. The textbook challenges readers to identify their own values and does not presume to tell readers what they should want or how they should behave. Instead, it invites them to determine if their beliefs or values are congruent with their behavior. If you agree that your primary role is to teach students how to think and decide for themselves, you will probably structure your course and your own participation in a similar way. We do not think it is appropriate for instructors to impose their values on their students.

Establish a supportive environment. Even though personal-growth courses typically involve personal sharing and exploration by students, it is certainly inappropriate to push students to disclose deeply personal issues that are opened up in a classroom and then left unaddressed. We hope students will be given the choice of what concerns they are willing to disclose and that care will be exerted to create a supportive climate within the classroom that will enable students to take the risks involved in personal learning.

WORKING WITH CULTURAL DIVERSITY IN THE CLASSROOM

In teaching a personal-growth course, it is essential to pay attention to the reality of cultural diversity. Chances are that students in your classes will come from diverse groups with respect to age, culture, ethnicity, and religion, to name a few. For some of your students, taking such a course is a significant step. Some individuals may be slow to disclose personal material because of cultural injunctions against sharing family matters or personal experiences.

Ethnic and minority students may display behavior that might look like resistance, when such behavior actually makes sense in the context of their cultural background. It is important to distinguish between resistance as a manifestation of uncooperative behavior as opposed to a sense of reluctance to fully participate in an experiential class or one dealing with personal concerns. Often these students are not so much *resistant* as they are *reluctant,* or, in some cases, simply politely respectful. It is important to respect this diversity and not insist that all students be equally ready to engage in personal disclosure or to explore such topics as family matters, interpersonal issues, and value concerns.

Silence in individuals should not always be interpreted as refusal to participate. Quiet students may be listening and not speaking because of their cultural conditioning. They may be waiting to be called on. Some may be very hesitant to talk about members of their family. Such hesitation should not necessarily be interpreted as stubborn refusal to be open and transparent. Rather, some individuals may be influenced by taboos against openly discussing family matters. Instructors who are open to understanding the worlds of their students are in a better position to help these individuals begin to speak. If such students feel they are respected, there is a greater chance that they will begin to challenge their hesitation.

It is especially important to prepare students for the kinds of tasks and the nature of the personal learning process that will take place in your course. Many culturally diverse students will need guidance to make the most of a course dealing with personal issues. Preparation is critical because many behaviors expected in a group class are foreign to what people do in their everyday lives. For example, their culture may value *indirect* communication. When they are in an experiential class dealing with personal concerns and interpersonal communication, they may be expected to be direct as they speak to one another. In your class they may be expected to abide by norms of openness, honesty, and directness, and they may be expected to make themselves emotionally available. Some of the behaviors expected in your class may be most demanding for certain students, depending on cultural background, and may go very much against the grain of their cultural conditioning.

It is important that students in your class know that a personal-growth class involves introspection, sharing of experiences, and change. Students should be made aware of the possible consequences of change, not only for themselves but also for others in their lives. Members of their family may shun some students if they become too outspoken or if they move toward becoming highly individualistic. We hope you will encourage your students to evaluate how the material in your course fits into their worldview and cultural framework. They should decide if they are interested in exploring the range of personal topics that will be addressed in your course. Again, your respect for their values will go a long way in encouraging them to challenge themselves.

PART 2

Some Hints and Guidelines for Using
I Never Knew I Had a Choice

USING CHAPTER FEATURES

In Chapter 1 of the text, there are some guidelines for getting the most from the book. We hope that students will make full use of the features in each chapter that are designed to enhance active and personal learning. Each chapter has a number of consistent features including: Where Am I Now?; Take Time to Reflect; Personal Stories; Where Can I Go From Here?; and Website Resources. In addition to those listed at the end of Chapter 1, following are some further suggestions regarding several key features of each chapter.

WHERE AM I NOW?

One of the features of *Choice* is the inclusion of pre-chapter self-inventories, entitled "Where Am I Now?" These brief inventories start each chapter and are designed to stimulate critical thinking about the topics in the chapter. They generally consist of personal statements to involve the students, help them identify their attitudes and beliefs, and think about what they want to change. There are no absolutely right answers that fit for all.

We suggest you encourage students to take each chapter's self-inventory *before* they read and study the chapter. This assessment gets students focused on key elements of each chapter. It can be useful to begin a class by asking students to pick out some items they strongly disagreed with. This can be a good lead-in to a short talk or lecture on the topic of the chapter. You might also encourage your students to have someone they are close to take the inventory. In this way, they may discuss the topic and get involved before they begin reading. Another suggestion is to have the class break into small groups and ask them to select three of the items on the Where Am I Now? sections and discuss these issues in their groups. These small-group sessions may last 15 or 20 minutes, and can serve to introduce the topic and to get the students actively engaged in it.

Since the students' views may change as the material is discussed in class, consider having students re-read their responses after reading the chapter and make changes if appropriate. These self-inventories can be useful as reviews of the entire course if students retake them at the end of the term. In this way, they can determine what changes, if any, have occurred in their attitudes and beliefs.

Scoring. Because these assessments are to stimulate students' honest thinking, we prefer not to impose any statement of right or wrong answers or to ask students to score themselves. Thus the directions in the text do not contain any objective scoring method, other than deciding on a five-point scale their degree of agreement or disagreement with each item.

TAKE TIME TO REFLECT

The goal of the "Take Time to Reflect" sections of the text is to help students become active learners who apply what they read to themselves. These sections and the responses they elicit are an integral part of the textbook. You might remind your student from time to time that completing these activities is an essential part of their learning experience. You can refer to these "Take Time to Reflect" exercises often during class lectures, and you set aside class time for small group sessions in which students can share their responses with one another. This encouragement can increase students' involvement in the class sessions.

PERSONAL STORIES

The book contains many first-person accounts, or Personal Stories, that are interspersed in the chapters. Encourage your students to single out the stories that they most identify with and that teach them the most about themselves.

The stories can be catalysts to get students thinking and talking about personal topics. You can have students discuss in small groups the Personal Story in each chapter that most spoke to them and to talk about lessons they can learn from these first-person accounts.

Have students write their own personal stories, not only to share an experience, but also to get perspective on it. Stories can be written in their journals for private reference or as brief optional assignments. Be sure to give students flexibility about the topics they write about and avoid causing students to disclose more personal information than they feel comfortable doing. Screen written personal stories and get the writer's permission before sharing them with the class.

JOURNALS

Many instructors who use this book and who teach personal growth courses encourage students to keep journals. From our perspective, the journals are the students' private records of the thoughts and feelings that may be stimulated by the course. In the text, we suggest that students take certain the "Take Time to Reflect" sections or end-of-chapter activities (Where Can I Go From Here?) that have the most meaning for them and write more fully about the relevant issues in their journals. The end-of-chapter activities suggest things students can do on their own to make the concepts in the book come alive for them. Again, consider giving time in class for students to work in small groups to discuss their reactions to these out-of-class exercises. It is important to stress to students the value of attempting to apply to their everyday lives what they discuss in class and what they read in the text. If the aim is for students to think about the topics in the chapters and then to translate what they learn about their behavior into daily life, the journal is an excellent tool for personal reflection and for monitoring oneself.

You might want to include regular journal writing as a requirement of your course. It is important to state your policy at the beginning about whether the journals will be completely confidential, or better, whether you will request to see the journals either weekly or less frequently during the course. Reassure students that they will not be forced to show any writing that they deem too personal to share.

Encourage students to purchase a separate notebook in which to write their responses. By using a loose-leaf notebook for their journal, they can add pages from other sources and move materials around. This will allow students to create their own textbook. Encourage students to personalize this book --- in doing so; they become co-authors by finishing the book as it applies to them.

Challenge students to take part in writing and revising this book. After they read the Personal Stories, encourage them to think about their reactions and write briefly in their journals about the one story that had the most impact upon them. Ask them to write about ways that they see themselves in selected stories in the chapters.

Some broad journal topics you may want to assign occasionally:
- What I learned about others and myself in a particular class meeting.
- Topics I want to talk about or have avoided talking about.
- Some of the things I am learning about myself in this course.
- Some concrete changes in my attitudes, values, or behaviors that I want to make.

Encourage students to write in their journals in a free-flowing and unedited style, rather than attempt to analyze or edit what they write. They might find it valuable to write what first comes to their consciousness. Encourage them to be honest and to use journal writings as an opportunity to get to know themselves better and explore their thoughts and feelings in more depth.

QUESTIONS FOR THOUGH, DISCUSSION, AND EVALUATION

We have included plenty of questions for thought and discussion in the body of the text and in the "Take Time to Reflect" sections. In addition to these, we have listed other questions for each chapter in this resource manual. Some or all of these questions can be used to prompt discussions, or they can be duplicated and distributed to the students for use as a study guide. The questions are also suitable for quizzes, short-answer essays, take-home essay exams, reaction papers, or in-class essay exams.

In some personal-growth courses, instructors tend not to give quizzes and examinations, either in class or out of class. Instead, they use the reaction-paper idea. Students might be asked to type two-page reaction papers in which they discuss how the required readings on a given topic apply to them. For example, if the topic is intimate relationships, ask them to read the chapter and then give *their* thoughts and reactions on some aspect of intimate relationships. It is a good idea to ask them to avoid merely summarizing what they read or writing in a detached and overly intellectual manner. The questions provided in this manual are ones that can be given to students to help them narrow down a given topic.

In this manual are multiple-choice test items, which are found in each of the chapters. A number of instructors requested that we add these objective-type items, since they like to use tests as well as papers and discussion.

WHERE CAN I GO FROM HERE?

Most of the exercises for group activity and experiential learning included in this manual were originally part of the textbook. Several instructors that we have spoken with recommended that we put most of the exercises designed strictly for in-class group participation into a separate instructor's manual. This gives you the freedom to use or not to use any of the exercises you wish. You may not want to use many exercises in class, or you may want to modify those you do use. We realize that we have presented many more exercises than anyone could ever do in a semester-long course, but we'd rather give you more exercises to select from than too few.

The exercises are simply additional tools that can help students get personally and experientially involved with the concepts in the textbook. We see them as means to an end, not ends in themselves. Before attempting to use an exercise in class, it is good to ask yourself why you are using it, what you want to accomplish, and whether the students are ready to handle it. In addition, we believe it's important to be thoroughly familiar with an exercise and ideally, to have experienced it yourself before you try to present it in class.

CAUTION: Some of the exercises described in this manual can lead to intense emotional experiencing. We've used some of them in small groups where the students knew in advance that the course would be conducted along the lines of a personal group. In those cases, we've interviewed each student beforehand, and a prerequisite for the class was that each student had had prior group or personal counseling. We would *not* use in an introductory class on personal growth many of the techniques or exercises that we use in a small-group advanced class.

SOME ETHICAL CONSIDERATIONS IN USING EXERCISES

There is sometimes a fine line between what is therapeutic and what therapy is. We do *not* believe that the classroom is an appropriate place for therapy, which includes dealing with unconscious material and working toward major personality change. We *do* believe that a class can combine educational aims (learning content) with therapeutic aims (becoming more aware of self and others and making choices based on this increased awareness). Thus, in one-exercise students write down some major turning points in their lives and think about how decisions they've made affect them now. This kind of exercise can combine thinking about one's experiences with a good deal of emotionality, and it can be a therapeutic or growth-producing experience. Students can achieve insights into their patterns, see how they limit their growth and effective functioning, and think about ways they might want to change current behavior. In class, they can experiment with new behavior, and they may practice their new behavior in their daily living. We'd call this kind of experience therapeutic. Simply becoming more aware of their attitudes and feelings may be growth producing in itself and can lead to significant changes. Such therapeutic gains are to be distinguished from working through deep personality conflicts in the classroom. It's essential that we assess our own level of competency and that we avoid going beyond the level of our training and professional experience.

A further consideration involves the reluctance some students may feel in regard to certain activities and exercises. It is crucial to stress to students that *they have the right to decline to participate at any time.* The freedom to participate or not to participate in-group exercises is critical. This freedom can be diminished by group pressure or a person's fear of saying "no" and being different from the others, and it is incumbent upon the instructor to create a climate in which these hindrances are minimized. The right to say "I pass" also extends to a student who does not wish to talk about certain topics or issues or who has already become involved in an exercise and doesn't want to go any further. As instructors, we should be sensitive to students' readiness and willingness to become emotionally involved. It is important to respect their judgment concerning how far they want to pursue an issue.

PART 3

Suggestions for Teaching the Course

In this section, I (Jerry Corey) would like to describe some of the ways I teach the kind of course for which *I Never Knew I Had a Choice* is designed, and how I integrate the exercises and activities into the course.

GOALS AND OBJECTIVES

At the outset it is essential to ask yourself what you most want to accomplish and what you hope my students will leave with at the end of the semester. You might find the following questions helpful as you formulate your own goals and objectives:

1. Do you want your students to learn theories of personality development? Is a knowledge of cognitive material important? Of primary or secondary importance?

2. Do you want the students to develop their own personal goals? If so, how?

3. Do you have your own expectations of what you hope your students will experience and learn?

4. Do you value discussion and the students' interaction with one another, as well as interaction between you and them?

5. Do you want primarily an interactive class? Would you like small group discussions, experiential exercises, and collaborative learning approaches daily? Once a week? Never?

6. Do you want them to challenge their attitudes, values, and beliefs? Do you hope they focus on their philosophy of life—what it is, how it was formed, and any modifications they want to make?

7. Do you want students to challenge their attitudes, values, and beliefs, especially as they pertain to education?

8. Do you want your students to open themselves up to new experiences and try some things they haven't tried? How much value do you place on experimenting with new behavior, taking risks, and trying out new behavior outside as well as inside the class?

9. What kinds of things do you want them to know by the end of the semester? What facts and concepts are important? What questions do you hope they'll raise? What questions would you like to pose to them? What topics do you consider most important to explore?

10. Do you want your students to examine their past decisions and reassess them? Are you interested in encouraging them to look at their choices and opinions now?

11. Do you expect them to improve their ability to express their thoughts and feelings both in writing and in speaking? Are you primarily interested in their communication skills?

12. What value do you place on journal writing? Do you want to allow time in class for spontaneous writing as a focusing device? Do you expect students to keep a journal out of class? How might you expect students to make use of their journals?

13. Are you concerned with creating a climate of trust in which personal self-disclosure can occur? Do you expect a personal sharing?

14. How important is critical thinking and creative thinking in your course? How can you best promote reflective thinking?

15. To what degree do you want your students to structure the course and assume responsibility for its direction? To what degree do you feel it's your job to do the structuring?

The goals and objectives of the courses we teach depend on the course and the type of students taking the class. All the questions of how to teach the course, how to structure it, and what and how to evaluate depend upon what the goals and objectives are.

APPROACH: LECTURE? DISCUSSION? GROUP?

The question of which approach to take in class directly relates to the goals and objectives you've developed. Many instructors use a combination of many approaches, particularly in my larger classes (40 or more students) for students who haven't had much group experience. Some instructors give informal lectures on key topics, invite guest speakers to talk to the class, ask students to put on certain presentations, to read books on personal growth, to write reaction papers, to keep journals, and to participate in small-group sessions in which they talk about the topics selected and apply these issues to their personal lives.

Some instructors share their experiences, struggles, and life choices. If self-disclosure is used, it is important to distinguish between self-disclosure that is facilitative and self-disclosure that is just storytelling. In part, appropriate instructor use of self-disclosure can model a way to reveal oneself in good taste. The important thing to keep in mind is that our main purpose is to get students to think about their lives, and not simply to tell them about ours.

PROBLEMS IN INTEGRATING DIDACTIC AND EXPERIENTAL APPROACHES

We may be very enthusiastic and spend hours preparing what we believe is exciting material, only to get to class and discover that we're talking to the wall. Despite all the things we bring in to stimulate students to think and interact, we may still find them sitting passively and being very unresponsive. This can be most discouraging! It would be natural for an instructor to conclude, "I'm doing something wrong. Maybe I'm talking too much, so I'll give the students more of a chance to talk." Perhaps the instructor will then initiate group exercises as catalysts for small-group discussion and interaction, only to find that most of the students now sit passively in their small groups and listen politely to the few who dominate the discussion. They may even protest that the instructor should take over and "teach them" and that they're uncomfortable with the lack of structure.

In the end, the problem may not be with the methods and approach we use. Perhaps we should look at the impact we are having as persons on our students and look at what they want (or don't want) and how much they're willing to invest to make the course meaningful to them. We can wear ourselves out by wanting a lot for our students and wanting something for them, they may not want for themselves. At times like this, it can be useful to remind yourself that this course is an *invitation* to personal growth and that, ultimately, students are free to accept or reject this invitation. Some students will not feel ready to say much about themselves in class, yet they may go home and think about the class and make decisions on their own. Some students may not be ready or willing to explore the personal issues raised in the course, regardless of what method and approach we use.

The choice of teaching style is not a simple matter of deciding on a lecture approach, an "experiential" approach, or an unstructured, student-initiated approach. Many factors are involved in selecting a teaching style, including our personal reactions to the students in our classes.

Before writing *I Never Knew I Had a Choice*, I visited many college classrooms and observed a variety of teaching styles. There were significant differences among instructors who taught classes in the general area of psychology of personal growth or adjustment. I have my own approach to teaching a psychology of personal-growth course—an approach that fits *me*. I'd like to describe it in some detail as a way of suggesting possibilities and stimulating your thinking about how *you* would like to teach the course.

11

PART 4

Organization of a
Personal-Awareness Course

The course I (Jerry Corey) will describe is an upper-division course at California State University at Fullerton, called "Character and Conflict." The main text for all sections of this course is *I Never Knew I Had a Choice*. The catalog description is as follows:

HUMAN SURVICES 300, CHARACTER AND CONFLICT (3 units)

Prerequisite: consent of instructor at first class meeting. An experiential, theme-oriented group class exploring life choices in the struggle toward personal autonomy. Themes include review of childhood and adolescence, adulthood and autonomy, work and leisure, body image, sex roles, sexuality, love, intimate relationships, marriage and its alternatives, loneliness, death and loss, meaning and values.

Credit/No Credit grading only.

This course is approved as one of the options for the General Education requirements under Category E (lifelong understanding and development). This course deals with an integrative perspective of the human being as it concerns social relationships, one's physical being, emotional development, and the exploration of psychological issues. The course does equip students for lifelong learning by dealing in some depth with critical areas of human behavior as listed in Category E, such as sexuality, nutrition, care of one's health and body, the relationship between psychological and physical health, learning how to cope constructively with stress in daily life, deepening one's understanding of personal and interpersonal issues (love, intimacy, being alone and being with others, the connection of facing one's death and living life fully, and the implications of death and dying on creating a meaningful philosophy of life).

Although this course is designed as an experience for personal and interpersonal growth, it is not an unstructured encounter group. Rather, it is a theme-oriented group experience in which students hear brief lectures, read selected articles and books, write reaction papers, discuss selected topics, work on their personal concerns, and learn the principles of group process. Each week there is a different topic for exploration. The topics for my particular course follow the order and content of *I Never Knew I Had a Choice*.

The primary purpose of the course is to help the participants increase their awareness of the values and attitudes that underlie their behavior in daily life. I encourage them to think seriously about how each theme applies to them personally. I feel that if I can create an atmosphere in which participants can openly and honestly explore their feelings, thoughts, and actions in these critical areas, they will be better able to make significant choices that can alter the courses of their lives. The course is *not* a substitute for intensive psychotherapy, which aims at uncovering unconscious material and working toward personality change, nor is it intended to provide group therapy. Rather, it focuses on strengths and the ways in which these strengths may be blocked. The course is essentially an *invitation* to self-exploration.

Lectures, talks by guest speakers, and talks given by the students themselves can be useful catalysts for group interaction. Generally, I begin a three-hour class with a lecture, demonstration, or some other type of prepared presentation. My purpose is to sharpen the students' focus on the topic of the week and to stimulate their interaction.

In most of my classes, there are at least 40 students. Since the class size would prohibit significant interaction, I divide the class into four groups. Two advanced students from another course I teach ("Practicum in Group Leadership") serve as facilitators and co-lead the groups, with my supervision. This gives me an opportunity to circulate among the groups during the class session. Afterward, I meet with the group leaders; they discuss their experiences during the session, and I give them feedback on what I observed. When group leaders from a training class were not available one semester, members of the class assumed facilitator positions on a rotational basis, and I met with these students in advance for some preparation. In this way, most of the students in the class shared in the responsibility for conducting the class.

FORMAT AND STRUCTURE OF THE COURSE: A SUMMARY

The following details summarize the format and structure of the class and clarify the procedures all of the instructors of this course use. Of course, each instructor brings his or her own ideas and methods to this course.

1.   Eight students are selected for the practicum in-group leadership, which is a separate but concurrent class with "Character and Conflict." The students in the practicum do their fieldwork by co-leading in the "Character and Conflict" class each week.

2.   As supervisor in the practicum and instructor of the class, all of the instructors of this course meet with these group leaders for a three-day workshop before the semester begins. The workshop is an intensive group experience designed to prepare the leaders for the responsibility of facilitating their own groups.

3.   Each week, the group leaders and the instructor meet an hour before class. During this session, the leaders discuss ideas related to the topic of the week and explore ways of opening their group and keeping the members focused on various aspects of the topic under consideration.

4.   Co-leader pairs stay together and stay with the same group all semester. The main functions of the group leaders are to introduce the topic, to get the members started on exploring the topic in a personal and meaningful way, and to help create an accepting (yet challenging) atmosphere in which participants are encouraged to relate freely with one another as they develop ways of realizing their goals.

5.   Immediately after the class, the leaders meet with the instructor for an evaluation session. The leaders discuss their experiences with their groups, including any problems they had, and the instructor offer a critique of what was observed when he or she visited the group.

6.   During the week, the co-leaders get together and discuss the progress of the group. They also read the reaction papers of the members of their groups, and they comment on these papers. They prepare to work with the next topic, agree on some approaches to use, and resolve any problems that have arisen between them.

There are other options if peer counselors or semi-trained leaders aren't available. Group leaders can be appointed from the ranks of the class, the class can be run like a leaderless group, or a recorder can keep track of the general proceedings of the group, to name a few options.

A DESCRIPTION OF THE PROCESS AND STAGES OF THE COURSE

Many students aren't prepared for a group-oriented course that deals with intimate themes such as autonomy, love, sex, intimacy, loneliness, death, and the meaning of life. They often expect a straight lecture class, and it takes some time for them to learn how to participate in small groups and talk about these personal dimensions of themselves. Many have anxieties about engaging in personal interactions in their groups.

During the initial phases of the class, the members may be excited over the prospect of a course that deals with personal issues and allows them to get involved with their peers in open discussion. More often than not, however, class members appear rather resistant. This resistance shows up even if they have enrolled in the course as an elective or are seeking a class that involves a personal learning experience. They wonder if the class experience will make any real difference to them, and they question their need to engage in self-exploration with others. In the beginning, the talk tends to be somewhat safe and relatively impersonal, since it takes some time to establish a level of trust. Trust is clearly being established when people openly express their mistrust if it exists, when they're willing to share meaningful aspects of themselves, when they begin to think of their own goals and purposes and show some initiative in class, when their self-disclosure is appropriate and they are willing to risk disclosing some personal material, when the interactions are honest, when conflict is recognized and openly discussed, when feedback is freely given, and when there is both caring confrontation and support in the class or group.

Until this climate of trust develops, people tend to wait for the instructor to get things moving and to keep them moving. Conflict is frequently characteristic of the beginning stages, and there is often some wrestling among the members for positions of dominance. Some look to the instructor to be more directives, while others resent attempts by the instructor to structure the class or to use interaction exercises.

Another characteristic of students during early stages of the class is the tendency to talk about others, instead of focusing on themselves and their reactions. Gradually they learn to focus on their own feelings and thoughts, and they tend to spend less time talking about others.

As the session's progress and class members get more into a "working stage," there is an increased sense of cohesion and feeling of belonging. They begin to care about one another, and they begin to talk more directly to one another. They focus more on the here-and-now, and they feel freer to deal openly with what they're experiencing. Leadership functions might become distributed among the participants, who may feel free enough to make suggestions and to initiate discussions of topics they want to explore. Their closeness tends to grow as they share common human struggles. People demonstrate a willingness to try on a new behavior, both in and out of class, because of the support they feel from others.

Sometimes a student will say, "I get the feeling that you always have to have a problem when you come to this class. We spend so much time talking about things that aren't going well for us, and I feel uneasy if I don't have a problem to share." Of course, this kind of statement can be a form of defensiveness if the person is avoiding looking with any depth at his or her own life. On the other hand, it can be an accurate statement of what does occur in some classes or groups. It isn't always necessary to dwell on problems for growth to occur, and the group can still be working even if people aren't being "heavy" and highly intense. Many members experience new facets of themselves when they play, or when they are humorous, or when they have an opportunity to simply share everyday things about themselves.

By the end of the class, many members have paused to take a personal inventory of their basic beliefs and assumptions about themselves and others; they have had the opportunity to express to others their thoughts, feelings, and experiences; they have reexamined decisions they made earlier regarding their worth and potential; they have given thought to ways they want to change; and they have tried new behavior outside of class.

As the class draws to a close, it isn't uncommon to observe some sense of sadness as the course comes to an end. As the participants realize that their class will end soon, their intensity sometimes tapers off. They are often reluctant to bring up new business to explore in the limited time that remains. They generally talk about their reluctance to part, particularly if they have been close and have worked together well. They talk about their feelings of loss, and they experience a sense of separation anxiety. But the process of learning how to say goodbye is also important, and it can be both sad and joyful at the same time. During the final week or two, I ask the class members to consolidate their gains and to recall the highlights of the course. In this way, they can give thought to specific things they will do to ensure some continuity in their learning, so that they can apply what they've learned in practical and specific ways outside of class.

As the participants review, what the experience has meant to them and what they learned that they want to take away with them, these are some of the more common learnings they express:

- I can trust others.

- I don't need to be liked by everyone.

- Others will care for me if I allow them to.

- It isn't too late for me to change if I want to.

- I'm not alone in what I feel.

- I can make choices, and I can trust these choices.

- Being spontaneous is fun.

- I have talents I didn't realize I had.

- I'll never be truly accepted unless I'm willing to accept rejection.

- I get from a class what I'm willing to put into it.

- My greatest fears didn't come true when I revealed myself.

- People can be beautiful and creative when they shed their masks.

Many classes don't fit the picture described above, but this discussion is an attempt to present some generalized trends that my colleagues and I frequently observe in our group-oriented classes on the college campus. The class described above is a combination of a lecture and group approach to personal, experiential learning. There are many ways of doing a course in self-development, however, and the way you design your particular class is a function of factors such as the number of people in your class, your style, and orientation as an instructor, and the type of class and needs of the students.

THE ISSUE OF GRADING AND EVALUATION

A difficult problem many of us face is that of giving grades in a course that deals with subjective issues and rests largely on personal experience. I have wrestled with the problem of grading for a long time and have tried a number of various approaches, some of which I'll describe here.

I find that students and teachers can get so hung up on the question of grades that it can interfere with the process of learning. This is especially true of courses dealing with personal growth. I like to make a distinction, therefore, between grading and evaluation. I very much believe in evaluation procedures. Students in my classes evaluate themselves on an ongoing basis through reaction papers, and I meet with them both privately and in small groups to evaluate how the course is going for them. This is as much an evaluation of the course and of me as it is of them. I read and evaluate their papers, and I give them periodic feedback in terms of how I see them. I also have my students evaluate the course and me before the middle of the term and again toward the end of the course. So, I find value in evaluation, and I see it as a necessary tool in deciding how well we (both students and I) are meeting the goals of the course, which include the personal goals of the students as well as my own expectations and requirements.

Although I believe in the value of evaluation—particularly self-evaluation—I think that issuing grades usually inhibits learning more than it facilitates it. However, since I am required to assign grades, I have developed approaches that I can live with in conscience. In one of our courses that deals with personal growth and uses a group orientation, we were instrumental in changing the grading from the traditional letter grades to Credit/No Credit. Many colleges offer the choice between a letter grade or a Pass/No Pass grade for self-awareness courses. The latter makes sense to me, and I support this type of global evaluation.

In most of my group-oriented courses, the only system of grading is Credit/No Credit. In some of these classes, the enrollment is usually restricted to 15. To obtain credit in these classes, students are generally expected to do the following:

- **Attend all the sessions.** I stress this requirement because absence affects the group as well as the person who misses the class. I expect a commitment from students, and a minimal evidence of commitment is attendance.

- **Participate in the class in an active way.** I don't mean that students must participate in all exercises or share what they would prefer to keep private, but I do stress the importance of being willing to talk about themselves and their concerns.

- **Write a number of reaction papers.** At times, I have asked for weekly reaction papers which I read and comment on and return to the students the next week. At other times, I have asked for longer papers every three to five weeks. If only three to five papers are assigned, I ask students to keep ongoing journals, with the understanding that I won't be collecting and reading them. The reaction papers give students an opportunity to express their thoughts and feelings on the topics we explore, to comment on their readings, to assess their own progress, and to evaluate the direction of the course or suggest modifications for it.

To be sure, there is a good deal of work involved in this group-oriented course, and quality work is expected. I don't see any inconsistency in expecting students to become fully involved in a course that deals with personal issues. Most of these group-oriented, personal-growth courses are electives, and students are given information about the course either before they enroll or at the first class meeting. In this way, they know in advance that they will be expected to work, and they have a good idea of the course structure, as well as the goals. The requirements are demanding, but I'm convinced that the students have plenty of options within the structure that enable them to define the course to meet their needs.

We spend the first few weeks in these small-group courses getting acquainted and together deciding some specific things we'll be doing and how we want to spend our time together to get the most from the experience. Although students may complain about the workload, I find that most of them appreciate a course in which they can genuinely learn and in which the focus is on their personal concerns.

Another Sample Syllabus for
Human Services 300   Character and Conflict
By Dr. Michael Russell

Dr. Michael Russell is Professor of Human Services and Philosophy at California State University, Fullerton. He has taught Human Services 300 for about 30 years and continues teaching this course on a regular basis. His syllabus is presented below as an alternative to the one presented earlier. You will note that Dr. Russell's syllabus contains a detailed list of expectations for students who enroll in the course. There is an emphasis on informed consent, which all of those who teach this course agree upon. Because this course deals with personal exploration and consists of group interaction, it is assumed that students need to know what they need to do in order to enroll in this course and to receive credit.

Course Description. Prerequisite: consent of instructor at first class meeting. An experiential, theme-oriented class exploring life choices in the struggle for personal autonomy. Themes include: body image, sex roles, love, sexuality, intimacy, marriage, alternative life-styles, loneliness, death, meaning, and values. [Credit/No Credit grading only]

Required textbook: Corey and Corey, *I Never Knew I Had a Choice* (9th edition, 2010).

Informed Consent. Students may only take this *Character and Conflict* course with the consent of the instructor. That consent is typically given at the first class meeting, and is contingent upon the student's becoming familiar with the nature and expectations of the course, as explained in this syllabus and as described by the instructor. You should not finalize your decision to take this course until you have had an opportunity to carefully review this information. Once in the course, at the complete and sole discretion of the instructor, you may be asked to discontinue participation in the class; in that case, at the sole discretion of the Department Head or her designee, arrangements may be made for alternative means for completing the course for credit.

Character and Conflict is a different and emotionally challenging sort of a course. The purpose of the course is to provide an opportunity for a more personal sort of self-understanding and expression than most of us usually get, with a focus on issues and conflicts that affect you directly in your daily lives; the readings and lectures are intended to contribute toward that end, but the emphasis will be on small group interaction in which you are expected to be an active participant in discussions of topics which will typically become personal, emotional, and intimate. Topics will include autonomy, masculinity and femininity, love, sex, marriage and relationships, one's body, one's family, loneliness, encountering others, death and loss, meaning, and other themes your group may develop on its own, including discussing frankly and openly the nature of your interactions with one another. It is very important for you to understand in advance that these discussions will be taking place on a personal rather than a detached or typically academic level. Of course, no one will or could force you to talk about any specific topic that you do not wish to disclose; but there will be "peer pressure" for you to have willingness. In general, to be a contributing participant will entail you actively focusing on and talking about areas of your personal life which involve conflict and emotional sensitivity for you. If you are not willing to do that, you will inhibit the readiness of others to fully participate. In that case, you should not be taking this course, are not welcome to take it, you do not have the required permission to take it, and you may be required by the instructor to discontinue attendance.

The class is intended for students who contemplate careers in one of the helping professions (such as counseling, psychotherapy, social work), on the reasoning that the ability to understand the struggles of others is rooted in the ability to find counterpart struggles within oneself. It is also presented as potentially contributing to the general education appropriate to a university, provided that the student elects to take it after being informed about its nature. If you feel that you are required to take this course and yet do not want to be part of this sort of personal interaction and disclosure, please discuss your reservations with the instructor to see whether there might be some alternative. But please do not deceive yourself by skimming over this attempt to caution and inform you about what to expect and conclude that "you have a right to be here" -- or you "need this course" because of some requirement, whether or not you feel like being an active participant in the course as described; you do not have that "right" any more than you would have the right to sign up for a basketball course and then squat in the middle of the court in everyone else's way. If you do not want to participate in the ways indicated you will inhibit others who do want this, and you will be in the way.

Early in the course the class will be sub-divided into groups. Most of a typical class meeting will be in the small groups, once the instructor has made some opening remarks on the theme for that meeting. Student leaders who are being supervised by the instructor will conduct the groups. The instructor will rotate among the groups. Student leaders and the instructor meet to discuss the groups before and after each class meeting. The student leaders are expected to be fallible human beings, typically working on their undergraduate degrees, whose job is to seek to encourage and facilitate a group environment conducive to honest and personal interaction. They will encourage you to participate, they will read and comment on the papers you write, and they will attempt to contribute to meaningful interaction within your group. The course is offered for a population that is presumed to be composed of relatively well-functioning individuals who wish to speak openly with one another. Once again, if you are not interested in being an open participant in this sort of an experiential setting you ought not to be taking this course. If you fear that you may not be emotionally prepared for this sort of experience, you should discuss your concern with the instructor.

You will be asked to promise to treat the personal disclosures of others as confidential. *Respect for confidentiality is an absolute requirement* of the course, and those who violate this are subject to being dropped from the course without credit. There are some important qualifications on this principle of confidentiality. There is no way to guarantee that everyone will respect this principle of confidentiality, but you are expected to commit yourself to it. Also, if I believe that you present a significant risk to yourself or others, or if I learn about a current risk of abuse to a child, I will have an obligation to make a report of this danger. I also reserve the right to confer with appropriate professionals should I believe that my work with you requires outside consultation. I may review content of group meetings in supervision meetings with the group leaders from other groups. Please feel free to discuss with me any concerns that may be raised by any of these considerations.

Requirements for Credit. Attendance is mandatory. Willingness to interact openly about personal issues is also mandatory. All written assignments are mandatory. The instructor's continued endorsement of your being a participant in the class is mandatory.

This course is offered only on a credit no credit basis. To get credit in the course you must turn in *each* of the reaction papers indicated on the syllabus. These are personal reaction papers and they are meant to provide a forum for you to express and learn about yourself, your own views and struggles and experiences. While the papers are written for you, the instructor and the group leaders will read them. The papers will not be acceptable if they are too brief, or insubstantial, or careless. You will not get credit in this course unless your instructor accepts all your work. Typing is preferred, but easily read longhand is acceptable. Papers may not be acceptable if they are especially messy, hard to read, brief, superficial, or continually focused away from yourself and your own reactions. The point is not to debate or critique what others say or write, but to use each section of each paper as a vehicle for expressing yourself, your own feelings about your own struggles. Papers are to be submitted in triplicate.

You are asked to provide more than one copy of your assignments, to facilitate their being read by group leaders and the instructor. Each assignment has at least 3 parts. All parts should be clearly identified and the top page should have your name or student number, the assignment number, the date and chapters discussed, and any information about extra or missing sections, stapled together (not just paper clip or folding).

(a) Lecture/whole class. Respond to something in the whole-class meeting in the instructor's introductory remarks or occasional "exercise" before or after the small groups meet. The point is for you to be looking at yourself, not to critique or debate the instructor. Find an opportunity to reflect on something about yourself that was evoked. Minimum length 75 words: suggested length, 200, but go on as long as you like.

(b) Respond to your small group, emphasizing events and reactions to the most recent meeting. Again, the point is for you to be reflecting on you, not to analyze or lament the experiences or ideas of others. This should be about you; hopefully you will find a way to let others know in person things you are thinking and feeling about them. Challenge your self to say in-group the things you write about. Minimum length 150 words: suggested length 250 words, but go on as long as you like.

(c) Respond to the chapter in *I Never Knew I Had a Choice* for the current meeting as a means of "getting primed" for the topic. Once again, the point is to find a vehicle for you to focus on you, not to debate the author of the text or to dryly review each and every point made there. Minimum length 75 words, but go on as long as you like.

Make-Up Work. You are expected to attend every class in order to get credit. If you must miss class, this can only be an excused absence if you clearly made every reasonable effort to notify the instructor that you would be absent. You are expected to do a reaction to an extra book to make up for **excused** absences ("excused" means, in part, that you made every effort possible to notify the instructor and your group that you would be absent), in substitution for parts (1) and (2) which you were unable to attend. The instructor should approve the book in advance, and be some sort of "self-help" book or book liable to further the introspective aims of this course. Your "Part 4" of the paper in which you make up for the missing assignment should contain the usual chapter response, and then, write in response to some book selected with the instructor's approval. Any of a large number of "self-help" books might be appropriate; you should choose a book which at this point in your life is likely to further your awareness of some area of conflict or something about you that would be worth looking into, perhaps relevant to the topic of the missing week. Minimum length for this section: 250 words. (This paragraph is 258 words long.) In addition, you are to provide a response to the chapter you were to have read for the meeting you missed (75 word minimum).

Timely Papers. You are also expected to turn in each paper on time, and in a reasonably neat and readable form. In the case of missing or late unacceptable portions of the assignments, when they are due, you should expect to be asked to provide an additional section, in your next paper, exploring the possible significance of the problem section -- e.g., what does it say about your life at the present, or your feelings about the topic or situation that didn't get written about as it was supposed to have been? Minimum length: 100 words.

Another Sample Course Outline for
Psychology 102
Instructor: Richard Kandus
Mount San Jacinto College

One of the reviewers (Richard Kandus) of *I Never Knew I Had a Choice* submitted his course outline for his course, Psychology 102 (Psychology of Personal Growth). We are describing parts of his approach to teaching the course because it represents yet another slant on the personal growth course for the community college. We think you might find his contract grading approach useful. Below we summarize some of the key points in Richard Kandus' course outline, but we are describing only some parts of his course material.

Course Description. It is hoped that this course will be a process of personal and group explorations and experiences in self-discovery, personal growth, and human interactions.

Classroom Work. In-class hours will consist mainly of discussions, explorations, and group exercises related to topic areas covered in the textbook. Regular and prompt attendance at class is expected. A large portion of the class time is devoted to discussion and other forms of experiential learning. Lectures explore alternative viewpoints and cover various topics in the chapters.

Evaluation and Grading. Students may choose to work toward an A, B, or C grade. Packets of work toward that grade are due three times during the semester. Each chapter requires at least a two typewritten page reaction paper to the readings. In addition, during the course of the semester, students are required to "try something they have never done before" with the purpose of expanding or "maximizing" some underdeveloped personal potential. During the last weeks of class, students are asked to share their experiences in brief (5 minutes) reports to the class. These reports are graded Pass/Fail. A Pass is earned by: (1) turning in "notes" in advance of giving the report, in the first packet; (2) including the following points in the report: a description of what potential you want to maximize; a discussion of how you tried to maximize that potential; and a discussion of how effective you were in maximizing that potential.

To qualify for a grade of "A" or "B" student are expected to participate in a fieldwork project that involves a service for someone else. Students are encouraged to select a project that they would enjoy. It should be something they are not already doing. The fieldwork will take about 1 to 2 hours each week. Students are expected to submit a one-page summary of their project with each of the three packets they turn in during the semester. In writing the fieldwork report, key points to address are: What service are you providing for someone? What impact does this project have on them? What effect are you having on them? What impact does this project have on you? What effects are you experiencing?

To qualify for a grade of "A" students are to do all that is required for the grade of "B" and they are also to select a total of 3 books to read (from the suggested reading list). In addition, they write a book report for each of these books.

To qualify for a "C" grade, students are expected to:

- complete chapter assignments
- complete the maximizing report
- have 4 or less absences

To qualify for a "B" grade, students are expected to:
- complete chapter assignments
- complete the maximizing report
- have 3 or less absences
- participate in a fieldwork project

To qualify for   "A" grade, students are expected to:
- complete chapter assignments
- complete the maximizing report
- have 2 or less absences·
- participate in a fieldwork project
- write 3 book reports (books of students' own choosing)

Again, we have selected one aspect of Richard Kandus' course outline, which is the contract grading aspect that he describes as a part of his syllabus.

PART 5

Some Guidelines for
Experiential Classes and Some Ways
to Maximize Personal Learning

In Chapter 1 on Personal Learning there is a brief discussion of choosing a new style of learning and some guidelines for getting the most from the course. What follows is a more detailed discussion of specific ways that students might enhance the quality of their personal learning in the course.

This is material that both Marianne and Jerry have developed for personal-growth classes, self-awareness groups, and workshops with college students. Both Marianne and Jerry continue to see the importance of helping students learn how to involve themselves in a personal way in these experiential classes and groups. Too often students are at a loss to know how to respond when they enroll in a course dealing with the personal concerns and topics described in *I Never Knew I Had a Choice*.

If you are designing your class along experiential lines, feel free to use the following material in any way that you think will work best for you and your students. Some colleagues reproduce these guidelines in modified form and give them to the students at the initial class session, and then follow up by discussing ways of deriving the maximum benefit from experiential groups. The following material is written directly to the students who are about to embark on a group-oriented personal-growth class.

Advantages of Experiential Learning and Group-Oriented Classes

Let us look at some of the values inherent in a group approach to learning about yourself and others.

1. The classroom can be a vehicle for personal learning. Often you are critical of much of your education because you see it as impersonal, abstract, and not related to your own life. An experiential approach offers the chance for you to get directly involved in the learning process, and it allows for an integration of thinking and feeling.

2. Experiential classes can be a way of coming to know ourselves. By revealing who we are to others, we begin to see new dimensions of ourselves and understand ourselves on deeper levels.

3. Personal learning can provide an opportunity to understand others more fully. In many lecture-oriented courses, you are lucky if you know the names of any fellow students by the end of the term. In an experiential course, you can come to know others in a very personal and meaningful way and thus develop close bonds with others.

4. By learning about others, you also see commonalities between them and you. You may no longer feel isolated and alone in your experiences. In dealing with interpersonal relations you have the chance to discover how you are unique, but at the same time how you are like others in universal concerns and struggles.

5. An experiential approach offers a supportive environment for expressing what you feel without being judged and also a place to experiment with new behavior. You can try out new ways and see how they fit for you; *then* you can decide to what degree you want to incorporate any new ways of behaving into your everyday life.

6. You can explore your style of relating with others in your classroom situations. You might insist that you are different in your class from the way you are in real life. However, participating in an experiential course that deals with human relations gives you a behavior sample of how you function in your everyday transactions. This feedback on how others experience you and are affected by you can be extremely important.

7.   If your class is heterogeneous (mixed) in terms of cultures, sexes, races, ages, socioeconomic status, etc., you have a good chance to view a part of the world outside. The feedback you get can be diverse and rich. This provides a good way for you to get to know a wider range of people—many of whom you'll have some contact with apart from your classroom situation.

8.   In many classes there are very few opportunities for getting feedback. Information comes at you, and there is little chance to apply this to yourself, or even to respond to the information you are acquiring. In a course that stresses interpersonal learning, you're expected to share and become an active part of the process. In doing so, you can get honest and useful feedback as to how others see you. They can point out obvious things about you that you may be missing. If you have consistent feedback from different people, then you can begin to seriously consider what others are telling you about yourself and *you* can then decide what you might do with this feedback.

9.   A real use of this type of class is to think about ways you might be able to translate what you've learned in this course to your daily life. This class can become a lab—a place to experiment in safety; now you can decide what new behaviors you'd want to make a part of your daily living.

10.   This course can provide valuable data that you can use in making decisions. Perhaps you thought you *had* to be a certain way and had no choice. You can discover that you have the power to change—that you don't have to be defined by others. This recognition of the power you have over your life can help you decide the ways you want to change outside of the classroom so that you can gain increasing control of your life.

The Importance of Establishing Goals for This Course

Experiential and group-oriented approaches are often criticized on the grounds that nobody knows what is expected and many are floundering while they wait for another to begin something. Not only do instructors need to be clear as to their learning objectives and expectations of students, but also you as a learner need to clarify what your goals and expectations are for this course. Some students do not spend enough time thinking about why they might be taking a particular course, and what they hope to leave with at the end of the course.

This class is an invitation to self-exploration, which can lead to a reevaluation of your values, attitudes, and behaviors. This invitation to look at your life and your relationships with others is a most important facet of the course. Since taking this honest look at yourself is not a command, it is up to you to decide what, how much, and when you wish to explore personal issues. There are some general goals that are relevant and common to an experiential class. The following are some goals for small group interactions:

- to explore in an open fashion personal issues that are significant to the class members

- to deal with the here-and-now interactions that occur in the class

- to confront others in a caring, yet honest, manner so that you will look at the impact you have on others

- to reveal yourself so that others can know you

- to learn to listen fully and to respond to what you hear

- to be able to clarify your personal goals and establish a level of trust on which these issues can be dealt with

- to search for alternatives and options

- to give feedback to others freely

Ways of Getting the Most from Your Group Experience

We think it is important that instructors prepare their students for deriving maximum benefit from an experiential class. If your course is conducted along the lines of a group experience, many students will not be familiar with how to involve themselves in the group process. You may want to use the guidelines given in the previous section, to use the guidelines given below, or to adapt some of these guidelines to the kind of class you teach. We find that it is important that we do some teaching early in the semester. If students do not have adequate preparation, we find that problems frequently emerge later on in the semester. We are convinced that the time it takes to orient students is time well spent.

How can students get the most from an experiential group-class experience? How can they maximize their learning? The recommendations that we offer below are adapted from two of our books, each of which have sections on teaching group members ways to participate fully in the group experience. These books are: Corey, Corey, Callanan, and Russell (2004), *Group Techniques*; and Corey, Corey, & Corey (2010), *Groups: Process and Practice*.

1. Recognize that trust is not something that "just happens" in a group; rather, you have a role in creating this climate of trust. If you are aware of anything getting in the way of a sense of safety, share your hesitations with the group.

2. Commit yourself to getting something from your group by focusing on your personal goals. Before each meeting, make the time to think about how you can get involved, what personal; concerns you want to explore, and other ways to use the time in group meaningfully.

3. Rather than waiting to be called upon, bring yourself into the interactions at the beginning of each session by letting others know what you want from this particular meeting. Although it is useful to have a tentative agenda of what you want to discuss, don't cling inflexibly to your agenda if other issues surface spontaneously within the group. Be open to pursuing alternative paths if you are affected by what others are exploring.

4. Realize that if the work other members are doing is affecting you, then it is crucial that you let them know how you are being affected. If you are able to identify with the struggles or pains of others, it generally helps both you and them to share your feelings and thoughts.

5. Decide for yourself what, how much, and when you will disclose personal facets of yourself. Others will not have a basis for knowing unless you tell them about yourself. If you have difficulty in sharing yourself personally in your group, begin by letting others know what makes it hard for you to self-disclose.

6. Don't confuse self-disclosure with engaging in storytelling. Avoid getting lost and overwhelming others with mere information about you or your history. Instead, express what is on your mind and in your heart presently. Reveal your struggles that are significant to you at this time in your life, especially as these concerns pertain to what others in the group are exploring.

7. Express persistent feelings you are having that pertain to what is emerging in the group in the here-and-now. For example, if you are feeling intimidated by other people in the group, announce that you feel this way. If you feel somewhat isolated, share this. If you do not want to be a part of the group, it is essential that you talk about this. Be willing to assume responsibility for what you feel, rather than blaming others for what you may feel.

8. Although silence may sometimes be golden, don't become a silent member. Realize that others will not know you if you do not let them know what issues are important to you, nor will they know that you identify with them or feel close to them, unless you let them know.

9. Practice your attending and listening skills. If you can give others the gift of your presence and understanding, you are contributing a great deal to the group process.

10. Try to challenge yourself if you sense that you are "taking too much group time for yourself." If you become overly concerned about measuring how much you are taking and receiving, you will inhibit the spontaneity that can make a group exciting and productive.

11. Use your group as a place to experiment with new behaviors. Allow yourself to try out different ways of being to determine ways that you may want to change. Discover how to carry out any new ways of thinking, feeling, and acting into your outside life. In between sessions, practice the skills you are learning in your group. Give yourself your own homework assignments and let others in your group know how you are applying in-group learnings to your behavior with family, friends, and associates.

12. Understand that making changes will not be instantaneous. You can expect some setbacks in the progress you make, also. Keep track of any progress you are making and remember to give yourself credit for your efforts and the subtle changes you are making.

13. Avoid giving others advice, or giving intellectualized interpretations of their behavior, or using questioning as your main style of interacting. It is possible to question others or to offer them advice yet keep yourself very distant in this process. If you are inclined to ask a question, let others know why you are interested in hearing their answer. If you want to give advice, reveal to others what your investment is in giving this advice. Learn to speak *for* yourself and *about* yourself.

14. Concentrate on making personal and direct statements to others in your group. Direct communication with a member is more effective than "talking about" that person through the leader.

15. In giving feedback to others, strive to avoid categorizing or labeling them. Instead of telling others who or what they are, tell them what you are observing and let them know how they are affecting you. Rather than judging them as persons, focus on how you respond to some of their specific behaviors in-group.

16. Pay attention to any consistent feedback you receive. If you hear that others perceive you as being somewhat judgmental and critical, don't be too quick to argue and convince them that you are open and accepting. Instead, take in what you are hearing and consider their input to determine the degree to which what they are saying might fit for you.

17. Respect your defenses and understand that they have served a purpose. However, when you become aware of feeling or acting defensively in your group, challenge your defenses by seeing what will occur if you strive to be less guarded. At least identify out loud that you are feeling defensive and begin exploring what you might be resisting.

18. Provide support for others by expressing your care for them, but don't quickly intervene by trying to comfort others when they are experiencing feelings; for instance, expressing pain over an event. Realize that people need to experience, share, and work through certain feelings; they do not need reassurance that "all will turn out for the best." Let them know how their pain may be touching you, but don't attempt to "cure" them of their pain.

19. Take responsibility for what you are accomplishing in your group. Spend some time thinking about what is taking place in these meetings and evaluating the degree to which you are attaining your goals. If you are not satisfied with your group experience, look at what you can do to make the group a more meaningful experience.

20. Be aware of respecting and maintaining the confidentiality of what goes on inside your group. Even though you may not maliciously breach others' confidences, recognize how easy it can be to talk inappropriately with persons not in the group, revealing what members have shared. The way you handle confidentiality says a great deal about your character. If you have any concerns whether what you are sharing is staying within the group, be willing to bring this matter up in a session.

21. Be prepared to be not always understood or accepted by significant others, especially as you make changes. Some people may not support the new directions you choose to travel, and your changes

may be threatening to them. It is a good idea to create a support system within your group. Contact selected members and ask them to help you remember the lessons you learned in the group. Reporting to others is an accountability procedure that will enable you to meet your personal goals.

22.   Keep a personal journal in which you record impressions of your own explorations and learning in your group. The journal is a good place to enter your reactions to books you read for your personal development. A journal will be invaluable in keeping track of your progress and noting changes in your ways of thinking, feeling, and acting.

PART 6

Chapter Outlines, Objectives, Questions, Key Terms Defined,

Test Items, Exercises, and Activities

For each of the chapters in the book, we have developed a series of catalyst questions for use in class discussions, small-group interactions, and individual review of the chapters. Many of these questions are also appropriate for quizzes, exams, take-home reaction papers, and other evaluation devices.

We've developed the following study guide for instructors who would like to offer their students structure in reading the chapters. The questions and guidelines provide students with a focus as they review, and students might find such a device very helpful as they attempt to pull the material together and to review for tests.

For those of you who want to administer tests covering the content of the chapters, we've provided both essay questions (which can also be used for class discussions) and objective test items. For this manual we've designed about 30 to 50 multiple-choice items for each chapter that you can use in a number of ways as weekly quizzes, as the basis for drawing items for a midterm or final examination, or simply as a comprehension check that you give to students to take at home for study purposes. This study guide is closely geared to the multiple-choice test items that you'll find in this manual. Students who use this study guide could be expected to do well on the chapter tests. **Note: There are five questions for each chapter that are on the Website, each of which will be found in Part 9 (On-line Quiz Items).**

If you favor this structured approach, or if you want to include objective testing on this book as a part of your evaluation procedure, your students will undoubtedly appreciate having the following study guide as a part of their course outline.

Suggestion for Final Examination. If you would rather not use separate chapter quizzes, you could simply pull together all these multiple-choice items (plus some short essays if you desire) and you will have a comprehensive final exam covering the main content of the complete textbook.

CHAPTER 1: INVITATION TO PERSONAL LEARNING AND GROWTH

Outline

Where Am I Now?
Choice and Change
    We Do Have Choices!
    Are You Ready to Change?
    What About Other People
Models for Personal Growth
    Adjustment or Growth?
    A Humanistic Approach to Personal Growth
    Overview of Maslow's Self-Actualization Theory
    Choice Theory Approach to Personal Growth
Are You an Active Learner?
Multiple Intelligences and Multiple Learning Styles
    Taking Responsibility for Learning
Getting the Most from This Book: Suggestions for Personal Learning
Chapter Summary
Where Can I Go From Here?
Website Resources

Chapter Objectives

- to introduce the philosophy and approach of this book

- to describe several models for personal growth

- to identify some of the key leaders in the development of humanistic psychology and describe some of their major ideas and contributions

- to encourage an active stance toward learning

- to explore a variety of learning styles

- to provide suggestions for how to use this book

Questions for Thought, Class Discussion, and Evaluation

1. Has your education taught you much about yourself? In your classes so far, has time been allowed to discuss values and matters of personal concern to you? Discuss and give examples.

2. When you look at the kind of college student you are now, how would you describe yourself as a learner? In what ways has your earlier education contributed to the kind of learner you now are?

3. In what ways might you want to change as a learner? Discuss and mention some specific things you'd like to be able to say about yourself as a learner.

4. Assume you could design the course you're about to take, using this textbook. Look through some of the major headings in each chapter. How would you set up the course? What methods would you use? What structure would you give the class? What requirements would you have, if any?

5. When you consider the course you're about to take, what are your personal goals? What do you most hope to leave the course with at the end of the semester?

6. In terms of your own hopes for the course, what are you willing to do to become an active and involved learner?

7. What are some specific things that you're willing to do in this course that are different for you? What risks are you willing to take?

8. Contrast the concepts of self-esteem with other-esteem. Do you see a way to integrate both of these concepts?

9. What are the values of self-exploration? Are there any risks attached to honestly looking at one's life?

10. What is the major emphasis of positive psychology?

11. Compare your view of freedom of choice with that of the Coreys.

12. State the essence of the philosophy underlying *I Never Knew I Had a Choice*.

13. What are the major differences between active versus passive learning? How would you describe your own learning style?

14. What are some of the basic differences between growth and adjustment? Would you rather be growing or adjusting?

15. What are the basic aspects of the self-actualization model for personal growth? Describe the main characteristics that Maslow found in his studies of self-actualizing people.

16. How is self-actualization a lifelong process as opposed to arriving at a finished place in one's life?

17. After reviewing the characteristics of the self-actualizing person, spend some time reflecting on each of the topics in this book with reference to how these topics might have applications to people who are functioning at this high level. At this time in your life, how would you describe your progress toward the self-actualizing process? What are some factors that might be blocking your own actualization?

18. What is your understanding of the concept of social interest? Contrast the Western concept of social interest with the Eastern concept of social interest.

19. Some writers contend that the good life cannot be lived alone and that people do not find themselves in isolation; rather, they find themselves through connectedness with others. Discuss the balance between becoming one's own person and being concerned with others. Do you see any contradiction in being concerned about both your own and others' welfare?

20. Alfred Adler contends that people are not the victims of fate, but are creative, active, choice-making beings whose every action has purpose and meaning. In light of your own personal experience, to what degree do you agree or disagree with this view of human nature?

21. Another of Adler's basic concepts is social interest. According to Adler, our happiness and success are largely related to our sense of belonging and to feeling connected to others. Discuss the quality of your own meaningful relationships with others. To what degree do your actions show your social interest?

22. What are some implications of Carl Jung's concept of the shadow?

23. What are some key ideas of the philosophy of Carl Rogers?

24. Natalie Rogers developed person-centered expressive arts therapy. What are some of the advantages of using expressive arts as a therapeutic approach?

25. The Coreys encourage readers to make their own decisions and determine the kind of person they want to become. They also emphasize the importance of the impact that their decisions have on the people around them. In your own experience, have you encountered any difficulty in thinking about your own personal growth and how your actions affect others in your life?

Glossary of Key Terms

The paradoxical theory of change holds that personal change tends to occur when we become aware of *what we are* as opposed to trying to become *what we are not*.

Self-esteem refers to having a positive view of one's self and a sense of confidence and self-worth.

Other-esteem involves respect, acceptance, caring, valuing, and promoting others, without reservation.

Adjustment involves the psychological processes through which individuals cope with the demands and challenges of daily life; it is a norm by which people can assess their level of mental health.

Self-exploration involves being honest with yourself and others, thinking for yourself, and making a commitment to live by your choices.

Personal growth can be viewed as a lifelong process rather than as a fixed point at which we arrive.

Self-actualization means working toward fulfilling our potential, toward becoming all that we are capable of becoming.

Humanistic psychology is an approach to the study of personal growth based on an actualizing model of what humans can become.

Positive psychology is an approach that focuses on positive emotions, health, hope, courage, contentment, happiness, well-being, perseverance, resilience, tolerance, and human strength.

Social interest is an Adlerian concept which involves identification and empathy with others and which includes a striving for a better future.

Community feeling is a sense of belonging to the ongoing development of humankind.

Individualism is a Western concept which affirms the uniqueness, autonomy, freedom, and intrinsic worth of the individual and emphasizes personal responsibility for one's behavior and well-being.

Collectivism affirms the value of preserving and enhancing the well-being of the group and emphasizes unity, unification, integration, and fusion.

Individuation is a process of moving toward a fully harmonious and integrated personality.

The shadow is the aspect of human nature associated with primitive impulses such as selfishness and greed.

Fully functioning person is a concept of humanistic psychology implying becoming a genuine and effective person.

Person-centered expressive arts therapy extends person-centered theory by helping individuals access their feelings through spontaneous creative expressions.

Psychodrama is primarily a humanistic and action-oriented approach to group therapy in which people explore their problems through role-playing, enacting situations using dramatic ways of gaining insight, discovering their own creativity, and developing behavioral skills.

Hierarchy of needs is a concept of Maslow's self-actualization theory holding that we must first meet our basic needs before we can satisfy our higher needs for actualization.

Reality therapy is a cognitive-behavioral approach to psychotherapy that aims at helping people satisfy their basic human needs.

Choice theory is the foundation of reality therapy that holds that we are social creatures who need to both give and receive love.

Total behavior is our best attempt to get what we want to satisfy our needs; it involves acting, thinking, feeling, and physiology.

WDEP is an acronym describing the basic procedures used in the practice of reality therapy. W= wants and needs, D = direction and doing, E = self-evaluation, P= planning.

Active learner is one who assumes responsibility for his or her own education.

Multiple intelligences, a theory developed by Howard Gardner, posits that intelligence is not a single, easily measured ability, but a group of complex multidimensional abilities. The eight types of intelligence and learning described by Gardner include: verbal-linguistic, musical-rhythmic, logical-mathematical, visual-special, bodily kinesthetic, intrapersonal, interpersonal, and naturalistic.

Emotional intelligence refers to the ability to control impulses, empathize with others, form responsible interpersonal relationships, and develop intimate relationships.

TEST ITEMS FOR CHAPTER 1
INVITATION TO PERSONAL LEARNING AND GROWTH

1. Positive psychology
   a. is a biological approach to humor and creativity.
   b. calls for increased attention and research on positive emotions.
   c. has no support in the empirical literature.
   d. is no longer a popular approach to the study of development.

2. In regard to change, Corey and Corey believe that
   a. we can expect that others will change as a result of the changes we make in our lives.
   b. change is a comfortable process.
   c. we find ourselves in isolation, meditation, and probing our unconscious for insight.
   d. if you are making change happen in your life, others may not appreciate all of the ways that you are changing.

3. The Coreys' basic point of view is that freedom of choice is
   a. doing whatever you want without regard for others.
   b. a basic part of our birthright.
   c. not something given to us but something we must actively achieve for ourselves.
   d. an illusion, since we are determined by our past experiences.
   e. something we acquire when we reach mature adulthood.

4. Personal growth is best viewed as
   a. a fixed point at which we arrive when we reach adulthood
   b. exactly the same thing as adjustment.
   c. a process rather than a fixed point at which we arrive.
   d. what we do on our own, not engaging other people in the process.

5. Self-actualization is best described as
   a. working toward fulfilling our potential, toward becoming all that we are capable of becoming.
   b. being pain-free, not allowing outside circumstances to affect our peace of mind.
   c. something that only the mature adult can accomplish if they have mastered all developmental tasks of earlier years.
   d. settling for a complacent existence, with neither challenge nor excitement.

6. A central concept of the humanistic approach to personal growth is
   a. self-actualization.
   b. determinism.
   c. active listening.
   d. social interest.

7. _____ is the psychologist most often credited with making the major breakthroughs in understanding self-actualization.
   a. Abraham Maslow
   b. Carl Rogers
   c. Alfred Adler
   d. Carl Jung

8. According to Maslow, self-actualization is possible only when
   a. we come to terms with our parents.
   b. our most basic needs are fulfilled.
   c. we resolve our mid-life crisis.
   d. we understand our dreams.

9. Maslow found that self-actualizing people had the following characteristics:
   a. a capacity to tolerate and even welcome uncertainty in their lives.
   b. spontaneity and creativity.
   c. a need for privacy and solitude.
   d. all of the above.

10. Carl Rogers's theory focused on
    a. social interest as the standard by which to judge psychological health.
    b. striving toward self-actualization.
    c. the importance of nonjudgmental listening and acceptance as a condition for people to feel free enough to change.
    d. the goal of individuation, or a fully harmonious and integrated personality.

11. Rogers built his entire theory and practice of psychotherapy on the concept of
    a. the fully functioning person.
    b. achieving individuation.
    c. striving for self-actualization.
    d. self-determination.

12. _____ made a choice to focus on the unconscious realm in his personal life, which also influenced the development of his theory of personality.
    a. Alfred Adler
    b. Carl Jung
    c. Abraham Maslow
    d. Carl Rogers

13. The process of achieving individuation implies
    a. being self-actualized.
    b. developing a harmonious and integrated personality.
    c. social interest based on identification and empathy with others.
    d. separating from the influence of early childhood experiences.

14. The primary goal of Jung's theory is
    a. rejecting the dark side of our nature.
    b. recognizing that we are creative, active, choice-making beings whose every action has purpose and meaning.
    c. overcoming the deterministic view of human behavior.
    d. achieving individuation, or a fully harmonious and integrated personality.

15. _____ developed a theory largely based on his early childhood experiences of struggling to overcome weaknesses and feelings of inferiority.
    a. Alfred Adler
    b. Carl Jung
    c. Abraham Maslow
    d. Carl Rogers

16. A basic concept of Alfred Adler's theory is
    a. self-actualization.
    b. individuation.
    c. determinism.
    d. social interest.

17. Adler's theory stresses self-determination in opposition to Freud's
    a. psychosexual stages of development.
    b. psychic structure composed of id, ego, and superego.
    c. defense mechanisms.
    d. deterministic view of human beings.

18. Adler equates his basic concept of social interest with
    a. identification and empathy with others.
    b. unity, unification, integration, and fusion with others.
    c. global responsibility.
    d. collectivism, which affirms the value of preserving and enhancing the well-being of the group.

19. Who is considered a pioneer in person-centered expressive arts therapy?
    a. Carl Rogers
    b. Natalie Rogers
    c. Zerka Moreno
    d. Virginia Satir

20. All of the following are humanistic principles that underlie person-centered expressive arts therapy **except** for which of the following?
    a. The creative process is transformative and healing.
    b. Most behavior is aimed at trying to conquer the shadow.
    c. All people have an innate ability to be creative.
    d. Personal growth is achieved through self-awareness, self-understanding, and insight.

21. Who is considered a pioneer in the development of psychodrama?
    a. Maya Angelo
    b. Natalie Rogers
    c. Zerka Moreno
    d. Virginia Satir

22. Who is considered a pioneer in the development of family therapy?
    a. Maya Angelo
    b. Natalie Rogers
    c. Zerka Moreno
    d. Virginia Satir

23. Which of the following is not true as it applies to psychodrama?
    a. Psychodrama is an action approach to group therapy.
    b. In psychodrama, people enact their problems rather than talk about their problems.
    c. Psychodrama is not concerned about the past, but is primarily oriented toward the future.
    d. In psychodrama, the past, present, and future are brought together through enacting scenarios.

24. Empirical studies conducted on what constitutes happiness have found which factors as being **very important ingredients** for overall happiness?
    a. money, gender, social status
    b. love and intimate relationships, work, personality
    c. parenthood and age
    d. intelligence and physical attractiveness

25. The process of self-actualization as viewed from a Western orientation
    a. rests on collectivism, which affirms the value of preserving and enhancing the group as the main principle guiding social action.
    b. emphasizes unity, unification, integration, and fusion.
    c. is grounded in individualism, which affirms the uniqueness, autonomy, freedom, and intrinsic worth of the individual.
    d. emphasizes cooperation, harmony, interdependence, the collective responsibility.

26. Eastern orientation emphasizes
    a. cooperation, harmony, interdependence, achievement of socially oriented group goals, and collective responsibility.
    b. personal responsibility for our behavior and well-being.
    c. the ultimate aim of personal self-actualization.
    d. uniqueness, autonomy, freedom, and intrinsic worth of the individual.

27. How is Maslow's hierarchy of needs organized?
    a. safety; physiological; love and belongingness; self-esteem; self-actualization
    b. self-esteem; safety; physiological; love and belongingness; self-actualization
    c. love and belongingness; physiological; self-esteem; safety; self-actualization
    d. physiological; safety; love and belongingness; self-esteem; self-actualization

28. Once our physiological needs have been met, our focus will then be meeting our
    a. security and stability needs.
    b. safety needs.
    c. esteem needs.
    d. love needs.

29. Ron is living on the streets. His alcoholism has brought him to this point and he is depressed. He is seeking help at a homeless shelter and has asked to see a counselor. According to Maslow's theory, the *first* goal of counseling would be to help Ron with
    a. the search for self-actualization.
    b. his safety needs, which include a sense of security and stability.
    c. working on his need for esteem, both from self and others.
    d. meeting his physiological needs.

30. According to Maslow, we are able to strive toward self-actualization once the following needs are met
    a. psychological, cognitive, spiritual, and emotional.
    b. physiological, safety, love, and esteem.
    c. belongingness, freedom, basic honesty and caring.
    d. autonomy, love, and self-esteem.

For numbers 31-34, match the category for self-actualization with the behaviors and traits listed below.

31. Self-awareness
32. Freedom
33. Basic honesty and caring
34. Trust and autonomy

    a. sense of social interest, interpersonal relationships, sense of humor
    b. efficient perception of reality, ethical awareness, freshness of appreciation
    c. search for purpose and meaning, autonomy and independence, acceptance of self and others
    d. detachment, creativity, spontaneity

35. Which of the following is *not* a characteristic of self-actualizing people?
    a. sense of social interest
    b. being completely independent
    c. having a capacity for real love and fusion with another
    d. possessing a sense of humor

36. Emotional intelligence pertains to the ability to:
    a. control impulses
    b. empathize with others
    c. form responsible interpersonal relationships
    d. all of the above

37. John is working in a helping profession. He enjoys being around people and has many friends. He seems to learn best by relating, sharing, and participating in cooperative group environments. These characteristics are associated with the following type of intelligence:
    a. intrapersonal.
    b. visual-spatial.
    c. interpersonal.
    d. verbal-linguistic.

38. For the most part, traditional approaches to schooling, including teaching methods, class assignments, and tests, have been geared to and measure the growth of
    a. visual-spatial and intrapersonal abilities.
    b. multidimensional intellectual abilities.
    c. verbal-linguistic and logical-mathematical abilities.
    d. both intuitive and cognitive abilities.

39. Michael likes to read maps, charts, and diagrams. He is able to visualize clear images when he thinks about things. He is planning to become an engineer and his favorite classes are those in which he can design and create things. Michael has the following intellectual orientation:
    a. intrapersonal.
    b. visual-spatial.
    c. logical-mathematical.
    d. verbal-linguistic.

40. If you are a kinesthetic learner, you prefer to learn by
    a. doing, by getting physically involved through movement and action.
    b. reading, watching videotapes, and observing demonstrations.
    c. listening to lectures, audiotapes, and discussing what you've heard.
    d. reciting information and teaching others.

41. If your intelligence is logical-mathematical, you probably
    a. have clear visual images when you think about things.
    b. like to explore patterns and relationships and enjoy doing activities in sequential order.
    c. prefer listening to music when you study or read.
    d. like being in cooperative group environments.

42. In choice theory, total behavior consists of all of the following components of behavior **except for**
    a. acting
    b. working
    c. thinking
    d. physiology

43. Examples of those who are naturalistic learners include
    a. speakers, attorneys, poets, and teachers.
    b. biologists, geologists, physicists, and researchers.
    c. painting, sculpting, and engineering.
    d. farmers, botanists, hunters, ecologists, and landscapers.

44. Self-disclosure is best described as
    a. adopting a direct communication style.
    b. sharing our deepest secrets with others.
    c. a way of deepening self-knowledge by sharing oneself with others.
    d. the act of telling others our unconscious motivation for our behavior.

45. Marge had problems with math when she was in grade school. She is now in college and fearful of taking the required math courses that will allow her to graduate. She tells herself that she will fail again, so why try? Marge is almost ready to quit school. This is an example of
    a. a self-fulfilling prophecy.
    b. individuation.
    c. a deterministic acceptance of fear.
    d. failing to take a risk.

ANSWER KEY FOR CHAPTER 1
INVITATION TO PERSONAL LEARNING AND GROWTH

1.	b	p. 9		26.	a	p. 21
2.	d	p. 6		27.	d	p. 19
3.	c	p. 7		28.	b	p. 19
4.	c	p. 8		29.	d	p. 19
5.	a	p. 9		30.	b	p. 19
6.	a	p. 9		31.	b	p. 19
7.	a	p. 17		32.	d	p. 20
8.	b	p. 17		33.	a	p. 20
9.	d	p. 18		34.	c	p. 20
10.	c	p. 12		35.	b	p. 20
11.	a	p. 12		36.	d	p. 29
12.	b	p. 11		37.	c	p. 31
13.	b	p. 11		38.	c	p. 29
14.	d	p. 11		39.	b	p. 30
15.	a	p. 10		40.	a	p. 30
16.	d	p. 10		41.	b	p. 30
17.	d	p. 9-10		42.	b	p. 23
18.	a	p. 10		43.	d	p. 31
19.	b	p. 13		44.	c	p. 33
20.	b	p. 13		45.	a	p. 33
21.	c	p. 14				
22.	d	p. 16				
23.	c	p. 14				
24.	b	p. 5				
25.	c	p. 21				

Activities and Exercises for Classroom Participation for Chapter 1

During the early stages of a class in personal learning, it is a good idea to focus on getting the students oriented toward the course, which will most likely be very different from most of the courses they've had. This can be done by discussing their expectations about the class, as well as my expectations of them. We find that a consideration of what their past schooling has been like is a valuable and non-threatening way to talk about how they can make this particular class a different kind of experience and how they can develop a new style of learning. The following are some exercises that we've used as "warm-ups" and as ways of allowing the students to introduce themselves and to get focused.

1.   Getting Acquainted. Break into dyads for about ten minutes, and talk with your partner about why you're taking this course. You might tell the person what you heard about the course and what you hope to get from it. Make contact with someone you don't know already.

2.   Sharing Expectations. The preceding exercise can be done several times, so that each student has a chance to contact several others. Then the group reconvenes, and students are asked to share why they took the class and what specific things they hope to learn.

3.   Brainstorming. You might ask your students during one of the first few sessions to share ideas they have concerning possibilities for the course. What are some things they might like to experience or do during the semester? A good way to lead off this exercise is to say: "Assume that you could structure this class any way you wanted. What are some possibilities that occur to you?"

4.   A Review of Past School Experiences. Students can be asked: "Think of a teacher you particularly liked, and see his or her face. What does that teacher tell you? What was it like to be in that person's class? Can you recall and relive some moments of joy?" After the guided fantasy, students can break into small groups of four and share the highlights of their remembrances. Then convene as a whole class, and anyone who wants to is invited to share his or her remembrances. This exercise can be a good way to stimulate recall of what the students' schooling has meant to them. *Caution*: In some people it can also evoke a great deal of emotion.

5.   Blocks to Learning. As students review their past school experiences, ask them to identify and explore some area in their life where they unfinished business. Encourage them, preferably in small groups, to talk about what holds them back or negative self-talk affects what they do in everyday life. How do they experience a block to learning? How do they experience a block to becoming the person they would like to become? In small groups, they can explore how life might be different for them if they were able to challenge this block, or if the block were absent. You might start the discussion as follows: Ask them to imagine that they are successful in discarding one particular block. How is their life different without this block? What does the block prevent them from doing or being? To what degree do they fear their own creativity?

6.   Giving Away a Block. Ask students to identify a block within them that could get in the way of being an effective person or a successful student. Then ask them to give this particular block away. They can do this by imagining they are actually giving their block to another person, who is willing to keep this block for them for a certain period of time. You might introduce this exercise thusly:

Consider what it would be like for you to feel free of your block. Discuss what it will take to realize your dreams of graduating and explore ways that you can overcome personal barriers. For example, if you tell yourself that you have to be the perfect student because you are the first person in your family to attend college, talk about how you might experience pressure to do well. Then give this pressure to another person (maybe for a week). Literally put this pressure into an envelope and hand it to another person saying that you will appreciate him or her keeping this block for you for a week. What ways might you be different if you were to act as if you gave some of your personal barriers away, even for a short period of time?

7. **Dealing with Fears.** If the course is structured along the lines of small groups in which students are expected to become personally involved, there are usually some fears, such as we described earlier. It often is useful to ask students to work in groups of about four or five and to express and explore any fears they might have about being in the course. After the groups have had enough time to focus on some specific fears, all the groups are asked to report some of their fears, which are listed on the chalkboard. We note how often some fears are mentioned, and we then explore some of the most commonly mentioned fears as a class.

8. **Being Willing to Make Mistakes.** Explore with your students the importance of seeing mistakes as an essential part of learning. Encourage them to use this course to experiment with new and more effective ways of learning. Making mistakes does not have to be problematic, unless students' fears about mistakes lead to inactivity. In small groups, ask students to identify any mistakes they have made in their previous learning experiences. What have they learned from these mistakes? Has the fear of making mistakes held them back from trying new things?

9. **Contracts.** The class members are asked to think about some changes they are each willing to make and what they are willing to do to make these changes a reality. Each class member writes a contract dealing with something new that he or she is willing to do within a specified time period. The contract might be related to behavior in the classroom. For instance, the person who rarely participates in class verbally but who would like to do so can decide "For the rest of this semester, I will verbally participate at least once in each class session." Of course, the contracts can be more personal. The object of the exercise is to make students think about concrete changes they'd like to make and to give them the experience of trying to stick to a contract.

10. **Sealed Contract.** Earlier we described an exercise in which participants are encouraged to think about a contract they are willing to work with in the class. This is a variation we have used. Members are asked to write down some things that they'd like to be able to say they have done and some changes they'd like to have made by the last class meeting. They write down their responses, seal them in envelopes and we collect them. They are returned at the last session, and at that time the students can read their contracts aloud to their group if they wish and comment on the degree to which they have fulfilled their expectations of themselves.

11. **Trust Building.** We think that the creation of a trusting climate is a *must* during the first few sessions. We also assume that most people don't walk into a classroom with a trusting attitude toward everyone else. It seems to us that trust must be earned and worked for. We therefore ask students to talk openly about what it is like for them to be in a class like this. Ask them to mention anything that might make them hesitant to participate.

12. **Learning Styles**. After students complete and score the RIMI, they can form small groups to explore ways that they learn best by discussing some of these questions: How do you learn best? What are some of the ways that you approach new tasks or a problem? Do you learn best by being told something? By reading it? By getting involved in figuring out something? Do you learn best by seeing what you are learning?

13. **Multiple Intelligences.** In the chapter is a discussion of the eight kinds of intellectual abilities. Ask students to identify which of these forms of intellectual abilities represents their strengths. They can form small groups in class based on their dominant intelligence. What implications do the students see for the way they might best learn based on their dominant intelligence?

14. Active Learning. Consider giving at least a brief lecture dealing with ways your students can become active learners in your class. Ask them to read the section on active learning and then ask students how they responded to the Take Time to Reflect. Ask students to read the section on taking responsibility for their learning and discuss the Take Time to Reflect section, which pertains to how they might get involved in this course in an active way.

15. Guest Speakers. Inquire about a person who has done extensive work with learning styles as a speaker. A faculty member from the Psychology Department or a counselor from the Counseling Center may have expertise in learning styles.

CHAPTER 2: REVIEWING YOUR CHILDHOOD AND ADOLESCENCE

Outline

Where Am I Now?
Stages of Personality Development: A Preview
Infancy
Early Childhood
Impact of the First 6 Years of Life
Middle Childhood
        Developing a Self-Concept
        Protecting the Self: Ego-Defense Mechanisms
Pubescence
Adolescence
Chapter Summary
Where Can I Go From Here?
Website Resources

Chapter Objectives

- to introduce the stages of development in childhood and adolescence

- to describe developmental tasks and choice points

- to provide a context for understanding present behavior based on past experiences

Questions for Thought, Class Discussion, and Evaluation

1. Discuss the life-span perspective of personality development.

2. How are the various life stage categories interrelated? Discuss how it is impossible to neatly separate the periods of life into compartments, and how each stage in life influences the others.

3. How accurate are the stages of personality development, in terms of major developmental tasks and crises of each period, when you apply them to your own life so far?

4. Outline Erikson's eight stages of development from infancy through the later years, describing briefly the major conflicts and developmental tasks at each stage.

5. Discuss the importance of receiving love as an infant with respect to developing a trusting view of the world. What are some of the possible effects on later development if love and caring are absent during infancy?

6. Briefly define the concept of emotional intelligence.

7. Discuss the effects of the events of the first six years of life on later personality development. Do you believe that, as adults, we're determined by our early childhood experiences? To what degree does earlier conditioning influence us now? What role do you think that choice plays in changing your current patterns?

8. When you look at whatever problems you might have now, do you see any evidence of the origin of these problems during the first few years of your development?

9. Be familiar with the core struggle of each of the eight stages in the life span, according to Erikson. For example, in one sentence, be able to describe the nature of the struggle between trust versus mistrust.

10. Carefully study the chart on the overview of the developmental stages, getting clearly in mind the differences between the self-in-context view of development and Erikson's psychosocial view.

11. Know the stages of development from infancy through old age, with respect to name of the stage, age span, core struggle of the period, potential personality problems that can arise if development task of the stage is not mastered, and differences between Erikson psychosocial view and the self-in-context view at each stage.

12. How do your own struggles in life compare with what you are reading in this chapter?

13. How important do you think the school years (ages 6 to 12) are in terms of their impact on adolescent and adult development? Select one event from your own school years, and show how this event has some significance for your life now.

14. What is your understanding of the term self-concept? How does it develop? How does one's self-concept influence one's behavior?

15. What is the meaning of a *psychological moratorium* during adolescence? Did you experience this in your own adolescence?

16. In what way is adolescence a time for searching for an identity?

17. What are a few choices you made as an adolescent that have an influence on the person you are today?

18. Describe some of the core conflicts associated with the adolescent period. Select at least one conflict that you experienced. How did you deal with this conflict? What decisions did you make? What impact does this decision have on your life now?

19. Discuss the process of identity formation during adolescence. Consider factors such as peer groups, parents, the role of school, and societal factors that influence the shaping of identity.

20. Discuss the idea that the mastery of developmental tasks in adulthood is related to the level of mastery of tasks during the childhood and adolescent years.

21. Discuss how the ego-defense mechanisms protect our self-concept. When is the use of such defenses a part of normal coping? What is the main problem in relying upon these defensive strategies in dealing with stress?

Glossary of Key Terms

Autonomy refers to mature independence and interdependence.

Systemic perspective is grounded on the assumption that how we develop can best be understood through learning about our role and place in our family of origin.

Psychoanalysis is a theory and approach to psychotherapy founded by Sigmund Freud that emphasizes unconscious psychological process and places importance on early childhood experiences.

Psychosocial theory stresses the integration of the biological, psychological, and social aspects of development.

Core struggles occur at every stage of development according to Erik Erikson. Depending on how successfully tasks are mastered at each stage, a person's development may be enhanced or hindered. From infancy through adolescence, the core struggles are trust versus mistrust, initiative versus guilt, industry versus inferiority, and identity versus role confusion.

Crisis pertains to a turning point in life, or a moment of transition characterized by the potential to go either forward or backward in development.

Self-in-context is a perspective that takes into account race, socioeconomic class, gender, ethnicity, and culture as central factors that influence the course of development throughout the individual's life cycle.

Feminist perspective of development emphasizes the social and cultural aspects influencing personality development.

Life-span perspective pertains to developmental stages from infancy to old age.

Infancy is a time from birth to age 2 with the core struggle being trust versus mistrust.

Attachment theory, an extension of psychoanalytic theory, emphasizes the emotional bonding between the infant and a caretaker who is perceived as a source of security.

Attachment styles are typical ways of interacting in close relationships.

A secure pattern is characterized by feelings of intimacy, emotional security, and physical safety when an infant is in the presence of an attachment figure.

An anxious-avoidant pattern involves the experience of an insecure attachment relationship because attachment figures consistently reject an infant.

An anxious-ambivalent pattern is characterized by an infant's intense distress at a caretaker's departure and inability to be comforted upon return of the caretaker.

Resiliency is an amazing ability to adapt to trauma or other adverse events in one's life.

Authoritative parents set high goals for their children, yet they are accepting and allow their children to explore.

Authoritarian parents are very strict, have high demands, and use threat of punishment to control their children.

Permissive parents tend to be indulgent and make few demands on their children.

Neglectful parents provide for their children's physical needs, but are not greatly involved in their children's lives.

Early childhood is a time between ages 2 to 6 when children learn independence and when they begin the journey toward autonomy by progressing from being taken care of by others to meeting some of their own physical needs.

Middle childhood is between the ages of 6 to 12 years when children expand their knowledge and understanding of the physical and social worlds, develop a sense of values, learn new communication skills, and engage in social activities.

Self-concept refers to our awareness of ourselves; it is the picture of self that includes perceptions about the kind of person we are.

Ego-defense mechanisms are psychological strategies we use to protect our self-concept from unpleasant aspects of reality.

Repression consists of sealing off from consciousness threatening or painful thoughts and feelings.

Denial involves distorting what we think, feel, or perceive to be a stressful situation.

Displacement involves redirecting emotional impulses from the real object to a substitute person or object.

Projection consists of attributing to others our own unacceptable desires and impulses.

Reaction formation is a form of defense against anxiety by expressing the opposite impulse.

Rationalization involves manufacturing a false but plausible excuse to justify unacceptable behavior and explain away failures or losses.

Compensation consists of masking perceived weaknesses or developing certain positive traits to make up for limitations.

Regression involves reverting to a form of immature behavior that an individual has outgrown.

Fantasy involves gratifying frustrated desires by imaginary achievements.

Self-deception involves softening harsh reality as a protection against anxiety.

Pubescence typically occurs between the ages of 11 to 14 and is characterized by major physical, psychological, and sexual changes.

Adolescence, a period of development from about 13 to 20, is a central time to formulate a sense of personal identity.

Individuation is a process of separating from our family system and establishing an identity based on our own experiences.

Psychological moratorium is a period during which society gives permission to adolescents to experiment with different roles and values before making major commitments.

TEST ITEMS FOR CHAPTER 2
REVIEWING YOUR CHILDHOOD AND ADOLESCENCE

1. The following is *not* a characteristic of the autonomous person:
   a. ability to function only with constant approval and reassurance.
   b. sensitivity to the needs of others.
   c. mature independence and interdependence.
   d. ability to effectively meet the demands of daily living.

2. The term *autonomy* refers to
   a. the need for privacy.
   b. mature independence and interdependence.
   c. being totally independent.
   d. an unconscious psychological process of letting go of the need for approval from others.

3. Freud developed a model for understanding early development based on _____.
   a. psychosocial factors.
   b. unconscious psychological processes.
   c. individuation and differentiation.
   d. maturation.

4. A concept of Erikson's theory of personality development is that
   a. psychosexual and psychosocial growth occur separately.
   b. human development occurs over the entire life span.
   c. crises need not be resolved at each stage.
   d. the id is the life force of human development.

5. Erikson's psychosocial theory stresses the
   a. integration of the biological, psychological, and social aspects of development.
   b. need to meet one's lower needs, in order to move towards self-actualization.
   c. resolution of psychosexual conflicts.
   d. integration of self-concept with the ideal self.

6. The self-in-context perspective takes into account _____ as being central to the course of development throughout the life cycle.
   a. race
   b. culture and ethnicity
   c. gender
   d. all of the above

7. The feminist perspective on development is
   a. strongly supportive of Erikson's focus on the individual.
   b. critical of Erikson's focus on the individual.
   c. critical of the Freudian psychoanalytic approach.
   d. both (b) and (c)

8. From the self-in-context view, _____ is a time of finding one's own voice and the beginning of developing a sense of autonomy.
   a. infancy
   b. early childhood
   c. middle childhood
   d. pubescence

9. According to Erikson, the core struggle during infancy is
   a. self-reliance vs. doubt.
   b. initiative vs. guilt.
   c. trust vs. mistrust.
   d. industry vs. guilt.

10. Children who do not develop secure attachments in infancy
   a. will not be able to develop a positive self-image in adulthood and will have dysfunctional relationships
   b. will be able to develop a positive self-image in adulthood and develop healthy relationships
   c. may still develop a positive self-image and healthy relationships, especially if they have access to social support and find a mentor during childhood
   d. will have plenty of time to develop secure attachments before they are affected in any way

11. From the self-in-context view, _____ is a time for developing emotional competence, which involves being able to delay gratification.
   a. infancy
   b. early childhood
   c. middle childhood
   d. pubescence

12. From the self-in-context view, _____ is a period of searching for an identity, continuing to find one's voice, and balancing caring of self with caring about others.
   a. middle age
   b. adolescence
   c. middle childhood
   d. pubescence

13. Barbara wants to be the "perfect mother." She tends to be overprotective, doing things for her 3-year-old daughter that the child can very well do for herself. According to Erikson, although Barbara thinks she is being an effective parent, her daughter is likely to develop a sense of
   a. shame and doubt about her capabilities.
   b. guilt over her inadequacies.
   c. low self-esteem.
   d. right and wrong.

14. From the self-in-context view, _____ is a time for increasing one's understanding of one's self in terms of gender, race, culture, and abilities and a time for developing empathy.
   a. pubescence
   b. early adulthood
   c. middle childhood
   d. adolescence

15. Parents who squelch any emerging individuality and who do too much for their children are indirectly saying
    a. "Let us do this for you, because you're too clumsy, too slow, or too inept to do things for yourself."
    b. "You are so special to us that we will do everything for you."
    c. "If you make mistakes, you will feel bad about yourself, so we will help you establish a healthy dependency on us."
    d. "We will do for you what you can't do for yourself, so you won't have to feel failure."

16. According to Erikson, during the preschool years children will
    a. initiate many of their own activities.
    b. widen their circle of significant persons.
    c. identify with their own gender.
    d. increase their capacity to understand and use language.
    e. d. all of the above.

17. According to Erikson, the conflict that characterizes the preschool years is
    a. initiative vs. guilt.
    b. autonomy vs. shame and doubt.
    c. industry vs. inferiority.
    d. trust vs. mistrust.

18. Attachment theory is an extension of
    a. cognitive behavioral theory
    b. gestalt theory
    c. psychoanalysis
    d. existentialism

19. Annie feels incompetent in many areas of her life. She is fearful of being seen as foolish, so she seldom initiates any action. During her preschool years, many of her actions were ridiculed by family members and she ultimately withdrew from taking an active stance. According to Erikson, Annie failed to overcome the barriers associated with the following stage of development:
    a. trust vs. mistrust.
    b. autonomy vs. shame and doubt.
    c. industry vs. inferiority
    d. initiative vs. guilt

20. According to Erikson, a child of preschool age who is unduly restricted or whose choices are ridiculed tends to experience
    a. an inability to know right from wrong.
    b. a sense of guilt and ultimately will withdraw from taking an active stance.
    c. a rebellious nature.
    d. difficulty being empathic with playmates.

21. From the self-in-context view, _____ is the period that is characterized by major physical, psychological, and sexual changes; it is also a time of expanded sense of self in relation to peers, family, and community.
    a. middle childhood
    b. late childhood
    c. pubescence
    d. adolescence

22. Jared recently made the decision to enter nursing school. Upon informing his parents of his decision, his father replied, "Why go into nursing? You should become a doctor." This statement reflects
    a. gender bias
    b. good judgment
    c. gender equality
    d. the feminist perspective

23. Feminist therapists view the early adolescent period as one of
    a. expanding relationships with parents.
    b. "getting rid" of parents.
    c. keeping these relationships stable.
    d. great rebellion against all parental values.

24. If during the first six years of our lives we reached faulty conclusions based on our life experience, we are likely to
    a. challenge them as we realize that they are faulty.
    b. change them during adolescence.
    c. ignore them in order to function effectively.
    d. still be operating on the basis of them.

25. Which of the following parenting styles outlined by Diana Baumrind is associated with the most positive behavioral traits in childhood development?
    a. authoritarian
    b. authoritative
    c. permissive
    d. neglectful

26. Iryna's parents have adopted an authoritarian parenting style. Which of the following statements would they most likely make?
    a. "Iryna has such strong aptitude in math and we want her to feel the satisfaction of accomplishing a challenging goal, so we will encourage her to take an advanced math course."
    b. "We insist Iryna take the most demanding math course and bring home an A+."
    c. "Whatever Iryna wants to do is fine with us. If she feels like taking an easier math class this semester, that's her choice."
    d. "It's up to the school to decide what classes Iryna should take. That's why we pay taxes—so parents don't have to deal with their child's education."

27. Kevin is a 32 year-old unemployed man who lives with his parents. He has no plans to look for a job and spends much of his time in bars using his father's credit card to buy himself and others alcohol. Based on this information, it is likely that his parents raised him using
    a. an authoritarian parenting style
    b. an authoritative parenting style
    c. a permissive parenting style
    d. a neglectful parenting style

28. _____ is typically a turbulent and fast-moving period of life, often marked by feelings of powerlessness, confusion, and loneliness.
    a. middle childhood
    b. pubescence
    c. adolescence
    d. late middle age

29. According to Erikson, the critical event during middle childhood (ages 6 - 12) is starting school. During this period, the child will face the following key developmental task:
    a. a relative decline in sexual interests and emergence of new interests, activities, and attitudes.
    b. developing autonomy and achieving competency.
    c. achieving a sense of industry vs. inferiority and inadequacy.
    d. forming a sense of identity and initiative.

30. According to Erikson, failure to achieve a sense of industry during middle childhood tends to result in
    a. a sense of inadequacy and inferiority.
    b. a strain on the child's sense of identity.
    c. feelings of self-hatred that can never be erased.
    d. failure to acquire individuation.

31. The term _____ refers to your cognitive awareness about yourself. It is your private mental image of yourself and a collection of beliefs about the kind of person you are.
    a. self-esteem
    b. ideal self
    c. self-concept
    d. personality profile

32. Defense mechanisms can be thought of as
    a. unhealthy reactions to stress.
    b. most effective when used as the primary means to cope with stress.
    c. psychological strategies that we use to protect our self-concept against unpleasant emotions.
    d. reactions used primarily by mentally distressed individuals.

For numbers 33-37, match the defense mechanism with the most appropriate definition below.

33. Regression
34. Reaction formation
35. Displacement
36. Projection
37. Rationalization

    a. attributing to others our own unacceptable desires and impulses
    b. redirecting emotional, usually hostile, impulses from the real object to a substitute person or object
    c. behaving in a manner contrary to one's real feelings
    d. exhibiting immature behavior that was earlier outgrown
    e. manufacturing a false, but "good," excuse to justify unacceptable behavior

38. Matt's parents claim that their teenage son is not using drugs, even though they found paraphernalia in his room. This is an example of
    a. rationalization.
    b. denial.
    c. repression.
    d. compensation.

39. Richard came home and yelled at his wife after his boss had chastised him for making an accounting error when doing the quarterly reports. This is an example of
    a. reaction formation.
    b. rationalization.
    c. displacement.
    d. projection.

40. Helen is a college student who suffers from test anxiety and fear of failure. These problems began during early childhood when she started school younger than her peers. She failed at tasks that were easily accomplished by most of her schoolmates. Although Helen knows she has problems taking tests, she does not remember the traumatic events that led to her fear of failure. She is using the following defense mechanism:
    a. regression.
    b. displacement.
    c. projection.
    d. repression.

41. Patrick likes to "party" on the weekends and recently got a ticket for driving while intoxicated. He explains his predicament by saying "Everyone does it! I just got caught!" This is an example of
    a. denial.
    b. rationalization.
    c. displacement.
    d. projection.

42. Harry has been unfaithful to his wife for many years, and yet he constantly accuses his wife of cheating on him. This is an example of
   a. reaction formation.
   b. displacement.
   c. rationalization.
   d. projection.

43. Sue was a passive teenager, but at age 30, she began to work hard at being an assertive woman. Recently, when faced with an angry husband, she reverted to her passive stance. Sue is using the following defense mechanism:
   a. regression.
   b. compensation.
   c. repression.
   d. projection.

44. Mary is getting a divorce from a man who cheated on her. She has two children who are reacting with chaos to the change in their lives. She recently started college and is succeeding as a student, so she puts most of her energy into her coursework. To avoid feelings of failure as a mother and a wife, she is using
   a. compensation.
   b. projection.
   c. displacement.
   d. reaction formation.

45. According to Erikson, a critical time for forming personal identity, finding meaningful life goals, and creating meaning in life is during
   a. early childhood.
   b. middle childhood.
   c. adolescence.
   d. young adulthood.

46. John is an adolescent who feels overwhelmed by the pressures placed on him to go to college and make an occupational choice that will lead to financial independence. His girlfriend wants to get married, and he doesn't want to lose her, so he feels pressured to make a commitment that he doesn't feel ready to make. According to Erikson, John is dealing with the following core struggle:
   a. industry vs. inadequacy.
   b. autonomy vs. shame and doubt.
   c. generativity vs. despair.
   d. identity vs. role confusion.

47. During adolescence, a crucial part of the identity-formation process requires individuation, which refers to
   a. finding meaning in living and coping with feelings of uselessness.
   b. separation from the family system and establishing personal identity based on one's own experiences rather than one's parents' dreams.
   c. expressing sexuality in ways that are congruent with one's value system.
   d. the development of primary sexual characteristics.

48. A *psychological moratorium,* recommended by Erikson, is a period
    a. during which children learn how to relate to others
    b. when adolescents are given permission by society to experiment with different roles.
    c. during adolescence when young people make major commitments in their personal life.
    d. during childhood when trust is formed by relying on parents to get basic needs met.

49. In response to their growing awareness of the systematic exclusion of people from their racial and cultural group from full participation in the dominant society, many young people of color develop _____, which protects them from the psychological assault of racism and keeps the dominant group at bay.
    a. an oppositional social identity
    b. a personality disorder
    c. a psychotic disorder
    d. a social justice mind set

ANSWER KEY FOR CHAPTER 2
REVIEWING YOUR CHILDHOOD AND ADOLESCENCE

1. a   p. 40
2. b   p. 40
3. b   p. 41
4. b   p. 41
5. a   p. 41
6. d   p. 42
7. d   p. 42
8. d   p. 45
9. c   p. 44
10. c   p. 48
11. b   p. 44
12. b   p. 45
13. a   p. 44
14. c   p. 44
15. a   p. 50
16. e   p. 49
17. a   p. 44, 49
18. c   p. 46
19. d   p. 44, 50
20. b   p. 44, 50
21. c   p. 45
22. a   p. 42
23. a   p. 63
24. d   p. 53
25. b   p. 51

26. b   p. 51-52
27. c   p. 52
28. c   p. 65
29. c   p. 44, 56
30. a   p. 44, 56
31. c   p. 57
32. c   p. 58
33. d   p. 59
34. c   p. 59
35. b   p. 58
36. a   p. 59
37. e   p. 59
38. b   p. 58
39. c   p. 58
40. d   p. 58
41. b   p. 59
42. d   p. 59
43. a   p. 59
44. a   p. 59
45. c   p. 61
46. d   p. 61
47. b   p. 62
48. b   p. 62
49. a   p. 65

Activities and Exercises for Classroom Participation for Chapter 2

With this topic—personality development during childhood and adolescence—we like to develop small-group activities that allow students to explore their own personality development during the various stages of life. We particularly like to focus on the turning points, important decisions, crises, methods of dealing with crises, and significant events of the various life periods. The exercises we are about to describe are all attempts to assist students to think about the impact that others have had on them (especially their parents), the choices they've made at different times in life, and the extent to which they are the products of earlier influences. Also, we hope that students will give some thought to ways they want to change, new decisions they want to make, and ways they can become more autonomous.

1. What effect do you think the first six years of your life have had on the person you are today? Are you aware of any unfinished business from these early years that still has an impact on you?

2. In small groups within the classroom, recall and share your experiences during the early years of school, from ages 6 to 12. What was school like for you? In what ways did you find success? Are there any failures that stand out for you? How do you suppose your elementary school years, especially the primary grades, have affected you now? How did these years and the experiences you had then affect your self-concept (the way you viewed yourself and how you felt about that self-image)?

3. Again, in small groups, discuss your adolescent years, using most of the same questions listed above. In what ways was your adolescence different from your early school years?

4. Take the eight developmental stages identified by Erikson, and apply the key ideas to your own development. Did you experience the crises and conflicts outlined by Erikson?

5. Write down through the course of a week some of your most pleasant childhood memories. Try to recapture some of the feelings you had then.

6. Interview several adolescents that you know. You could ask them about the concerns they are facing, how they see their future, and what they'd like to be different in their lives. Of course, the degree to which you deal with personal issues will be a function of how well you know these adolescents and of your relationship with them. You could interview your brothers and sisters, or your own children, if they are in this age range. The general patterns could be summarized and perhaps brought to class. Compare your findings with your own adolescent years.

7. Develop a chart in which you review the choices that were available to you as an adolescent. What are a few significant choices you made then, and how do you think these choices have an impact on you today?

8. In small groups, discuss the topic: "If I could live my adolescent years over again, what I'd most like to change would be. . . ."

Suggested Class Activities

1. In small groups, discuss your level and degree of self-acceptance. Talk with others about specific ways that you are able to accept yourself and ways that you discount yourself.

2. Explore specific ways that each of you could work toward becoming more self-accepting. For example, you may have rated yourself as being able to accept compliments only rarely. Assuming that you'd like to be able to believe positive feedback from others, explore the things you usually do that prevent you from accepting positive responses. Do you make jokes about yourself? Do you tell others that they really don't know you? What could you say to others instead of your usual self-depreciating remarks?

Ideas for Practicing Self-Acceptance Outside of Class

1. For a week pay particular attention to situations in which you either *appreciate* or *depreciate* yourself. For example, assume you complete a project that was important to you. Are you able to enjoy the outcome? Did you enjoy the process? Did you tell yourself that what you accomplished was not good enough? Is there something you did that interfered with your feeling of success? Note the situation in your journal, and write down how you responded to it.

2. After you have become aware of how you limit your acceptance of self, especially through statements that you are making, experiment with making positive statements about yourself and your abilities. For example, if you play a musical instrument and get enjoyment from it, you may at the same time tell others that you're really not that good. You may put yourself down even though many others have told you they think you play the instrument well. You could experiment with a different sentence, such as: "I enjoy making music, and I play the instrument well."

Self-Concept—How We See Ourselves and How We Feel About That View

We are more than a description of roles and traits. How we *feel* about the way we describe ourselves is a basic part of our self-concept. Thus, you may define yourself by many of the things you do, which could include being a student, a worker, a husband or wife, a musician, an athlete, etc. You also have evaluations attached to these roles. Take the role of being a student. How *do* you see yourself in this role? Are you passive? curious? motivated? bright? Thus, you have some evaluation of each of your roles.

What are the roles you exhibit in your everyday life, and how do you generally feel about yourself in each of these roles? List the *most* important roles, and then list how you evaluate yourself in each of these.

_____   _____
_____   _____
_____   _____
_____   _____
_____   _____
_____   _____

After you have listed the above roles, rank them in terms of their importance to you. Consider the roles that account for most of your time. Is this the way you want it to be? Are there any changes you'd like to make?

Class Exercises

1. In small groups discuss the roles you deem *most* important and *least* important in your life. Be specifically aware of how much time you devote to each role. Share with others the degree of satisfaction/dissatisfaction you derive from each role. Also, spend time in your group discussing possible competing roles. For example, you may be a mother of young children and a college student. What is it like for you to have these dual roles and how do you manage these roles? Are both roles fulfilling to you?

2. Imagine yourself in an ideal role that would lead to good feelings about yourself. Now form dyads and share with your partner what this role is and how it would be for you to actually *be* in this ideal role. Share how you think your life would be different if this role were a reality. Do you have any ideas of how you can go about bringing your actual roles in line with ideal roles?

CHAPTER 3: ADULTHOOD AND AUTONOMY

Outline

Where Am I Now?
The Path toward Autonomy and Interdependence
      Recognizing Early Learning and Decisions
      Learning to Dispute Self-Defeating Thinking
      Learning to Challenge Your Inner Parent and Your Inner Critic
Stages of Adulthood
Early Adulthood
      Provisional Adulthood
      Emerging Adulthood
      Entering the 20s
      Transition From the 20s to the 30s
Middle Adulthood
      The Late 30s
      Life During the 40s
Late Middle Age
      The 50s
      The 60s
Late Adulthood
      Themes During Late Adulthood
      Stereotypes of Late Adulthood
      Challenging the Stereotypes
Summary
Where Can I Go From Here?
Website Resources

Chapter Objectives

- to describe key tasks of development in adulthood

- to examine the context of early decisions and present-day influence

- to provide a framework for understanding the meaning of autonomy

- to demonstrate that autonomy and interdependence are related

Questions for Thought, Class Discussion, and Evaluation

1. Define and explain what achieving personal autonomy means to you.

2. Do you agree or disagree with the concept that many of our present-day attitudes are formed by earlier decisions? Explain. What are some early decisions you made in your life, and how do these decisions influence your behavior now?

3. To what degree do you think you've become psychologically independent? Discuss some ways in which you haven't become your own person, and also some steps you've taken toward independence.

4. Discuss what you understand by the phrase "challenging one's inner parent." Do you think it is possible to become an autonomous person without critically evaluating parental messages? Discuss.

5. Do you think it is ever possible to "become one's own parents"? If so, in what sense? Discuss some of the problems involved in learning to "become our own parents."

6. What is transactional analysis? Who developed this theory?

7. Have a clear understanding of the following terms from the perspective of transactional analysis. In a single sentence, be able to define each of these terms: ego state, Parent, Adult, Child, life-script, injunctions, early decisions, redecisions, early messages.

8. Drawing upon transactional analysis, apply some of the concepts to yourself.

9. Discuss the concept of life scripts. Do you think we are passively scripted by our parents, and thus our lives are programmed? Or do you think we cooperate in accepting parental messages and thus write our own scripts? Discuss.

10. List some of the common injunctions described in the text, along with possible decisions that could be made in response to them.

11. What are some of the injunctions that have had the most powerful impact on your life? Explain. Discuss some of the decisions that you've made in response to these injunctions. Are there any redecisions, or new decisions, that you are considering now?

12. What is rational emotive behavior therapy, and who developed it?

13. How are irrational beliefs related to our behavior? How can people learn to dispute irrational beliefs?

14. Describe the A-B-C theory of personality that explains how we form negative self-evaluations.

15. What is the core struggle during early adulthood, according to Erikson?

16. When people enter their twenties, what are some of their main concerns? How does this apply to your life?

17. What are some main concerns of individuals as they make the transition from the twenties to the thirties?

18. According to Erikson, what is the core struggle during middle adulthood?

19. What are a few of the events that might contribute to the midlife crisis?

20. How typical is it to change careers in midlife? Does it necessarily mean that the person made a poor vocational choice earlier?

21. According to Erikson, what is the core struggle of later adulthood?

22. What is the best way to prepare for a satisfying life during our later years? What are some steps you can take now toward this goal?

23. What are some of the major problems facing the elderly? What choices are open to them?

24. How can retirement be either a traumatic or a joyful time?

Glossary of Key Terms

Autonomy involves accepting responsibility for the consequences of one's choices, rather than holding others accountable.

Maturity involves the development of a mature, interdependent self.

Connection is an interaction between two or more people that is mutually empathic and mutually empowering.

Disconnection is an encounter that works against mutual empathy and mutual empowerment.

Transactional analysis (TA) is a theory of personality and a method of counseling, developed by Eric Berne, that is based on the assumption that adults make decisions grounded on past premises that were at one time appropriate for survival needs, but which may no longer be functional.

Life script is an unconscious plan for life made in childhood, reinforced by parents and by subsequent events, and culminating in a chosen alternative.

Injunctions (or early messages or parental injunctions) are messages telling children what they have to do and be to get recognition.

Decisions consist of how people view themselves based on the injunctions they accept or reject.

Cognitive-behavioral therapies are theories of personality and approaches to counseling that involve a set of procedures that attempts to change feelings and behavior by modifying faulty thinking and believing.

Rational emotive behavior therapy is based on the premise that emotional and behavioral problems are originally learned from significant others during childhood.

Self-defeating thinking is supported and maintained by negative and dysfunctional statements that we repeatedly make to ourselves.

A-B-C theory of personality is based on the assumption that people's problems do not stem from activating events, but rather from their beliefs about such events.

Inner parent refers to the attitudes and beliefs we have about ourselves and others that are a direct result of things we learned from our parents or parental substitutes.

Inner critic refers to our inner voice that criticizes us and makes constant judgments about our worth.

Mindfulness is a process through which people become increasingly observant and aware of external and internal stimuli in the present moment and adopt an open attitude of accepting *what is* rather than judging the present situation.

Acceptance involves a process of connecting with your present experience without judgment or self-criticism, but with curiosity and kindness, and becoming aware of your mental activity from moment to moment.

Core struggles occur at every stage of development according to Erik Erikson. Depending on how successfully tasks are mastered at each stage, a person's development may be enhanced or hindered. From early adulthood through late adulthood, the core struggles are intimacy versus isolation, generativity versus stagnation, and integrity versus despair.

Early adulthood in the period between ages 21 through 34 that involves developmental tasks such as establishing a gender-identity, finding an occupation, separating from family of origin, and developing a personal worldview.

Emerging adulthood is a period of life from roughly ages 18 to 25 that is characterized by change and exploration of possible life directions.

Middle adulthood, a period of roughly from 35 to 49, is a time when people tend to engage in a philosophical reexamination of their lives.

Midlife crisis is a turbulent period of doubts and reappraisals of one's life.

Individuation, or integration of the unconscious with the conscious and psychological balance, is achieved for middle-aged people when they can let go of preconceived notions and patterns that have dominated the first part of their lives, and become open to deepening the meaning of their lives.

Late middle age, between the early 50s and the mid-60s is a time when many adults are beginning to consider retirement, pursue new interests, and think about what they want to do with the rest of their lives.

Late adulthood, from the mid-60s onward, is a time to put our life in perspective and accept who we are and what we have done.

Ageism refers to prejudice toward or stereotyping of people simply because they are perceived as being old.

TEST ITEMS FOR CHAPTER 3
ADULTHOOD AND AUTONOMY

1. As we leave adolescence and enter young adulthood, our central task is to
    a. assume increased responsibility.
    b. develop effective coping mechanisms.
    c. challenge our early childhood assumptions.
    d. rebel against our parent's values.

2. Transactional analysis is a theory of personality and a method of counseling that was originally developed by
    a. Albert Ellis.
    b. Carl Jung.
    c. Eric Berne.
    d. McGoldrick and Carter.

3. _____ is grounded on the assumption that we make current decisions based on past premises that were appropriate at one time but may no longer be valid.
    a. Freud's psychosexual theory of development
    b. Erikson's psychosocial theory of development
    c. Transactional analysis
    d. Jung's theory of personality development

4. The life script, or plan for one's life, is an important contribution of TA and is made up of
    a. both parental teaching and early decisions we made as a child.
    b. injunctions that cannot be changed once they are formed.
    c. genetic predisposition and psychological conditioning.
    d. transactions and parental interactions.

5. According to TA, life scripts
    a. begin in infancy with subtle nonverbal messages.
    b. are made up of parental teachings.
    c. are the early decisions we make as children.
    d. all of the above.

6. It would be most accurate to say that parents give their children _____ life scripts.
    a. only positive
    b. only negative
    c. positive and/or negative
    d. neutral

7. Practitioners of TA would say that your life scripts were largely formed by your _____ and _____ experiences.
    a. educational; recreational
    b. family; cultural
    c. oedipal; pre-oedipal
    d. religious; educational

60

8. According to TA, early messages that we pick up from our parents are called
   a. conjunctions.
   b. life scripts.
   c. injunctions.
   d. redecisions.

9. When children hear and accept the parental injunction "Don't make mistakes," they may
   a. equate making mistakes with being a failure.
   b. believe that they are not important.
   c. accept the message not to seek success.
   d. play down any accomplishments.

10. When adults focus on taking care of others at the expense of their own needs and have trouble having fun, they may have received the following parental message:
    a. "Don't be important."
    b. "Don't be a child."
    c. "Don't make mistakes."
    d. "Don't be you."

11. The parental message that suggests to the child that he or she is the wrong sex, shape, size, or color, or has ideas or feelings that are unacceptable to parental figures, is
    a. "Don't belong."
    b. "Don't be you."
    c. "Don't be close."
    d. "Don't be a child."

12. Which of the following concepts in not associated with the feminist approach?
    a. connection
    b. disconnection
    c. mutual empathy and mutual empowerment
    d. life scripts

13. The concept of autonomy includes the concept(s) of:
    a. self-in-relation.
    b. self-in-context.
    c. rewriting one's life script.
    d. both (a) and (b).

14. In TA, the theory is built on the assumption that adults make decisions:
    a. only after they have explored their unconscious wishes and fears.
    b. based on past premises.
    c. in accordance with the demands placed on them by society.
    d. in early childhood, which once made, are unable to be changed.

15. Rational emotive behavior therapy and other cognitive-behavioral therapies are based on the premise that emotional and behavioral problems are:
    a. based primarily on the exploration of how people think.
    b. based on exploring early childhood trauma as a way to understand present problems.
    c. based on intense feelings that need to be expressed.
    d. based on changing behavior by changing our feelings toward given situations.

16. According to the self-in-context view, the major aim during _____ is being able to engage in intimate relationships and find satisfying work.
    a. early adulthood
    b. middle adulthood
    c. late middle age
    d. late adulthood

17. _____ was the developer of rational emotive behavior therapy.
    a. Abraham Maslow
    b. Eric Berne
    c. Albert Ellis
    d. Carl Rogers

18. According to rational emotive behavior therapy, our emotional upsets are
    a. caused by traumatic events in life.
    b. caused by rejection from those we love.
    c. caused by regression into childhood behavior.
    d. the result of our faulty thinking.

19. Rational emotive behavior therapy teaches people how to
    a. evaluate early childhood survival roles.
    b. dispute irrational beliefs.
    c. challenge faulty injunctions.
    d. control actual life events that upset us.

20. According to Ellis, most of our irrational ideas that create emotional problems are due to "musts" such as
    a. "I must perform well and win the approval of important people, or else I am an inadequate person!"
    b. "Others must treat me fairly and considerately."
    c. "My life must be easy and pleasant. I need and must have the things I want, or life is unbearable!"
    d. all of the above.

21. The attitudes and beliefs we have about ourselves and others are a direct result of things we learned from our parents or parental substitutes. The willingness to challenge this _____ is the mark of autonomy.
    a. authority figure
    b. inner child
    c. inner parent
    d. authoritative parent

22. The term "inner parent" refers to the
    a. attitudes and beliefs we hold that we've learned from our parents.
    b. values we choose for ourselves, which may differ from our parents' values.
    c. type of parent we wished we had when we were children.
    d. parental values we pass on to our children.

23. When challenging the early childhood messages that have influenced our lives, it is important to
    a. recognize that many of the values we incorporated from our parents may be healthy standards for guiding our behavior.
    b. passively accept as truth the messages we learned when we were children.
    c. blame our parents for the psychological pain we suffer.
    d. expect our parents to be different from who they are and wait for their approval.

24. The inner critic reflects the concerns of your
    a. parents.
    b. church.
    c. significant others.
    d. all of the above.

25. What is the process called that involves becoming increasingly observant and aware of external and internal stimuli in the present moment and adopting an open attitude of accepting *what is* rather than judging the present situation?
    a. self-care
    b. congruence
    c. hyperawareness
    d. mindfulness

26. People moving in the direction of autonomy
    a. find themselves in isolation and are not bound up with the quality of their relationships with others.
    b. have a desire to become both free and responsible and to do for themselves what they are capable of doing.
    c. are able to "do their own thing" irrespective of the impact of those actions on others.
    d. seek answers primarily outside themselves, looking for what others expect of them and seeking their approval.

27. The struggle toward autonomy entails
    a. sorting out our values.
    b. understanding the ways our early decisions influence our present behavior.
    c. working for our own approval, rather than living according to someone else's design.
    d. all of the above.

28. The following is characteristic behavior of people who have achieved a sense of intimacy:
    a. establishing a clear sense of their own identity.
    b. being tolerant of differences in others.
    c. trusting others and themselves in relationships.
    d. all of the above.

29. The provisional adulthood stage of development is a period in which
    a. young adults make an initial attempt to create a place for themselves in a new world and a new generation.
    b. young adults who are deemed immature for their age are given privileges on a provisional basis, which can be revoked.
    c. provisions are made for older adults to maintain privileges they have enjoyed for many years (e.g., holding a driver's license) even if their ability decreases to exercise those privileges in a safe and responsible manner.
    d. middle-aged adults are faced with providing for their aging parents and for their own children.

30. The transition from the 20s to the 30s is a time
    a. of changing values and beliefs.
    b. when inner turmoil increases for many.
    c. when people may reevaluate their life plans and make significant changes.
    d. all of the above.

31. The period in life when we reach the top of the mountain and become aware that we must begin the downhill journey is
    a. early adulthood.
    b. middle adulthood.
    c. later adulthood.
    d. not associated with any adulthood period of life.

32. Which of the following statements is *not* true with regard to aging?
    a. Being involved with family and friends is one contributing factor to leading a long and rewarding life.
    b. There is a formula for growing old with grace and dignity.
    c. Being interested in doing good for others is associated with leading a long and full life.
    d. Regular physical exercise contributes to overall good health for older adults.

33. For Erikson, the stimulus for continued growth in middle age is the core struggle of
    a. intimacy vs. isolation.
    b. identity vs. identity confusion.
    c. generativity vs. stagnation.
    d. integrity vs. despair.

34. Angela is a middle-aged woman who is a devoted parent. She is also able to balance her life with a creative career, leisure-time activities, and meaningful volunteer work. According to Erikson, Angela has successfully resolved the following psychosocial struggle:
    a. generativity vs. stagnation.
    b. integrity vs. despair.
    c. intimacy vs. isolation.
    d. identity vs. role confusion.

35. People who have a sense of generativity
   a. show little interest in making the world a better place.
   b. tend to focus more on what they can give to others than on what they can get.
   c. focus on what they can get from others.
   d. avoid risks by choosing the security provided by a routine existence.

36. A major crisis that often occurs during middle adulthood is
   a. facing retirement.
   b. establishing one's identity.
   c. coming to the realization that some of our youthful dreams will never materialize.
   d. getting established in a career.

37. Jung found that many of his clients were concerned about
   a. finding meaning in projects that had lost their meaning.
   b. resolving guilt over sexual experiences.
   c. dealing with fears of controlling their aggression.
   d. being comfortable with feelings of emptiness and flatness of life.

38. Jung believed that major life transformations were an inevitable and universal part of the human condition at
   a. late adolescence.
   b. early adulthood.
   c. middle adulthood.
   d. late adulthood.

39. According to Jung, a condition of integration of the unconscious with conscious and psychological balance is
   a. individuation.
   b. differentiation.
   c. individualism.
   d. the persona.

40. For Jung, people can bring unconscious material into awareness by paying attention to their
   a. rational thought patterns that drove them during the first half of life.
   b. emotional upsets that were caused by difficult life events.
   c. dreams and fantasies and expressing themselves through poetry, writing, music and art.
   d. inner child.

41. In *The Silent Passage*, Sheehy states that menopause
   a. represents a midlife crisis.
   b. means losing youthful looks.
   c. inevitably leads to feelings of depression.
   d. is a gateway to a second adulthood.

42. James looks back on his life with regrets, wishing that he could relive his life in such a way that he would devote more time to his family and less time to his work. According to Erikson, James has not successfully resolved the psychosocial crisis of
    a. intimacy vs. isolation.
    b. identity vs. identity confusion.
    c. generativity vs. stagnation.
    d. integrity vs. despair.

43. According to Erikson, the central issue of late adulthood is
    a. intimacy vs. isolation.
    b. integrity vs. despair.
    c. identity vs. identity confusion.
    d. generativity vs. stagnation.

44. On Ray's 63rd birthday, he mentioned to his wife that since he was approaching retirement from the company he had worked for over 30 years, he had come to terms with the fact that he was not going to reach his lifelong goal of being Vice President of the company. Ray's attitude suggests
    a. he is adapting to the challenges that are common during late middle age
    b. he is depressed about the fact that he didn't achieve his goal and is deluding himself to think he has come to terms with it.
    c. he has low self-esteem and he would not give up his dream if he had high self-esteem.
    d. he is trying to get his wife to feel sorry for him, which is a common phenomenon among men who are about to retire.

45. According to Erikson, persons who have succeeded in achieving ego integrity
    a. yearn for another chance, even though they realize that they cannot have it.
    b. view death as natural, even while living rich and meaningful lives.
    c. approach the final stage of their lives with a sense of personal fragmentation.
    d. feel that they have a lot of unfinished business.

46. _____ predisposes us to discriminate against the elderly by avoiding them or in some way victimizing them because of their age alone.
    a. Ageism
    b. Age prejudice
    c. Stereotyping
    d. Age discrimination

1. a   p. 70
2. c   p. 73
3. c   p. 73
4. a   p. 73
5. d   p. 73
6. c   p. 73
7. b   p. 74
8. c   p. 75
9. a   p. 75
10. b   p. 76
11. b   p. 76
12. d   p. 71
13. d   p. 72
14. b   p. 73
15. a   p. 78
16. a   p. 85
17. c   p. 78
18. d   p. 78
19. b   p. 79
20. d   p. 78
21. c   p. 80
22. a   p. 80
23. a   p. 80

24. d   p. 81
25. d   p. 81
26. b   p. 71
27. d   p. 72-73
28. d   p. 85, 87
29. a   p. 87
30. d   p. 89
31. b   p. 91
32. b   p. 101-102
33. c   p. 85
34. a   p. 92
35. b   p. 92
36. c   p. 91-92
37. a   p. 94
38. c   p. 94
39. a   p. 94
40. c   p. 94
41. d   p. 96
42. d   p. 86
43. b   p. 86
44. a   p. 96
45. b   p. 98
46. a   p. 98

Activities and Exercises for Classroom Participation for Chapter 3

1. Fold a good-sized piece of construction paper into thirds, and draw a picture or write a representation of your *past*, *present*, and *future*. Use any symbols you want, and design your poster in any way that seems to best represent the past as you remember it, the present as you experience it now, and the future you think you might have. Take about 20 minutes to draw your poster, and then share it in your group.

2. As a variation of the preceding exercise, draw the past that you *wish* you had experienced, the present you'd *like* to have, and the future you *hope* for. Compare this chart with the earlier one.

3. As a "homework assignment," make a collage of things that you feel represent yourself—the person that *you* see yourself as being. Try to stay with pictures only; try not to use many words. After you complete your collage, bring it to your group and discuss why you chose the pictures, colors, background, and organization.

4. Write down several of the important turning points in your life. Briefly describe how you have been affected by these turning points—the choices you made, and so on. Discuss them in your group.

5. Write your own book about yourself! Begin with yourself as an infant, and project your life through to the end. Poetry, pictures, drawings, and key phrases can be used to describe your life as you see it from beginning to end. As a variation, recreate a segment of your life (or your whole life, if you wish) that you would like to have experienced differently. In your small group, discuss how you could make this recreation a reality.

6. Use various collected objects to represent yourself. Several variations are possible. You might bring a cherished object from home that you feel tells something important about who you are. Another idea is to take 10 to 15 minutes alone and find something in nature or on the campus that you feel represents you in some way. Bring the object to your group, and share it with the others. What do you imagine your father, mother, sister, brother, or best friend might have picked to represent you?

7. Discuss with your group how free you feel at this time in your life. How do you think you could be a freer person? Who or what hinders you in making decisions that affect your life? You might discuss some of the most important choices you've made and tell how these choices have affected you. In what ways are you the person you are today as a result of the choices you've made or failed to make?

8. Reflect on some specific ways you would like to be the same as (and different from) your parents, particularly in regard to the ways that you would like to relate to your own children. Discuss your thoughts in your group.

9. Imagine your own children speaking about their relationship with you. If you don't have children, imagine that you do. What would you most want them to say about you? What do you most fear that they might say?

10. This exercise in role reversal is designed to help you "become your parents"—that is, enter their psychological worlds. Each class member decides whether he or she wants to become his or her mother or father. After the roles are assumed, the group talks about life in terms of such questions as "What do I have in life? What do I treasure? How do I feel about living? What are my values and basic beliefs? What concerns me the most? What are the joys in my life? What ways do I like myself? Dislike myself? What hurt do I experience? How close do I feel to my children? What do I think my future might be?" The idea is for students to become the parent of their choice and to speak in the manner they imagine their parent would. Then they can consider how much they are like or unlike their parents. In what ways have they identified with their father or mother? After the exercise, they can discuss what they felt during the exercise and what they learned from it.

11. Develop a chart summarizing some of the main areas of concern you have faced or are now facing in young adulthood. This chart can highlight choices pertaining to education, career, religion, lifestyle, intimate relationships, and so forth. Along with some of the choices you are faced with (or were faced with at this time in your life), write down how earlier experiences have influenced these later choices. This could make for valuable discussion material in small groups.

12. Summarize the main injunctions you received as a child. Bring your list to class, and in a small group explore the injunctions that have had the *greatest* impact on you. What are the circumstances surrounding these injunctions? In what ways have you helped to keep these injunctions alive through a self-indoctrination process? How do you think they have negatively influenced your self-concept? Elect a recorder in your group to summarize the most commonly mentioned injunctions and their effects.

13. List some of the early decisions you made. What decisions did you make as a child or adolescent that you still live by? Have you examined most of your early decisions? Some examples of early decisions are "It's better not to feel, so that I won't hurt," "I'll do what they expect so they'll approve of me."

14. Compare the struggles between women and men during the time of young adulthood. One idea would be to have small groups (all women and all men in separate groups) with the task of discussing ways they see pressures and conflicts unique to gender-roles. The groups can then form as an entire class and share their results.

15. A panel could be formed to discuss each of the topics covered in this book, as related to the young adulthood period. What are some major concerns of young adults (say in the 18 to 27 age bracket) in areas such as sexuality, dealing with loneliness, career choice, meaning and values, lifestyle choices, and so forth? How does this compare with the young adulthood period from ages 27 to 35? Each panelist could focus on one area and present some ideas for a few minutes. The panel could then interact as a panel, and the rest of the class can get involved in the discussion stimulated by the panel presentation. (This is a good way to tie this chapter into most of the topics that will be discussed in the book and the course.)

16. Look at the examples of elderly people who are challenging the stereotypes. What do these people have in common? Do any of them offer you inspiration and hope as you think about your aging?

17. If you have not yet reached middle age, interview or simply talk with several people you know in this age bracket. What are some of their concerns? Are there any things that stand out they wished they had done differently? How do they see their future? Thinking about how others are living during these years could be instrumental in helping you make choices now that will influence what you will someday say about your own middle-age years.

18. Observe and talk with some people in their later years. You can ask them some of the same questions as above. It may also be useful to simply ask them to tell you whatever they'd like and what it is like to be the age they are. and get a picture this way.

19. Project yourself into old age. Select an age and imagine your life at this time. In small groups, discuss how you imagine your life might be then. How would you like your life to be? What do you have to do now to make this happen? How do you fear your life might be like during your old age?

CHAPTER 4: YOUR BODY AND WELLNESS

Outline

Chapter Objectives

- to put wellness in the context of making life choices

- to provide an overview of sound health practices

- to challenge readers to make decisions about health and wellness

- to encourage readers to evaluate their thoughts and feelings about bodily identity

Questions for Thought, Class Discussion, and Evaluation

1. An examination of the choices you are making about your body and your overall wellness can reveal a great deal concerning your feelings about your life. What resources do you have to modify those aspects of your lifestyle that affect your bodily well-being?

2. What does the phrase "choosing wellness as a lifestyle" mean to you? In what way is wellness an active lifestyle choice, rather than a one-time decision?

3. What are some differences between wellness and the absence of illness?

4. How is wellness related to a balanced life involving our physical, emotional, social, mental, and spiritual needs?

5. How is sleep related to overall health?

6. If you have problems sleeping, what are some suggestions for preventing and coping with insomnia?

7. What are some of the main benefits of regular exercise?

8. What are some risks associated with exercise?

9. Designing an adequate program of physical activity is difficult for many people. Do you experience difficulties in exercising? Is so, what are these difficulties?

10. Discuss your thoughts about the axiom "You are what you eat." How would you describe your eating patterns?

11. Dr. Andrew Weil believes *what* and *how* we eat are critical determinants of how we feel and how we age. What are your thought about this?

12. Spirituality has many meanings and plays greater or lesser roles in different people's lives. What does spirituality mean to you? Do you see spirituality related to a balance in your life? What does spirituality mean to you?

13. What does the concept of accepting responsibility for your body mean to you? What are your thoughts about physicians who prescribe pills to alleviate bodily symptoms? What does this say about choice and responsibility? Can you think of any ways that you might be a victim of your body? Are there some ways that you'd like to assume a greater share of control of your body?

14. What are the components of your bodily identity?

15. How can the chronic practice of "swallowing" emotions take a physical toll on your body?

16. What is meant by "experiencing your body"? How can people do this through dance and movement?

17. What is the importance of touch, from the perspective of both physical and psychological health?

18. What is the meaning of the concept of body image? How does your view of your body have an impact on choices in other areas of your life? Where did you acquire your attitudes about your body image?

19. Do some of your present feelings and attitudes about your body have anything to do with decisions you made about your body during adolescence?

20. What are some ways that weight is associated with one's body image in this culture?

Glossary of Key Terms

Holistic approach is based on the assumption that the mind and body are an integral unit that cannot be separated.

Holistic health focuses on all facets of human functioning --- psychological, social, intellectual, and spiritual --- and a process whereby both physician and patient share responsibility for health decisions.

Wellness is an active process consisting of conscious choices we make in fashioning a healthy lifestyle.

The wellness process involves identifying personal goals, prioritizing these goals and values, making an action plan, and making a commitment to follow through on these plans.

Eating disorders are severe disturbances in eating behavior that are characterized by reoccupation with weight and unhealthy efforts to control weight.

Nutrition pertains to our food consumption and the processes involved by which we use the nutrients required for growth and survival.

Anorexia nervosa is an eating disorder characterized by intense fear of gaining weight, disturbed body image, and dangerous methods to lose weight.

Sleep deprivation involves not getting adequate sleep, which results in moodiness, continuing tiredness, difficulty in concentrating, and falling asleep at inopportune times (e.g., while attending a class, at work).

Bodily identity refers to one's awareness of how they experience their body through movement and touch.

Body image is the way in which one perceives his or her body in terms of size, appearance, health, proportion of body parts, etc.

Spirituality encompasses our relationship to the universe and is an avenue for finding meaning and purpose in living.

Religion refers to a set of beliefs that connect an individual to a higher power or a God.

TEST ITEMS FOR CHAPTER 4
YOUR BODY AND WELLNESS

1. According to the Coreys, accepting responsibility for our body entails
   a. choosing a lifestyle to maintain the body we want.
   b. realizing that we can control our body to a great extent.
   c. realizing we are active agents, not passive victims.
   d. all of the above.

2. Holistic health tends to focus on
   a. identifying symptoms of illness and curing disease.
   b. the relationship between our body and the psychological, social, intellectual, and spiritual aspects of ourselves.
   c. discovering the appropriate medicine for a given ailment.
   d. healing with herbs.

3. The following is *not* a factor that characterizes a wellness lifestyle:
   a. assuming responsibility for the actions and quality of health for both yourself and your loved ones.
   b. having a genuine concern for others and being tolerant of imperfections in others.
   c. being willing to devote time and energy to developing a sound basis for making good decisions about health.
   d. assuming personal responsibility for one's actions and the quality of one's health.

4. In their *Wellness Workbook*, Travis and Ryan describe wellness as
   a. a bridge that is supported by two piers, self-responsibility and love.
   b. simply the sum of separate parts.
   c. the absence of illness and low illness risk.
   d. something that merely happens to you.

5. Physicians report that it is common for patients to be more interested in _____ than
   a. getting pills and removing symptoms; changing a stressful lifestyle
   b. changing a stressful lifestyle; getting pills and removing symptoms
   c. having surgery; taking pills
   d. over-the-counter drugs; prescription medications

6. Concerning physical illness, with which statement would Bernie Siegel most likely *disagree*?
   a. When we are not meeting our emotional and spiritual needs, we are setting ourselves up for physical illness.
   b. One of the most common precursors of cancer is a traumatic loss or a feeling of emptiness in one's life.
   c. A physician's role is simply finding right treatments for healing his or her patients from disease.
   d. Illness serves some function, and illness makes sense if we look at what is going on with people who become physically ill.

7. Kevin had thrown himself completely into his work as a CEO of a large corporation until he had a series of heart attacks that had him reevaluating his self-destructive path. The following patterns of living can help Kevin move towards a healthy lifestyle:
   a. taking the time to seriously reflect on the direction he is going with his life.
   b. making a decision to take an active part in changing his life on many levels.
   c. seeking balance between his work life and leisure time.
   d. all of the above.

8. More health insurance companies are providing payment for
   a. faith healers.
   b. herbal medicine and vitamin therapy.
   c. preventive medicine as well as remediation.
   d. changing problematic lifestyles.

9. Tracey wants to get a healthier lifestyle but keeps telling herself that she doesn't have time to eat three balanced meals a day or exercise on a regular basis. She is using the following defense mechanism for not changing patterns of behavior that are affecting her health:
   a. denial.
   b. projection.
   c. rationalization.
   d. reaction-formation.

10. Which of the following statements is *not* true?
    a. Spiritual practices may be as important to your overall well-being as eating and exercising.
    b. A comprehensive view of health includes nourishing both your body and your spirit.
    c. Getting adequate rest and sleep is not related to overall health.
    d. Exercise is essential for cardiovascular fitness.

11. Exercise has a number of benefits. Which of the following is *not* one that is listed in the text?
    a. Releasing anger, tension, and anxiety
    b. Slowing down the aging process
    c. Preventing hypertension
    d. Decreasing the supply of endorphins

12. Research has shown that people who consistently sleep less than _____ hours or those who sleep more than _____ hours show elevated mortality risk.
    a. 5; 9
    b. 7; 8
    c. 6; 10
    d. 7; 10

13. One form of exercise that most people can do on a regular basis, which helps their heart, lungs, and circulatory system is
    a. running
    b. Pilates
    c. brisk walking
    d. playing baseball

14. Which of the following statements is *false*?
    a. The quantity of sleep matters more than the quality.
    b. The amount of sleep that is normal for different individuals can vary.
    c. It is possible to get more sleep than you need.
    d. Most people experience difficulty in falling asleep at least occasionally.

15. Which of the following statements is *false*?
    a. Spirituality is a key ingredient in a balanced life.
    b. Spirituality often helps us discover unity in the universe.
    c. It is not possible to be deeply spiritual without being religious.
    d. Feeding your soul may be as important as feeding your body for your overall health.

16. Our bodies express themselves through the
    a. chest, which can develop armor that inhibits the free flowing of crying, laughing, and breathing.
    b. neck, which can hold back expressions of anger or crying, as well as holding on the tensions.
    c. diaphragm, which can restrict the expression of rage and pain.
    d. all of the above.

17. According to the Coreys, the chronic practice of "swallowing emotions"
    a. can take a physical toll on our body.
    b. is a good way to deal with grief and anger.
    c. is a desirable way to deal with stress.
    d. generally will lead to experiencing more joy.

18. The following is *not* true concerning unexpressed emotions:
    a. Unexpressed emotions can manifest themselves in physical symptoms.
    b. Over time, unexpressed emotions will simply disappear.
    c. There is a direct relationship between a person's physical constipation and his or her emotional constipation.
    d. When we seal off emotions such as grief and anger, we also keep ourselves from experiencing intense joy.

19. Experiencing your body can be accomplished by
    a. paying attention to your senses of touch, taste, smell, seeing, and hearing.
    b. taking time to be aware of how your body is interacting with the environment.
    c. treating yourself to a massage.
    d. expressing yourself through dancing.
    e. all of the above.

20. Regarding the need to be touched,
    a. some research shows that it is necessary for healthy development.
    b. it is the same across all cultures.
    c. it is almost always sexually motivated.
    d. it has little to do with family of origin.

21. When Harlow and Harlow studied the effects of maternal deprivation on monkeys, they found that when infant monkeys were reared in isolation during the first six months after birth, they
    a. immediately fit in socially when introduced to other monkeys.
    b. adapted socially after some initial hesitation.
    c. showed serious inadequacies in their social and sexual behavior in later life.
    d. had the same sexual behavior as monkeys not raised in isolation.

22. According to the Coreys, our body image
    a. has little to do with our adjustment in other areas of life.
    b. is determined mainly by how others perceive us.
    c. has nothing to do with cultural messages about our body.
    d. is an important part of our self-concept.

23. Elaine is self-conscious about her body and thinks "If I don't have the ideal body, people won't like me." She also believes there is nothing she can do to change her appearance. She is exhibiting
    a. common self-defeating thoughts about body image.
    b. a judgmental view of how others perceive her.
    c. the first step towards challenging self-defeating patterns.
    d. a realistic view of how her looks affect her relationships with others.

24. If you feel that you are basically unattractive, you may
    a. tell yourself that others will see your defects and not want to be with you.
    b. contribute to the reactions that others have towards you by the messages you send them.
    c. be perceived by others as aloof, distant, or judgmental.
    d. want to get close to others but be frightened of the possibility of meeting rejection.
    e. all of the above.

25. When we unquestioningly accept certain cultural messages about our bodies, we are
    a. prone to develop feelings of shame.
    b. likely to set and meet goals in keeping with cultural expectations.
    c. being realistic in what we need to look like in order to be successful in our society.
    d. making decisions about our bodies that cannot be changed.

26. People who find that their weight is significantly affecting the way they feel about their body, yet are unable to lose weight, may give the following reason for their failure to do so:
    a. "I've tried every diet program there is, and I just can't seem to stick to one."
    b. "Every time I've lost weight, I've put it on again."
    c. "I don't particularly like the way I look, but it takes too much effort to change it."
    d. all of the above.

27. Regarding weight problems and body image,
    a. the same standards for ideal weight holds true across all cultures.
    b. anorexia and bulimia are frequently linked to the internalization of unrealistic standards.
    c. there are no "payoffs" to being overweight.
    d. overweight people overeat simply because they get too hungry between meals.

28. Making a change in one's lifestyle
    a. almost always happens shortly after recognizing the need to change
    b. is a process, not a single event
    c. almost always is related to a significant loss
    d. will not be permanent in the vast majority of cases

29. Which of the following statements is *not* true about weight problems?
    a. A basic change in attitude and lifestyle is important in successfully dealing with a weight problem.
    b. People with weight problems eat simply because they are hungry.
    c. People with weight problems may eat in response to external cues in their environment.
    d. There is no injunction that you must change your lifestyle even if you have a problem with weight.

30. Samantha, who is taking a heavy course load this semester, has been falling asleep in class and at home when she studies. She also seems moody, irritable, overly sensitive to criticism, tense, and she has difficulty concentrating and remembering things. A likely cause of these symptoms is
    a. a boring instructor.
    b. course material that is too difficult for her to comprehend.
    c. sleep deprivation.
    d. early onset Alzheimer's Disease

1. d p. 108
2. b p. 108-109
3. a p. 109
4. a p. 109
5. a p. 111
6. c p. 110
7. d p. 111
8. c p. 111
9. c p. 112
10. c p. 114
11. d p. 115-116
12. b p. 114
13. c p. 115
14. a p. 114
15. c p. 119-120
16. d p. 121
17. a p. 121
18. b p. 121
19. e p. 122
20. a p. 123
21. c p. 123
22. d p. 123
23. a p. 123
24. e p. 123-124
25. a p. 124
26. d p. 125
27. b p. 127
28. b p. 130
29. b p. 128
30. c p. 114

Activities and Exercises for Classroom Participation for Chapter 4

1. You may have become motivated enough to want to actively work at changing a pattern of behavior that is related to the health of your body. Some examples of self-directed programs are eliminating tobacco (or alcohol or some other drug); designing an effective exercise program; developing a systematic approach to maintaining an appropriate weight; and reducing stress. Be sure to keep observational records in your journal. After looking over a week's records, decide on a plan for action and then keep track of your progress. Begin your program of change by consulting a book such as *Self-Directed Behavior: Self-Modification for Personal Adjustment,* by Watson and Tharp (2007) for the details of setting up a program. What follows is an adaptation and modification of these authors' systematic model for self-directed change:

   a. **Observe your behavior** by focusing your awareness on what you're doing. Keep a record of your behavior. You might carry in your pocket a small notebook to keep track of behaviors (and feelings associated with them) that you want to change.

   b. **Develop a contract.** After you've increased your awareness of a particular behavior pattern, you can devise a plan for change. This involves, first, negotiating a working contract with yourself, your counselor, or another person and, second, actually doing things to change. These two steps make up the action phase of the program.

   c. **Select your goals.** What do *you* want for yourself? How do you want to be different? Make them specific rather than vague.

   d. **Translate your goals into target behaviors.** What are the behaviors you need to change or acquire in order to reach your goal? What specific behaviors would you like to increase? What behaviors do you want to decrease? How might you reach your goal?

   e. **Arrange to get information and feedback.** If you want to know how effective your new behavior is, it's essential to get reactions from others and think about them. Is your changed behavior working for you?

   e. **Revise your plan of action as needed.** The more you learn about yourself and the impact you have on others, the more you can refine your plans to change.

The following exercise is an alternative one that employs a behavioral approach to making changes in health habits.

2. We know what is healthy and unhealthy for us, yet we often have difficulties in committing ourselves to a plan for change. Even if you are determined to change certain lifestyle patterns, taking the first step is often difficult. You can find support groups and clinics to help you develop a course of action. If you are interested in making these changes on your own, consider getting involved in a self-directed behavior modification program, which involves the application of the principles of learning to changing specific behavior. The assumption is that any behavior that is learned can also be unlearned. Behaviors in that are not working effectively for us can be reduced or eliminated and then replaced by a set of attitudes and behaviors that will work.

Behavior modification is particularly appropriate if you are working at weight control or smoking control. Below is a summary of the essence of a behavior-modification program:

(a) The first step is to specify the target behavior. Vague statements about problematic behavior must be changed into clear statements about specific behaviors that you are willing to change.

(b) Next comes the process of simply monitoring your present behavior so you can become aware of what you are doing.

(c) The third step consists of designing a program, or a plan for change. It is essential that your plan be systematic and clear and that you reward yourself for carrying it out. A written contract can be of value here.

(d) As you carry out your plan, you will need to revise and fine-tune your program. This will entail finding strategies for dealing with setbacks and the discouragement that comes from meeting barriers to change.

(e) The final step consists of evaluating how effective it has been.

3. Introduce the topic of the importance of personal wellness for class discussion. Emphasize to your students the link between wellness and life choices – that personal wellness is not simply something that happens to them, rather it is the result of life choices. Students might well know that they *should* take care of themselves, yet not translate what they know into action. Encourage students to make an assessment of their current attitudes and behaviors in the area of personal health and to understand the effect of their habits on their academic success and well-being.

4. Ask students to take the Where Am I Now? and use their responses as the basis for a class discussion. After students take this inventory, ask them what it indicates about their priorities about wellness. Ask what wellness means to them.

5. Suggest to your students that they make an assessment of their overall health patterns [rest, exercise, diet, and nutrition]. The discussion of maintaining sound health practices can be the focus of either entire class activity or a small group activity. To make this assessment, ask your students to discuss the following questions:

Rest. Are you currently getting adequate sleep? If you are not, what gets in your way? How is this affecting different aspects of your life?

Exercise. What kind of exercise might you want to incorporate into your lifestyle? What campus or community resources are available (fitness center, gymnasium, exercise rooms)?

Diet. Do you think your diet contributes to the way you feel? How do your nutritional habits help or hinder you in being the kind of student you would like to be? How can campus resources help you in establishing and maintaining a good diet?

Spirituality. What does spirituality mean to you? What contributes to a meaningful life for you? What do you want to do about finding meaning and purpose in your life that you are not currently doing? Are there any resources on campus or in your community that address spiritual needs?

Once students make this assessment of their patterns of rest, exercise, diet, and spirituality, they can pinpoint some changes in specific areas that they might want to make. Most students will need some guidance and structure in establishing an action plan.

If your students decide they want to take better care of themselves, emphasize that it is good to avoid overwhelming themselves with doing everything at once. Suggest that they select a few target behaviors (such as eating balanced meals, or exercising, or taking some time for fun) and develop a self-directed action plan (which is outlined in the first exercise above). Ask students to write down what they are willing to change, how they will go about making the changes, and who they will use for support. Tell your students they are likely to find it more effective if they include others in helping them follow through with the commitments they make.

6. Arrange four small groups, one for each area pertaining to overall wellness: rest, exercise, diet, and spirituality. Ask students to join the group whose topic is of particular interest to them. As them to explore in the small group issues such as:

- What do you particularly like about some of your current behavior?

- What are you doing that you'd like to build upon?

- What is one behavior that you'd like to change?

- What ideas do you have for ways that you could go about making the change?

- If you were now doing what you'd like to be doing in this area, how would your life be different?

7.   Ask students to go to the student cafeteria and take note of the fast food that is readily available. This could stimulate a discussion of the responsibility we have for keeping ourselves well or sick.

8.   Suggest to students that they form a panel on the topic of the value of exercise. Each person on the panel could select one form of exercise and make a brief presentation of its values and provide some hints for successfully maintaining the program.

9.   If students decide that exercise if of value in their life and that they are willing to make it a priority, have them write down a plan for the next two weeks including the kind of exercise and approximate length of time they'll spend doing it each day. Then, for this two-week period ask them to chart their actual exercising activity on their calendar and to report on this in their journal.

10. Introduce the topic of body image. Have the class bring pictures from magazines and talk about what the images tell us we should look like. Discuss how the media defines beauty. Talk about how we buy into its pressures and the effects on us. Do your students have any reactions to the personal stories in the chapter that describe individuals' struggles with body image and weight?

11. Students often do not pay attention to the messages of the body. After reading the section dealing with your bodily identity suggest the following exercise to your class as a way to pay attention to what their bodies could be telling them.

If you have a headache or a stomachache, let your body reveal its message to you. In your journal, actually have a dialogue between some part of your body – or a symptom – and write what that body part or symptom might be telling you. Your aches may be telling you, "I can't take being overworked anymore." Or an upset stomach may be saying, "I am torn between wanting to do well and fearing that I'll do horribly." This dialogue with a body symptom can help you realize how you might be converting anxiety into a physical symptom.

CHAPTER 5: MANAGING STRESS

Outline

Chapter Objectives

- to examine the sources of stress

- to understand that we have control over stress

- to explore the relationship of our beliefs to the experience of stress

- to understand the basic causes and treatments for posttraumatic stress disorder

- to provide a context for understanding sexual abuse and harassment

- to describe various approaches to managing stress

Questions for Thought, Class Discussion, and Evaluation

1. Give your interpretation of this quote: "Either you control your stress, or stress controls you."

2. List and describe the major sources of stress.

3. What are some examples of environmental sources of stress that you face in a typical week? What are some ways you might reduce these stresses?

82

4. How are frustration, conflict, change, and pressure key elements of psychological stress? Write down some of the major conflicts, frustrations, and pressures that you deal with, and think about some ways that you might cope differently with these psychological stresses. How do they affect you emotionally and physically? How are these stresses related to your ability to form interpersonal relationships?

5. Discuss the notion that you don't have to allow yourself to be victimized by the psychological and physiological effects of stress. How does your interpretation of life events define what is and is not stressful? If you cannot always change or control external reality, how can you at least respond to stress in different ways?

6. What is the relationship of emotions (and stress) to the development of psychophysiological (psychosomatic) disorders?

7. Discuss the notions of depressing, angering, and headaching—as opposed to getting depressed, becoming angry, and having a headache. In what way can we have control over what we do, even though it may be difficult to control our feelings and thoughts?

8. In what ways might a life-threatening illness be a "wake-up call" to change the way you are living?

9. In your own life, can you think of any examples of how your body has paid a price for not coping with stress effectively?

10. What are the characteristics of people with a hardy personality? What are some of the distinguishing characteristics of hardiness as a personality style as it applies to dealing with stress? How can hardiness act as a buffer against distress and illness in coping with the stresses associated with change?

11. What are some of the basic differences between destructive reactions to stress and constructive responses to stress?

12. What is burnout? How can burnout result from chronic stress? Have you experienced any key signs of burnout, either as a student or in your work? What are some coping skills you can use to deal effectively with the effects of burnout?

13. What are the characteristics of constructive coping as behavioral reactions to stress? List as many different kinds of stress buffers as you can think of that could be of value to you in dealing creatively with everyday stress.

14. In what ways might the effects of early childhood incestuous experiences carry over into adulthood? How can psychotherapy be of value in helping incest victims work through early psychological scars?

15, What are some of the ways that posttraumatic stress disorders (PTSD) have increasingly become a topic of central concern?

16. How might your self-talk and your beliefs contribute to your experience of stress? What cognitive techniques could you use to lessen the impact of stress in your life?

17. How can acquiring a sense of humor be a powerful antidote to physical illness and stress?

18. What are some of the key principles of yoga? How can it be a useful way to prevent the negative impact of stress?

19. How is meditation a constructive response to stress? In your own words, describe the essence of meditation.

20. What are the basic attitudes associated with the practice of mindfulness?

21. List as many forms of relaxation as you can and state how relaxation is a stress buffer.

22. How is therapeutic massage a good way to deal with the negative impact of stress?

Glossary of Key Terms

Stress is an event or series of events that leads to strain, which often results in physical and psychological health problems.

Eustress is "good stress" that provides individuals with the necessary motivation to strive for the best.

Distress pertains to the negative effects of stress that can deplete individuals and lead to fragmentation.

Frustration entails something blocking attainment of one's needs and goals.

Conflict is a source of stress that occurs when two or more incompatible motivations or behavioral impulses compete for expression.

Approach/approach conflicts occur when a choice must be made between two or more attractive or desirable alternatives.

Avoidance/avoidance conflicts arise when a choice must be made between two or more unattractive or undesirable goals.

Approach/avoidance conflicts are produced when a choice must be between two or more goals, each of which has attractive and unattractive elements.

Change can be a source of stress when it involves readjustment in our living circumstances.

Pressure can be a source of conflict when it involves expectations and demands for behaving in certain ways.

Fight-or-flight is a response whereby the body goes on alert status and ready for aggressive action to meet a threatening situation.

Psychosomatic illness is some kind of physical illness that is largely caused by psychological factors (such as stress).

Posttraumatic stress disorder (PTSD) is an anxiety disorder resulting from a traumatic event and characterized by symptoms of reexperiencing the trauma, avoidance and numbing, and hyperarousal.

Critical incident stress management is a comprehensive, integrative, multicomponent crisis intervention system that is cost-effective, yet powerful.

Incest involves any form of inappropriate sexual behavior that is brought about by coercion or deception between two people who are related.

Child sexual abuse involves an adult engaging in sexual contact of any kind with a child.

Sexual harassment involves unwelcome sexual advances, gestures, requests for sexual favors, and other verbal or physical conduct of a sexual nature in the workplace or in the academic setting.

Acquaintance rape is a sexual assault by a friend or date; committed by someone whom the victim knows.

Date rape is forced and unwanted intercourse with someone in the context of dating.

Resilience is the capacity of individuals to bounce back from major stress events with minimal negative effects.

Constructive coping strategies are relatively healthful behavioral reactions to stress.

Hardiness is a personality pattern characterized by an appetite for challenge, a sense of commitment, and a strong sense of being in control of one's life.

Hardy personality implies being resistant to the effects of stress because of certain personal characteristics.

Burnout is a state of physical, emotional, intellectual, and spiritual exhaustion characterized by feelings of helplessness and hopelessness.

Time management is a strategy to managing stress by learning how to effectively schedule tasks.

Meditation is a process of directing our attention to a single, unchanging or repetitive stimulus aimed at personal transformation; it is a tool to increase awareness, become centered, and achieve an internal focus.

Mindfulness helps us to slow down and experience what we are doing by clearing out our mind and calming our body; it is aimed at keeping us in the here and now, focusing on *what is* rather than *what if*.

Progressive muscular relaxation is a technique to be practiced that leads to deep relaxation.

Relaxation response is a simple meditative technique designed to control blood pressure, body temperature, respiration rate, heart rate, and oxygen consumption; it is a self-regulatory technique to prevent stress-related illnesses.

Yoga is a way of life that involves practice of certain mental states and physical stretching exercises; it enables us to use the strengths we already have and build on them.

Massage therapy is a treatment that teaches people how to release muscular tightness often associated with facing stress; it is aimed at reducing pain, increasing alertness, reducing depression, and enhancing immune function.

TEST ITEMS FOR CHAPTER 5
MANAGING STRESS

1. Stress can be considered
   a. an inevitable part of life.
   b. something that we must learn how to cope with.
   c. something that can threaten our physical and psychological well-being.
   d. all of the above.

2. Concerning the relationship between stress and your body, with which statement would Bernie Siegel most likely *disagree*?
   a. Chronic patterns of intense stress lead to lowering of the efficiency of the body's disease-fighting cells.
   b. Cultures that place a high value on cooperation and collectivism produce the least stress.
   c. Cultures that emphasize competition and individualism produce the least stress.
   d. The level of stress is largely determined by cultural factors.

3. PTSD is an acronym for
   a. Posttraumatic Stress Disorder
   b. Posttraumatic Stress Diagnosis
   c. Post Tragic Stress Disorder
   d. Post Tragic Shock Disorder

4. Mary got up late and drove through congested traffic to register for classes. When she arrived at her college campus, she had to wait in a long line, only to find that many of the courses she wanted to take were filled. Mary was dealing with the following source of stress:
   a. psychological.
   b. life changes.
   c. environmental.
   d. routine.

5. All of the following are considered psychological sources of stress *except*
   a. frustration.
   b. conflict.
   c. pressure.
   d. psychosomatic disorders.
   e. change.

6. Joe has been looking for a job ever since he graduated from college. After a long search he was offered two jobs, both having excellent pay, good benefits, and opportunity for advancement. Joe was torn between two desirable alternatives and was facing the following type of conflict:
   a. approach/avoidance conflict.
   b. approach/approach conflict.
   c. multiple approach/avoidance conflict.
   d. avoidance/avoidance conflict.

7. Mary has been looking for a position since graduation and was offered a challenging job that can lead to advancement in a field she is eager to enter. The only problem is the fact that the job entails moving and she is reluctant to leave friends and family. In attempting to make a decision, Mary is struggling with the following type of conflict:
   a. approach/avoidance conflict.
   b. approach/approach conflict.
   c. multiple approach/avoidance conflict.
   d. avoidance/avoidance conflict.

For numbers. 8–10, match the type of conflict with the appropriate description below.
8. Approach/avoidance conflict
9. Approach/approach conflict
10. Avoidance/avoidance conflict

   a. arises when a choice must be made between two or more unattractive or undesirable goals.
   b. is produced when a choice must be made between two or more goals, each of which has attractive and unattractive elements.
   c. occurs when a choice must be made between two or more attractive or desirable alternatives.

11. The "fight-or-flight" response
    a. helps us get ready for aggressive action.
    b. involves biochemical changes that can lead to chronic stress and anxiety.
    c. can lead to a variety of psychosomatic disorders.
    d. all of the above.

12. Psychosomatic, or psychophysiological, disorders are
    a. real bodily disorders manifested in disabling physical symptoms yet caused by emotional factors and the prolonged effects of stress.
    b. caused by irrational thinking.
    c. illnesses suffered only by people who are hypochondriacs.
    d. likely to occur when our defense mechanisms are shattered.

13. Sex is abused when it
    a. is manipulative.
    b. is aimed at dominating another person.
    c. evokes guilt.
    d. is the tool of aggression and control.
    e. all of the above.

14. In the following case, the abuse of sexuality is indicated by the fact that power is misused, or a trusting relationship is betrayed for the purpose of gaining control over the individual:
    a. incest.
    b. date and acquaintance rape.
    c. sexual harassment.
    d. all of the above.

15. In the case of sexual abuse, a common denominator lies in the reluctance of victims to disclose that they have been wronged. This reluctance has often been due to
    a. the "blaming the victim" syndrome.
    b. victimization.
    c. Denial.
    d. betrayal of trust.

16. The effects of incest that takes place in early childhood
    a. are often carried over into adulthood.
    b. are generally forgotten and do not affect the victim in adult life.
    c. make it almost impossible to form intimate relationships during adolescence.
    d. always leads to promiscuity.

17. A reason children who have been sexually abused give for not telling others about the abuse is
    a. feeling ashamed.
    b. hoping to protect other siblings from the incest.
    c. fearing the consequences of telling.
    d. fearing that others might not believe them.
    e. all of the above.

18. Carey was victimized by her father when she was a little child. As an adult, she may experience the effects of incest through
    a. an inability to form sexually satisfying relationships.
    b. having difficulty trusting men who express affection for her, thinking they will take advantage of her.
    c. blaming all men for her feelings of guilt and her betrayal and victimization.
    d. all of the above.

19. Veronika Tracy conducted a research study to determine the impact of childhood sexual abuse on women's sexuality. She found that women with a reported history of sexual abuse in childhood—compared with women who were not sexually abused—tended to have
    a. fewer sexual problems.
    b. more interest in engaging in sex.
    c. higher propensity for sexual fantasies that involved force and guilt feelings about these fantasies.
    d. more satisfaction with sexual partners.

20. In the Coreys' work with women who have a history of sexual abuse, they found it was therapeutic for the women to
    a. simply share the burden associated with the abuse that they have been carrying alone for many years.
    b. accept the reality that they were indeed victims and learn to direct their anger inward.
    c. confront the victimizer in-group.
    d. cut off their feelings as a survival tactic.

21. In her therapeutic practice with female victims of incest, Susan Forward attempts to achieve the following goal:
    a. to assist the client to internalize the guilt, rage, shame, hurt, fear, and confusion that has surfaced.
    b. to help the client realize that she will probably remain psychologically victimized for the rest of her life.
    c. to help the victim place responsibility for the incest primarily with the aggressor.
    d. to help the victim take responsibility for her part in the incest.

22. Women who are raped by people they know
    a. generally do not feel guilt over the incident.
    b. are never able to psychologically recover and trust again.
    c. do not take responsibility for what occurred.
    d. take responsibility for the incident and are generally embarrassed or afraid of reporting the rape.

23. _____ is considered to be repeated and unwanted sexually oriented behavior in the form of comments, gestures, or physical contacts.
    a. Sexual abuse
    b. Sexual harassment
    c. Incest
    d. Pre-rape behavior

24. The following is *not* true about sexual harassment:
    a. Sexual harassment reduces people to objects to be demeaned.
    b. Sexual harassment is an issue of abuse of the power differential between two people.
    c. The person doing the harassing may not see his behavior as problematic and may even joke about it.
    d. Men experience sexual harassment more frequently than women.

25. The following is *not* an example of sexual harassment:
    a. repeated and unwanted staring, comments, or propositions of a sexual nature.
    b. conversations tinted with sexually suggestive innuendoes or double meanings.
    c. asking someone in the workplace for a date.
    d. questions about one's sexual behavior.

26. Which of the following events would be least likely to cause PTSD?
    a. a natural disaster
    b. sexual assault
    c. a disagreement with a friend
    d. a terrorist attack

27. _____ are _____ symptoms of PTSD.
    a. Intrusive thoughts, flashbacks, and nightmares; not
    b. Intrusive thoughts, flashbacks, and nightmares; common
    c. Alienation, avoidance, and agitation; rare
    d. Alienation, avoidance, and agitation; not

28. Which of the following statements is NOT true?
    a. Women are diagnosed with PTSD more often than men.
    b. Women encounter fewer traumatic events than men.
    c. The vast majority of people who experience traumatic or tragic events do not develop PTSD.
    d. Developing PTSD can be greatly reduced for most people if help is available within six months after the incident.

29. Adult survivors of childhood trauma
    a. need to tell their story and be heard if healing is to occur.
    b. should not tell their story since it will stir up painful feelings and memories.
    c. should avoid group psychotherapy as a treatment modality due to their vulnerabilities.
    d. have a relatively easy time separating their past trauma from their current realities.

30. Researchers have addressed the question of who stays well and why. Kobasa identified a personality pattern that is characterized by an appetite for challenge, a sense of commitment, and a strong sense of being in control of one's lives. This personality style is considered
    a. confrontational.
    b. energetic.
    c. hardy.
    d. motivated.

31. The results of Kobasa's study of high-stress executives who remained healthy, indicate that hardy individuals exhibited all of the following characteristics *except:*
    a. liking for challenge.
    b. strong sense of commitment.
    c. external locus of control.
    d. resistance to stress.

32. Individuals with an internal locus of control
    a. believe they can influence events and their reactions to events and accept responsibility for their actions.
    b. believe that what happens to them is determined by factors such as luck, fate, or chance.
    c. need reassurance when making life changes.
    d. encode stress-producing situations as compounding pressure.

33. Joseph is an executive in a large corporation that has shown continuous growth since he was hired. Joseph believes that his success has been determined by his abilities and the actions he has taken. According to your text, he has
    a. an external locus of control.
    b. an internal locus of control.
    c. problems giving credit to others.
    d. an obsessive need for recognition.

34. John experienced failure in school as a result of not taking the remedial classes that were suggested by his counselor. On top of this, his girlfriend decided that she wanted to break up their long-term relationship. John reacted by denying what was happening. This ineffective way of dealing with stress is known as
    a. conflict resolution.
    b. self-efficacy expectations.
    c. defensive behavior.
    d. habituation.

35. When using defensive behavior to alleviate stress, it's important to remember that this behavior
    a. does not have any adjustive value.
    b. will result in a reduction of stress over the long run.
    c. reduces the source of stress.
    d. may have an adjustive value resulting in reducing the impact of stress, but can actually increase levels of stress in the long run.

36. A drawback to depending on drugs and alcohol to reduce stress is that
    a. we numb ourselves both physically and psychologically.
    b. it compounds our problems rather than solving them.
    c. once the effects of drugs and alcohol wear off, we are still confronted by the painful reality that we sought to avoid.
    d. all of the above.

37. _____ is a state of physical, emotional, intellectual, and spiritual exhaustion as a result of repeated pressures, often associated with intense involvement with people over long periods of time.
    a. Burnout
    b. Stress
    c. Apathy
    d. Cognitive dissonance

38. People who burn out
    a. typically strive to set realistic goals in order to avoid frustration.
    b. tend to experience feelings of helplessness and hopelessness.
    c. tend to "work smarter" rather than working harder.
    d. work at conquering feelings of helplessness, since such feelings lead to frustration and anger.

39. Janet has a high potential for burnout since she feels trapped in a job that feels meaningless. In order to balance her life, Janet needs to
    a. create a variety of leisure pursuits that will give meaning to her life.
    b. start taking some "mental health" days off from work.
    c. disassociate mentally when she is at work.
    d. use defensive strategies to alleviate job stress.

40. Perhaps the best way to cope with the effects of burnout is to
    a. acquire skills in dealing with the impact of burnout.
    b. direct our energies to preventing the condition.
    c. avoid any type of stress that will lead to burnout.
    d. find a new line of work if your present job is stressful.

41. Robert is in a job that can be highly stressful. His behavioral reaction to job stress tends to be relatively healthy and adaptive, as he uses the following constructive coping mechanism:
    a. He confronts problems indirectly.
    b. He can realistically appraise his situation and make rational efforts to evaluate alternative courses of action.
    c. He uses wishful thinking to escape his predicament.
    d. He has learned to recognize and repress harmful emotional reactions to stress.

42. According to the Coreys, time management is a key strategy in managing stress. They suggest taking charge of your time by using all of the following strategies *except*
    a. reflecting on your long-range goals, prioritizing the steps you will take in reaching them.
    b. being realistic in deciding what you can accomplish in a given time period.
    c. creating a schedule that helps you get done what you want to accomplish.
    d. trying to be productive every moment and accepting new projects with energy and enthusiasm.

43. Jane experiences a great deal of pressure to perform on her job. She tells herself that "I must do this job perfectly." This stress-producing statement is
    a. a self-defeating belief.
    b. an irrelevant statement.
    c. based on the truth.
    d. passive/aggressive.

44. Studies exploring the physiological changes caused by laughter show the following benefits to individuals:
    a. lowered heart rate and blood pressure.
    b. stimulation of respiratory activity and oxygen exchanges.
    c. enhancement of immune and endocrine functions.
    d. all of the above.

45. The following statement is *not* true concerning the use of humor and laughter as an antidote to stress:
    a. Laughing at our own folly, our own inconsistencies, and some of our pretentious ways can be highly therapeutic.
    b. Humor not only acts as a buffer against stress, it also provides an outlet for frustration and anger.
    c. Laughter produces healing forces within our bodies and can be a powerful antidote to physical illness and stress.
    d. We need to take life seriously and humor is a way of avoiding reality.

46. _____ is a process of directing attention to a single, unchanging or repetitive stimulus as a way of quieting "internal noise" or "mind chatter."
    a. Daydreaming
    b. Hypnosis
    c. Meditation
    d. Progressive relaxation

47. The meditative state has been shown to
    a. induce profound relaxation but also reduce physical and psychological fatigue.
    b. relieve anxiety and stress-related disease.
    c. reduce the frequency of stress-related symptoms in people who consistently practice meditation.
    d. all of the above.

48. An attitude of practicing mindfulness would *not* include
    a. judging thoughts that pass through your mind.
    b. being open to each moment, realizing that some things can't be hurried.
    c. focusing on accepting things as they are.
    d. learning to trust your intuitions.

49. Progressive muscular relaxation technique is a method of deep relaxation that *starts* with the following step:
    a. Pay attention to your breathing, breath slowly through your nose and exhale slowly through your nose.
    b. Tense and relax, proceeding through each muscle group.
    c. Get comfortable, be quiet, and close your eyes.
    d. Clench and release your muscles on each part of your body two or more times.

50. Therapeutic massage is an excellent way to
    a. develop awareness of the differences between tension and relaxation states.
    b. learn ways to release the muscular tightness that often results when you are encountering stress.
    c. discover where and how you are holding onto the tension produced by stressful situations.
    d. all of the above.

ANSWER KEY FOR CHAPTER 5
MANAGING STRESS

1. d p. 134
2. c p. 134
3. a p. 144
4. c p. 135
5. d p. 136
6. b p. 137
7. a p. 137
8. b p. 137
9. c p. 137
10. a p. 137
11. d p. 138
12. a p. 138
13. e p. 146
14. d p. 146
15. a p. 146
16. a p. 147
17. e p. 148
18. d p. 148
19. c p. 148
20. a p. 148
21. c p. 149
22. d p. 150
23. b p. 150
24. d p. 150
25. c p. 151

26. c p. 144
27. b p. 145
28. d p. 145
29. a p. 145
30. c p. 140
31. c p. 140
32. a p. 140
33. b p. 140
34. c p. 143
35. d p. 143
36. d p. 143
37. a p. 142
38. b p. 142
39. a p. 142
40. b p. 142
41. b p. 153
42. d p. 157-158
43. a p. 153
44. d p. 155
45. d p. 155
46. c p. 158
47. d p. 159
48. a p. 161
49. c p. 161
50. d p. 164

Activities and Exercises for Classroom Participation for Chapter 5

1. Invite a guest speaker to talk about stress-management techniques covered in this chapter. You might have someone address deep relaxation methods, breathing techniques, and approaches to meditation.

2. Ask students to pay attention to specials on television that deal with stress-management strategies. Bring in some techniques or describe some programs aimed at helping people cope more effectively with stress.

3. Ask students to keep a record of the environmental stresses they are subjected to in the space of one week. How do they handle these stresses? What do the students think these external stresses do to one's physical and emotional health?

4. As a small-group discussion topic, ask students to identify specific situations they find most stressful. Once students know when they feel most stressed, they can do something to change a stressful situation. Ask students to discuss questions such as: What does stress do to them physically? How does stress affect their ability to learn? How does stress affect the quality of their relationships? What skills would they like to learn to handle stress better?

5. Consult the section of the text in which the relaxation-training exercise is given. Someone can study and practice this exercise and then lead the rest of the group in the relaxation exercise. Try the exercise at home for practice for at least a week or so.

6. Invite a physician to come to class and talk about the relationship between high-stress behavior patterns and the risk of getting heart disease. The physician can also talk about the psychological aspects of treatment, and about the emotional causes of certain physical illnesses.

7. Look at the news for one evening and write down the numbers and kinds of stresses that people are subjected to in a given day.

8. If someone in class is skilled in meditation, ask the person to present some suggestions to the rest of the class on how to meditate. The speaker could focus on steps involved, problems involved, and the values of the practice, as well as commenting on how this practice affects him or her personally.

9. Most colleges employ a number of people considered knowledgeable about time management. Identify one or more of these resource people and have them serve as guest speakers or as a parent of a panel on time-management techniques.

10. Ask students to monitor how they use their time for at least a week. After students have done a self-assessment regarding their use of time, have them choose one aspect of time management they are willing to commit themselves to doing more effectively. Help them focus on a few specific areas and concentrate on working out a strategy.

11. Currently, many college campuses offer education directed at the prevention of date and acquaintance rape. This education emphasizes the importance of being consistent and clear about what an individual wants or does not want with his or her dating partner and provides information about factors contributing to date rape. Many prevention programs are designed to help women increase their awareness of high-risk situations and behaviors and learn how to protect themselves. A guest speaker can present useful information to your students.

12. A way of monitoring stress in your life is to review the following Social Readjustment Rating Scale and evaluate the degree to which life changes have affected you. The scale was developed by Holmes and his colleagues (1967, 1970) as an objective method of measuring the stress resulting from life events. Stress is measured in terms of "life change units" (LCUs). Each life change is given a numerical value. For example, pregnancy is assigned 40, change in school is given 20, change in sleeping habits is given 16, and so on. To determine the severity of stress you have experienced, total up the LCUs that

relate to you. Keep in mind that it is the demand to adjust that a life change places on you that is important, rather than the type of life change alone. Holmes and his colleagues found a strong relationship between the likelihood of physical illness and the total LCU score. Their results suggested that a score in the 200s was associated with about a 50% chance of illness and that a score above 300 was associated with about an 80% chance of illness. It is important to interpret your score as a rough estimate of the stresses you have experienced through changing life situations, rather than as an exact measure. There is a great deal of individual variability with respect to the impact of specific life events. If your score indicates that you have been subjected to a high degree of stress, it is a good idea to consider ways in which you can reduce your exposure to stress and more efficiently deal with the stress that is inevitable in your life.

Social Readjustment Rating Scale

Life Change	Scale of Impact (LCUs)
Death of spouse	100
Divorce	73
Marital separation	65
Jail term	63
Death of close family member	63
Personal injury or illness	53
Marriage	50
Dismissal from job	47
Marital reconciliation	45
Retirement	44
Change in health of family member	44
Pregnancy	40
Sexual difficulties	39
Gain of a new family member	39
Business readjustment	39
Change in financial state	38
Death of a close friend	37
Change to a different line of work	36
Change in number of arguments with spouse	35
Mortgage or loan for major purchase	31
Foreclosure of mortgage or loan	30
Change in responsibilities at work	29
Son or daughter's leaving home	29
Trouble with in-laws	29
Outstanding personal achievement	28
Wife's beginning or quitting work	26
Starting or completing school	26
Change in living conditions	25
Revision of personal habits	24
Trouble with boss	23
Change in work hours or conditions	20
Change in residence	20
Change in school	20
Change in recreation	19
Change in church activities	19
Change in social activities	18

Mortgage or loan for lesser purchase	17
Change in sleeping habits	16
Change in number of family get-togethers	15
Change in eating habits	15
Vacation	13
Christmas	12
Minor violation of the law	11
Total LCUs	

Reprinted with permission from *Journal of Psychosomatic Research, 11,* 213–218, T. H. Holmes and R. H. Rahe, "The Social Readjustment Rating Scale," Copyright 1967, Pergamon Press, Inc.

13. One of the best and most practical ways of dealing with stress is by daily practice of a relaxation exercise such as the one described below. You can practice relaxation in many situations, and doing so can help you assume control of your own behavior, instead of letting yourself be controlled by situations that produce tension within you. For a period of at least a week (and preferably much longer), engage in relaxation training for approximately 20 to 30 minutes daily. The purpose of the exercise is to teach you to become more aware of the distinction between tension states and relaxation states. A further objective is to reduce unnecessary anxiety and tension. The strategy for achieving muscular relaxation is to repeatedly tense and relax various muscle groups. To deepen your relaxation, auxiliary techniques such as concentrating on your breathing and imagining yourself in peaceful situations can eventually be added. Here are some guidelines for your relaxation exercise. Make sure you're in a peaceful setting and in a relaxed position. Tighten and relax the various parts of your body, beginning with your upper extremities and progressing downward to your lower extremities.

a. Clench your fists tightly— so tightly that it hurts. Let go of the tension and relax.

b. Stiffen the lower part of the arm. Tense it. Feel the tension. Let go of the tension.

c. Tense the upper part of the arm. Tighten it until it begins to hurt. Relax it.

d. Repeat the last two steps for your other arm.

e. Wrinkle up your forehead. Wrinkle it tighter and tighter. Then relax and smooth it out. Picture your entire forehead and scalp becoming smoother and more relaxed.

f. Raise your eyebrows as high as you can. Hold this position. Relax.

g. Close your eyes as tightly as you can. Feel the tension. Close them even tighter, and feel that tension. Let go, and feel the relaxation around your eyes.

h. Wrinkle your nose as tightly as you can. Relax.

i. Clench your jaw, and bite your teeth together hard. Feel the pressure. Increase the tension in your jaw. Let your jaw and mouth become increasingly relaxed. Enjoy this relaxation.

j. Smile in an exaggerated way, and hold it. Let go. Purse your lips as tightly as you can. Tighten your mouth muscles, and feel the tension in your entire face. Let go of the tension. Relax.

k. The exercise progresses with the neck, shoulders, and upper back; then the chest, abdomen, and lower back; then the rest of the body, down to the toes; and finally the entire body. During the entire exercise, keep your eyes gently closed. Cover all the major muscle groups. For each group, tense the muscles for several seconds and then relax them. Note the difference between the tension and relaxation states, and repeat the tension/release cycles at least once or twice for each muscle group.

With practice, you can become aware of tension in every part of your body, and you can learn to relax all the areas of your body, separately or together, without first having to tense them. Ultimately, the goal is to teach you to control your tension states by choosing to switch to a deep muscular-relaxation state. Even closing your eyes for a few moments, concentrating on your breathing and the tension within your body, and telling yourself to "let go" are valuable tools in dealing with stress when you feel its effects on your body. It may take several weeks of practice to really feel the tension in your body and to release it. However, once you master some skills of progressive relaxation, it will be possible to relax your entire body in a few moments.

CHAPTER 6: LOVE

Outline

Where Am I Now?
Love Makes a Difference
Learning to Love and Appreciate Ourselves
Authentic and Inauthentic Love
Barriers to Loving and Being Loved
   Myths and Misconceptions About Love
   Self-Doubt and Lack of Self-Love
   Our Fear of Love
Is It Worth It to Love?
Chapter Summary
Where Can I Go From Here?
Website Resources

Chapter Objectives

- to identify meanings of authentic love

- to differentiate between authentic and inauthentic love

- to reflect on what gets in the way of loving others and being loved

- to understand the ways self-love is related to loving others

Questions for Thought, Discussion, and Evaluation

1. Summarize in a few sentences our dual needs to love others and to be loved by others.

2. Mention some of the major barriers to loving and being loved.

3. Identify some of the thoughts on love by writers such as Leo Buscaglia, Erich Fromm, Marshall Hodge, and Kahlil Gibran.

4. What are a few prerequisites to being able to genuinely love others?

5. Marshall Hodge claims that love and trembling seem to go together. Explain how the two are related. Mention some key fears people have about love.

6. Be familiar with the myths and misconceptions about love. What are your own reactions to the barriers that inhibit our ability to fully love and to be loved?

7. Differentiate between authentic and inauthentic love.

8. The authors describe their vision of the meanings of authentic love. Mention a few of the points they discuss. What are your own views on this topic?

9. The question is raised in this chapter—Is it worth it to love? What are your reactions to this question?

10. Briefly discuss the relationship between love and sexuality.

11. What importance do you place on self-love as a prerequisite to loving others? What are some ways that you appreciate yourself and have self-respect?

12. Discuss and mention at least two common myths associated with love.

13. Discuss the problem of looking to another person to confirm your worth and value as a person.

14. Discuss five common myths about love.

15. List and discuss three common ways in which people destroy intimacy and love.

16. Discuss the contention that, in order to be a whole person, one must fulfill one's need for love.

17. Comment on the idea that we don't fall in love but, rather, choose to love.

18. What are the meanings love has for you? Discuss in specific terms what it means to love another person.

19. How are love, sex, and intimacy related, in your view?

20. In what ways do you think you can nurture the love and caring you have for the significant people in your life? What can you do to express to these people the degree of your caring?

21. Discuss the issue of how lovable you see yourself as being. Why would another person want to love you? What do you have to offer? What characteristics do you have that are attractive? How could you become more lovable?

22. What are some important barriers within you that prevent you from loving others fully? What about the barriers that prevent others from fully loving you? What do you see that you can do about these barriers?

23. Do you believe that we choose to open ourselves to love? What does this choice have to do with our position on the question of whether it's worth it to love?

Glossary of Key Terms

Authentic love implies a set of characteristics pertaining to feelings and actions towards others (such as care, respect, and commitment).

Inauthentic love is love that is not genuine and which can be expressed in a number of ways including possessiveness and a need to be in charge.

Impaired givers have a high need to take care of others, yet a limited capacity to accept what others want to give to them.

Self-fulfilling prophecy is the process whereby expectations about a person cause the person to behave in ways that confirm such expectations.

Self-love entails valuing and caring for oneself.

TEST ITEMS FOR CHAPTER 6
LOVE

1. There is _____ evidence that people who lack love and commitment are_____
   a. scant; at high risk for becoming ill
   b. considerable; at high risk for becoming ill
   c. compelling; antisocial
   d. much; not likely to become ill

2. Frankl noted that in the Nazi concentration camp where he was imprisoned, some prisoners who survived while others perished
   a. kept alive the images of those they loved and retained some measure of hope.
   b. lost memories of love and didn't have to feel the pain of longing.
   c. identified with their captors and loved their fellow prisoners.
   d. were able to transcend their situation by praying for their captors.

3. By remembering loved ones who are now deceased in conversations, we create new relationships with them, which is
   a. indicative of major denial.
   b. indicative of psychosis.
   c. referred to as "continuing membership."
   d. referred to as "creative bereavement strategies."

4. Which of the following is NOT identified in the chapter as an essential ingredient in a long-term love relationship?
   a. self-acceptance
   b. realistic expectations
   c. collaborative decision making
   d. interests that differ from one's partner's interests

5. According to the Coreys, love does *not* involve
   a. risk, especially the risk of loss or rejection.
   b. emotional disengagement, which is needed in order to take space from each other during difficult times.
   c. free choice, for people who love each other are able to live without each other yet choose to remain together.
   d. commitment, which is the foundation of any genuinely loving relationship.

6. Rose is angry at her spouse because he refuses to take a vacation. She is so angry that she is shunning him, refusing to talk to him and ignoring his requests to discuss the matter. Rose's tactics are
   a. a cry for help, since their relationship is deteriorating.
   b. her way of getting separateness within the relationship so her identity can be maintained and preserved.
   c. deliberate and aimed at controlling her spouse.
   d. an expression of her need to be loved.

7. In order to harden ourselves so that we won't experience a need for love, we can
    a. close ourselves off from needing anything from anybody.
    b. isolate ourselves by never reaching out to another.
    c. refuse to trust others or to make ourselves vulnerable.
    d. cling to an early decision that we are basically unlovable.
    e. all of the above.

8. Many people try to present themselves to others in a favorable manner, and in doing so, put on "masks," metaphorically speaking. If others love us with our "mask," we will likely conclude
    a. that they will love what is underneath the mask
    b. that they really don't love the person behind the mask
    c. that we can trust their love
    d. that they have really good taste

9. The following is a misconception about love:
    a. In most intense, long-term relationships there are times when the alliance is characterized by deadness, frustration, strife, or conflict.
    b. When we love someone, we do not need to have other relationships.
    c. One of the signs of genuine love is that it is expansive rather than exclusive.
    d. Despite our need for love we often put barriers in the way of our attempts to give and receive love.

10. The following is a rebuttal to the myth of eternal love:
    a. When the relationship fades, this is a sure sign that love never really existed.
    b. The notion that love will endure forever without any change is realistic.
    c. While love can last over a period of time, it is to be expected that it will take on different forms as the relationship matures.
    d. With genuine love, you and your partner will never outgrow the love you share.

11. The Coreys identify all of the following as "myths and misconceptions about love," *except* for the assertion that
    a. love implies constant closeness.
    b. we fall in and out of love.
    c. love is an active choice.
    d. love is exclusive.

12. Buscaglia criticizes the phrase to "fall in love" and contends that it's more accurate to say that
    a. we grow in love, which implies choice and effort.
    b. we must have constant closeness in order to nourish our relationship.
    c. we need to passively wait for the right person to come along and sweep us off our feet.
    d. when love strikes, it is so powerful that it renders people helpless and unable to control what they do.

13. An "impaired giver" is a person who
    a. has a high need to take care of others, yet little tolerance in accepting what others want to give to them.
    b. creates a relationship in which the receiver has a feeling of security.
    c. expresses love unselfishly while being aware of meeting his or her own needs.
    d. lives up to the fact that love is selfless.

14. In regard to love and anger,
    a. denied or unexpressed anger can lead to the death of a relationship.
    b. anger needs to be dealt with in a constructive way before it reaches explosive proportions.
    c. love and anger can be compartmentalized, for when you deny your anger; you are nurturing your relationship.
    d. they are incompatible.

15. The following is a barrier to our attempts to give and receive love:
    a. the type of message we send to others when we are convinced that nobody could possibly love us.
    b. belief that our ability to receive love from others is based primarily on a single trait.
    c. imagining that other people have expectations we must meet in order to be loved.
    d. all of the above.

16. A common barrier to loving and being loved is
    a. lack of self-love.
    b. allowing yourself to be vulnerable.
    c. having responsibility toward the person you love.
    d. letting go of fear.

17. As a child, Ann got the message that she needed to be successful in order to be loved. She has a barrier to love based on the assumption that receiving love from others is based on
    a. putting her own needs before others.
    b. a single characteristic of her personality.
    c. a need for recognition.
    d. a belief in her ability to achieve.

18. A common fear of taking a risk with love is related to
    a. the fact that love doesn't comes with guarantees.
    b. fear of rejection and loss.
    c. uneasiness with intensity.
    d. all of the above.

19. According to the Coreys, an indirect way of getting clients to express self-appreciation when they are not accustomed to doing so is to
    a. have them write a balance sheet stating both their negative and positive points.
    b. ask how their best friend would describe them.
    c. confront their reluctance.
    d. have them describe their "ideal self."

20. In *The Art of Loving*, Erich Fromm describes the condition of self-love within a relationship as
    a. having respect for our own integrity and uniqueness.
    b. becoming selfless, losing ourselves in the one we love.
    c. looking for love in order to feel love for ourselves.
    d. having a 50/50 relationship.

21. A person whose love is inauthentic
    a. does not need to be in charge or make decisions for the other person.
    b. perceives personal change as a threat to the continuation of the relationship.
    c. is unlikely to be dishonest in the relationship.
    d. has responsibility toward the person loved.

22. Jeff is in a relationship in which he has unrealistic expectations of how his girlfriend must act in order to be worthy of his love. He is unwilling to share his thoughts and feelings when she tries to discuss the situation with him. According to the Coreys, Jeff is most likely to be a person whose love is
    a. inauthentic.
    b. romantic.
    c. controlling.
    d. authentic.

23. From the Coreys' perspective, all of the following are signs of authentic love *except*
    a. having respect for the dignity of the person who is loved.
    b. being vulnerable in the relationship.
    c. growth for both ourselves and the person we love.
    d. being focused on changing others so they will conform to our expectations of how they should be.

24. According to the Coreys, love
    a. is equated with physical attractiveness.
    b. involves total commitment and selflessness.
    c. means trusting the person I love.
    d. cannot tolerate imperfection.

25. According to the Coreys, love means
    a. that we are totally and exclusively wedded to each other.
    b. needing the person I love in order to feel complete.
    c. taking the person as they are, instead of treating them as if they already were what they ought to be.
    d. letting go of the illusion of total control of ourselves, others, and our environment.

26. Mary is asking the question "Sure, I need to love and to be loved, but is it really worth it?" When struggling with this question, her first task is to decide
    a. whether she prefers isolation to intimacy.
    b. if she is lovable or not.
    c. if she is capable of having a healthy relationship.
    d. whether or not she wants to be vulnerable.

27 Love means making a commitment to the person I love, which
    a. entails surrendering our total selves to each other.
    b. implies that the relationship is permanent.
    c. entails a willingness to stay with each other in times of pain, uncertainty, struggle, and despair, as well as in times of calm and enjoyment.
    d. all of the above.

28. If I am overly dependent on my relationship for meaning and survival, then I am
    a. free to challenge our relationship.
    b. able to challenge and confront when I feel unhappy with what is going on within the relationship.
    c. likely to settle for less than I want for fear of losing the person I am involved with.
    d. likely to encourage personal growth on an equal basis for both myself and the person I love.

29. In Hodge's book *Your Fear of Love*, he states that loving another person entails recognizing that
    a. we need to stay in relationships that may not be satisfying, in order to work out our intimacy issues.
    b. rejection means that we are fundamentally unlovable.
    c. it is worth the risk to love, even though we tremble and know that there is a possibility of being hurt.
    d. we have a guarantee that nobody will get hurt if our love is authentic.

30. Self-love is
    a. egotistic.
    b. an impediment to loving others.
    c. essential, since we are not able to love others unless we love and appreciate ourselves.
    d. a characteristic of inauthentic love.

ANSWER KEY FOR CHAPTER 6
LOVE

1. b p. 173
2. a p. 174
3. c p. 173
4. d p. 176
5. b p. 176-178
6. c p. 185
7. e p. 173
8. b p. 186
9. b p. 181
10. c p. 181
11. c p. 181-183
12. a p. 181
13. a p. 182
14. a p. 183-184
15. d p. 184-185
16. a p. 184
17. b p. 185
18. d p. 186
19. b p. 174
20. a p. 175
21. b p. 179
22. a p. 179
23. d p. 176-178
24. c p. 178
25. d p. 178
26. a p. 188
27. c p. 177
28. c p. 179
29. c p. 189
30. c p. 175

Activities and Exercises for Classroom Participation for Chapter 6

We recommend dividing the class into dyads for the purpose of working with some of the following material. After the pairs have shared some of their reactions to the questions and problems, the class or groups can reconvene for an in-depth exploration of the issues that most concern class members.

1.   Each person gives a list of all the conscious reasons for not allowing himself or herself to love others or receive love from them.

2.   Each person discloses what he or she imagines it would be like to have a loving relationship with him or her. Share your fantasy of the good things you could do for the other person, the risks of the relationship for the other person, and how he or she might feel about loving you.

3.   What are some ways you could change so that you would be more lovable?

4.   Where did you learn how to love? What standards do you have, or what model have you followed?

5.   Share with one other person fears that prevent you from experiencing love. In what ways do you keep yourself from getting close?

6.   *This is a suggestion for group interaction:* Since the theme you're exploring is love, look at this factor in your own group, if you have been meeting together for some time. Have each member address himself or herself briefly to the following questions: How much caring do I feel in this group? Are any of the people in this group special to me? Can I tell them so? Have I? Do I feel a sense of trust within this group? Can I express negative feelings in the group, as well as positive feelings? What can I do as a participant to be more caring in this group?

7.   What stages or patterns do you see in your significant relationships? What initial assumptions do you make as you enter a relationship?

Love and Sexuality

Although we treat the issues of love, sexuality, and intimacy in three different chapters, these topics cannot be completely separated. So we hope you'll try to make some connections by integrating the ideas of these chapters and applying them to yourself. The following personal inventory should help get you started.

After you've worked through the questions and indicated the responses that actually apply to you now, you might want to take the inventory again and give the responses that indicate how you'd like to be. Feel free to circle more than one response for a given item or to write your own response on the blank line. You may want to take the inventory again at the end of the course to see whether, or to what degree, any of your beliefs, attitudes, or values concerning love and sexuality have changed.

1.   As far as my need for love is concerned,
     a.   I can give love, but it's difficult for me to receive love.
     b.   I can accept love, but it's difficult for me to give love.
     c.   Neither giving nor accepting love is especially difficult for me.
     d.   Both giving and accepting love are difficult for me.
     e.   _____.

2.   I feel that I have been loved by another person
     a.   only once in my life.
     b.   never in my life.
     c.   many times in my life.
     d.   as often as I've chosen to open up to another.
     e.   _____.

3. When it comes to self-love and appreciation of myself,
   a. I have a healthy regard and respect for myself.
   b. I find the idea of self-love objectionable.
   c. I encounter great difficulty in appreciating myself.
   d. I'm generally able to love myself, but there are parts of myself that I dislike.
   e. _____.

4. I love others because
   a. I want their love and acceptance in return.
   b. I fear being alone if I don't.
   c. I like the feeling of loving another.
   d. I derive joy from giving to another person.
   e. _____.

5. To me, love is best described as
   a. giving to another out of my fullness as a person.
   b. thinking more of the other person than I do of myself.
   c. relating to another in the hope that I'll not feel so empty.
   d. caring for another to the same degree that I care about myself.
   e. _____.

6. My greatest fear of loving and being loved is
   a. that I will have nothing to give another person.
   b. that I will be vulnerable and may be rejected.
   c. that I might be accepted and then not know what to do with this acceptance.
   d. that I will feel tied down and that my freedom will be restricted.
   e. _____.

7. In regard to commitment in a loving relationship, I believe that
   a. without commitment there is no real love.
   b. commitment means I love that person exclusively.
   c. commitment means that I stay with the person in times of crisis and attempt to change things.
   d. commitment is not necessary for love.
   e. _____.

8. For me, the relationship between love and sex is that
   a. love often develops *after* a sexual relationship.
   b. sex without love is unsatisfying.
   c. the two must always be present in an intimate relationship with another person of the opposite sex.
   d. sex can be very exciting and gratifying without a love relationship.
   e. _____.

9. I could become more lovable by
   a. becoming more sensitive to the other person.
   b. learning to love and care for myself more than I do now.
   c. doing what I think others expect of me.
   d. being more genuinely myself, without roles and pretenses.
   e. _____.

10. If I loved a person who did not love me in return, I would
    a. never trust another love relationship.
    b. feel devastated.
    c. convince myself that I really didn't care.
    d. feel hurt but eventually open myself to others.
    e. _____ .

11. In love relationships I generally
    a. settle for what I have with the other person as long as things are comfortable.
    b. constantly seek to improve the relationship.
    c. am willing to talk openly about things I don't like in myself and in the other person.
    d. am able to express positive feelings but unable to express negative feelings.
    e. _____ .

12. When it comes to talking about sexuality,
    a. I encounter difficulty, especially with my partner.
    b. I feel free in discussing sexual issues openly.
    c. I usually become defensive.
    d. I'm willing to reveal my feelings if I trust the other person.
    e. _____ .

13. My attitudes and values toward sexuality have been influenced principally by
    a. my parents.
    b. my friends and peers.
    c. my church.
    d. my school experiences.
    e. _____ .

14. I think that social norms and expectations
    a. encourage the dichotomy between male and female roles.
    b. impose heavy performance standards on men.
    c. make it very difficult to develop one's own ideas about what constitutes normal sexuality.
    d. clash with my own upbringing.
    e. _____ .

15. I think that sexual attitudes could be improved by
    a. giving children more information while they are growing up.
    b. teaching principles of religion.
    c. increasing people's knowledge about the physical and emotional aspects of sexuality.
    d. allowing people to freely discuss their sexual values and conflicts in small groups.
    e. _____ .

Here are a few suggestions of things you can do after you've finished this inventory:
1. You can use any of the items that strike you as points of departure for your journal writing.
2. If you're involved in an intimate relationship, you can ask the other person to take the inventory and then share and compare your responses. Your responses can be used as a basis for dialogue on these important issues.
3. You can write down other questions that occurred to you as you took this inventory and bring these questions to class.
4. Your class can form small groups in which to discuss the items that had the most meaning for each person.

CHAPTER 7: RELATIONSHIPS

Outline

Where Am I Now?
Types of Intimacy
Meaningful Relationships: A Personal View
Anger and Conflict in Relationships
     Expressing Anger Constructively
     Addressing Conflict and Confrontation Effectively
Dealing with Communication Barriers
     Effective Personal Communication
     Communicating with Your Parents
Gay and Lesbian Relationships
     Psychological Views of Homosexuality
     Prejudice and Discrimination Against Lesbians and Gay Men
Separation and Divorce
     Finding New Ways of Being in Relationships
     When to Separate or Terminate a Significant Relationship
     Leaving Abusive Relationships
     Coping with Ending a Long-Term Relationship
Chapter Summary
Where Can I Go From Here?
Website Resources

Chapter Objectives

- to identify the different types of intimacy

- to conceptualize the nature of a meaningful relationship

- to understand common blocks to communications

- to learn principles of dealing with anger and conflict in relationships

- to acquire an understanding of gay and lesbian relationships

- to provide guidelines for dealing with separation or termination of relationships

Questions for Thought, Discussion, and Evaluation

We generally give the following instructions for these questions: Try to answer these questions as they apply to you. Reach into yourself and try to give honest responses that reflect how you really feel and think. Try to avoid giving the response you think you "should" be giving or you think is "expected." Many of these questions are intended for people who are presently involved in a couple-type relationship. If you're not now involved in such a relationship, you might apply the questions to a past relationship or else answer them as you'd like to be able to if you do become involved in such a relationship.

1. If you're presently in an intimate relationship and you had the option to "do it all over again," would you get involved with the same person, knowing all that you know now?

2. What are some of the best features of your intimate relationship? What are some features that you would most like to change? What are you doing about changing them?

3. How often does boredom become a part of your relationship? Can you recognize and accept this boredom? Can you speak with your partner about the boredom you experience? What do you do with your boredom?

4. To what degree do you express your feelings about your relationship with your partner? Do you spend much time together talking about the quality of your relationship? Do you ask yourself and your partner what you want from your relationship and how satisfying the current state of things really is?

5. In what ways and directions is each of you growing? *Are* you growing? Are you growing closer together or more distant and separate?

6. Do you have an identity separate from that of your partner? How much do you need and depend on your partner? What would become of you if you were to lose him or her?

7. Are you able to form other relationships with both men and women that also meet your needs? How do you feel about having close friendships with persons of the opposite sex? of the same sex?

8. What are some specific things you do to keep your intimate relationships alive and vital?

9. How do you imagine your life might be different if you were (were not) married or involved in an intimate relationship?

10. What are some of the things you most frequently talk about with your partner? Can you think of certain areas that you avoid discussing with your partner but that you think you need to talk about? What prevents you from doing so?

11. Expressing anger or dealing with conflict may be difficult for you because of what you have learned and the messages you have heard about anger, conflict, and confrontation. What messages, if any, have you received from your family of origin about feeling and expressing anger that you might you want to challenge?

12. How well do you deal with anger and conflict in your relationships? What difficulties, if any, do you have in dealing with anger and conflict?

13. Are you able to take responsibility for yourself in relation to your own personal growth, or do you find yourself adjusting to the expectations of your partner? Do you blame him or her for what you're not? Do you have a need to shape your partner according to a certain mold?

14. What's your picture of the ideal intimate relationship you'd like to have?

15. Why do you think you stay married (or involved in an intimate relationship)? Make a list of as many reasons as you can and have your partner do the same. Then compare notes.

16. Review the discussion in the text of unrealistic expectations, unreasonable ideals, and myths concerning marriage. How does each of these apply to you? Select the myths that you see as most pertaining to you. Have your partner or spouse do the same and then compare notes.

17. Do you feel that love and sex without jealousy is possible and desirable? Do you believe that a lack of jealousy concerning your partner's loving and sexual feelings toward others is indicative of indifference, or a sign of genuine caring? Is jealousy evidence of insecurity on the part of the jealous one? Is jealousy something we learn, or is it innate?

18. Describe and discuss briefly various types of intimacy: physical intimacy, emotional intimacy, intellectual intimacy, spiritual intimacy.

19. What are some of your views on friendship? What constitutes a friend? How important is friendship in your life?

20. Do you have any close friends of the same sex? The opposite sex? What is the difference, if any, between these friendships?

21. Discuss some of the problems faced by the single parent. Do you know a single parent? If so, describe some of the difficulties this person might have experienced in rearing a child or children alone.

22. Mention some of the main barriers to effective communication that inhibit interpersonal relationships.

23. Why is it important to forgive others who have hurt you? What is the importance of forgiveness?

24. Why is forgiving oneself critical in forming meaningful relationships with others?

25. Mention some of the reasons for the prejudice that still exists against homosexuals.

26. Mention some of the more common stereotypes, prejudices, and misconceptions regarding gay people. What are your thoughts about such notions?

27. What are some of the major sources of conflict in intimate relationships?

28. Before people decide to divorce or separate, what are some questions to consider?

29. Discuss choosing of the single lifestyle as a viable and acceptable option to marriage. Mention a few of the advantages and disadvantages of being single as opposed to being married.

Glossary of Key Terms

Intimate relationships are relatively long-lasting relationships in which frequent interactions occur in various situations.

Heterosexuals are people whose sexual desires and behaviors are directed toward members of the opposite gender.

Homosexuals are people who seek emotional and sexual relationships with same-gendered individuals.

Heterosexism is a bias against gay males, lesbians, and bisexuals; it is a belief system that values heterosexuality as superior to homosexuality.

Lesbians are women who are psychologically, emotionally, and sexually attracted to other women.

Gay men are psychologically, emotionally, and sexually attracted to other men.

Sexual orientation refers to the gender or genders that a person is attracted to physically, emotionally, sexually, and romantically.

Bisexuals are psychologically, emotionally, and sexually attracted to both women and men.

Discrimination involves behaving differently, usually unfairly, toward a specific group of people.

Gay-affirmative therapy, practiced by most therapists, helps individuals accept their sexual identity and learn strategies to deal with those in society who harbor prejudice toward them.

Hate crimes often include assault and murder and are directed against a victim because he or she is of a certain race, ethnic group, religion, or sexual orientation.

Homophobia is the irrational fear of homosexual people and strong negative attitudes about homosexuality.

Communication barriers are factors that get in the way of effective interpersonal relating.

Commitment is the choice to stay in a relationship, even though difficulties and challenges may arise.

TEST ITEMS FOR CHAPTER 7
RELATIONSHIPS

1. _____ is the dominant relationship in our society, especially if we broadly define it to include couples who are committed to each other even though they are not legally married.
   a. Marriage
   b. Singlehood
   c. Cohabitation
   d. Dating

2. Erikson maintains that the major task of early adulthood is the challenge of
   a. developing an independent identity.
   b. becoming self-directive.
   c. forming intimate relationships.
   d. being comfortable with isolation.

3. Donald was raised with a father who was a workaholic and paid little attention to his son. When Donald decided to talk with his father about his childhood, he was not satisfied with the results. What Donald needs to remember is that
   a. he has the power to bring about change in the other person if only he tries hard enough.
   b. he needs to take a passive stance and hope that his dad will change as he gets older.
   c. he should seek counseling and focus on how his dad is not meeting his expectations.
   d. he has the power to bring about change if he focuses on his own changes.

4. When we avoid intimacy, we
   a. may pass up the chance to really get to know others.
   b. will be able to save ourselves from pain.
   c. are being cautious, since closeness can only occur in a long-term relationship.
   d. are taking care of ourselves.

5. According to the Coreys, each of the following is characteristic of meaningful relationships *except*:
   a. Although each person desires the other, each can survive without the other.
   b. Each person expects the other to take responsibility for his or her happiness.
   c. The two persons are equal in the relationship.
   d. Each person finds meaning and sources of nourishment outside the relationship.

6. In speaking about intimate relationships, Kahlil Gibran suggests that
   a. the parties involved should do almost everything together.
   b. there be spaces in their togetherness.
   c. intimacy means losing oneself in the other.
   d. each person assumes responsibility for the other's happiness.

7. Janet is not satisfied with her relationship with her mother. She would like to develop a relationship that is more intimate and talk to her mother on a personal basis. Janet can take the first step toward changing the situation if she
   a. tells her mother how unsatisfied she is with her lack of personal conversation.
   b. lets her mother know, in a nonjudgmental way, that she would like to talk more personally.
   c. suggests that her mother take a class in interpersonal communication.
   d. goes to counseling with her.

8. If we hope to keep a relationship vital, we must
    a. reevaluate and revise our way of being with each other from time to time.
    b. rely on others for our personal fulfillment and confirmation as a person.
    c. be free of conflicts.
    d. meet all of our needs within the relationship.

9. Robert and Nancy have a meaningful, sexual relationship. They are aware that the intensity and novelty of their relationship has lessened after a period of being together. They can attempt to keep the romance alive by
    a. going to places they haven't been to before.
    b. varying their routine in some ways.
    c. asking for what they want and need during lovemaking.
    d. all of the above.

10. Physically assaulting a person on the basis of his/her sexual orientation is referred to as
    a. a hate crime
    b. homophobia
    c. agoraphobia
    d. a crime of passion

11. Commitment is a vital part of an intimate relationship. It means that the people involved
    a. expect the other person to make them feel alive, take away their boredom, and make them feel valued and important.
    b. do not need to find meaning and sources of nourishment outside the relationship.
    c. have an investment in their future together and are willing to stay with each other in times of crisis and conflict.
    d. repress their anger and frustrations in order to avoid conflict.

12. All the following are barriers to communication *except*
    a. silently rehearsing what you will say next while you are listening.
    b. telling others how they are, rather than telling them how they affect you.
    c. making genuine contact by openly expressing what you think and feel.
    d. selective listening.

13. The language we use as we are growing up is influenced by our
    a. gender.
    b. ethnicity.
    c. class and cultural background.
    d. location.
    e. all of the above.

14. Empathy, which is a basic component in any interpersonal relationship, is best understood as
    a. offering sympathy for another.
    b. having the ability to attribute meaning to statements without checking them out.
    c. entering another's world by listening with respect and understanding.
    d. showing pity for another.

15. Gay, lesbian, and bisexual individuals are frequently confronted with
    a. heterosexism
    b. interpersonal discrimination
    c. verbal harassment
    d. institutional discrimination
    e. all of the above

16. When should a couple terminate a significant relationship?
    a. Only after they have been in couples counseling for one year.
    b. If one of the partners is unfaithful and refuses to end the affair.
    c. After a major disagreement.
    d. No categorical answer can be given to this question.

17. The Coreys' discussion of the content and process of communication is influenced by the Euro-American slant that prizes
    a. indirect communication.
    b. harmony within the family, which makes it inappropriate for adult children to confront their parents.
    c. avoidance of direct eye contact.
    d. direct communication and making eye contact when speaking.

18. From the Coreys' perspective, each of the following statements describes meaningful conversation between two persons, *except*
    a. The language is specific and concrete.
    b. Each makes "You" statements in order to include both points of view.
    c. The speaker makes personal statements instead of bombarding the other with impersonal questions.
    d. There is a congruency between the verbal and nonverbal messages.

19. The following statement is specific and concrete:
    a. "I feel manipulated."
    b. "You never pay attention to me."
    c. "I don't like it when you don't call if you are going to be late because I worry about you."
    d. "You are self-centered and never think about anybody but yourself."

20. In dealing effectively with anger and conflict in relationships it is best to avoid
    a. expressing persistent annoyances.
    b. expressing feelings in a direct and honest way.
    c. stuffing feelings to preserve harmony.
    d. telling others feelings and thoughts that may be difficult for them to hear.

21. Lois and her parents usually communicate on a superficial level. Lois would like to talk more intimately with her parents and feels angry when they don't respond the way she anticipated. She needs to
    a. wait for her parents to make the first move.
    b. withdraw when her expectations are not immediately met in order to avoid the pain of rejection.
    c. put aside her need to remake her parents and accept any small changes they may make.
    d. confront them with their reluctance to change.

22. The Coreys' guidelines for meaningful relationships can be applied to
    a. friendships.
    b. parent-child relationships.
    c. relationships between couples who are married or unmarried, gay or straight.
    d. all of the above.

23. Concerning the origin of homosexuality,
    a. it is clear that one's sexual preference is the function of genetic or physiological factors.
    b. it is entirely a learned behavior.
    c. it is a matter of choice.
    d. experts have differing views on the issue.

24. Same-sex sexual orientation can be regarded as
    a. another style of expressing sexuality.
    b. a form of mental illness.
    c. an unhealthy choice brought about by disappointments in opposite-sex relationships.
    d. faulty resolution of the Oedipus or Electra complex during Freud's phallic psychosexual stage of development.

25. Paula and Beth are having conflicts in their lesbian relationship and are seeking counseling with a heterosexual counselor. Paula is open about her relationship with Beth, while Beth is reluctant to let others know she is a lesbian. An effective way of dealing with this couple would be to
    a. actively try to convert them to a heterosexual lifestyle.
    b. help them clarify their own values and decide for themselves what course of action to take.
    c. convince Beth to come "out of the closet."
    d. confront Paula for staying in the relationship.

26. Homosexual relationships are *not*
    a. becoming the avowed preference of an increasing number of people in our society.
    b. gaining total acceptance in today's society.
    c. considered to be a viable alternative to a heterosexual lifestyle.
    d. confronted with similar issues as heterosexual relationships.

27. The gay liberation movement
    a. was instrumental in eliminating discrimination in the military.
    b. has removed the stigma of homosexuality.
    c. has changed public perception, allowing lesbians, gay men, and bisexuals to be open about their relationships.
    d. is actively challenging the stigma attached to this sexual orientation.

28. The American Psychological Association
    a. no longer refers to homosexuality as a form of mental illness.
    b. backs the military's "Don't ask, don't tell" policy.
    c. believes that the general public is well educated about gay and lesbian lifestyles.
    d. has taken the stand that the origin of homosexuality involves both genetics and learning.

29. Being involved in a gay or lesbian relationship
    a. is simply a matter of sexual preference.
    b. involves many of the same interpersonal conflicts that any couple will eventually face and need to resolve.
    c. is acceptable to most of the heterosexual society.
    d. is a result of early childhood sexual abuse.

30. When a couple experiences a crisis in their marriage, this is likely to mean that they
    a. should get a divorce.
    b. should get a separation and consider a divorce.
    c. have the chance to create a new life together.
    d. never should have gotten intimately involved with each other in the first place.

31. Before getting a divorce, the Coreys suggest that a couple consider
    a. personal counseling just for the one seeking a divorce.
    b. getting a good lawyer for each person as soon as possible.
    c. mediation through the courts before getting a divorce.
    d. personal counseling for each person and relationship counseling as a couple.

32. Frequently, problems in a marriage are
    a. reflections of internal conflicts within the spouses.
    b. caused by differences in money management.
    c. the result of the women's movement.
    d. due to external forces.

33. Harry has been married for fifteen years to a woman who consistently rejects any attempts to improve their relationship. He wants to get a divorce, but tells his counselor that he can't leave until his children graduate from high school. This kind of thinking
    a. is realistic since children need both parents.
    b. is based on the fact that a troubled marriage is better than being alone.
    c. often burdens children with unnecessary guilt.
    d. is characteristic of a "giver" who is willing to sacrifice his or her own happiness for the sake of the children.

34. Doris is hesitant to terminate her abusive marriage because she may
    a. rationalize that her situation is not really so bad.
    b. excuse the partner's behavior and find fault with herself for bringing about the abuse.
    c. believe her husband's promises to reform.
    d. all of the above.

35. The following behavior could indicate that a couple is in an abusive relationship:
    a. withholding love and affection.
    b. making promises, yet never keeping them.
    c. showing extreme jealousy and possessiveness.
    d. using physical or psychological threats.
    e. all of the above.

36. The following is *not* true concerning abusive relationships:
   a. All abusive relationships involve physical violence.
   b. Subtle emotional abuse over a period of time can erode a relationship.
   c. People sometimes remain in an abusive relationship in the hope that their situation will change.
   d. It is difficult for the victim in an abusive relationship to reach out and form new friendships.

37. Joe is attempting to leave his long-term relationship with Susan. She is feeling a great deal of stress that is intensified by the irrational belief that
   a. she needs to take responsibility for her part in the break-up of the relationship.
   b. her relationship didn't work out and it proves that she is a failure and unlovable.
   c. although she is in pain over the situation, she will be able to survive.
   d. she needs to take time to grieve the loss.

38. The Coreys would *not* agree with the following suggestion for living with and learning from the termination of a meaningful relationship:
   a. Personalize your partner's actions.
   b. Express your anger.
   c. Find a support network.
   d. Get closure.

39. Sandy recently ended a five year relationship with Tom, who spent much of his free time at bars with his coworkers while they were together. Sandy's friends keep telling her that she needs closure before she moves on with her life. To seek closure, it would be appropriate for her to
   a. embrace her anger and think of ways to sabotage Tom's future relationships with women.
   b. try to forget that the relationship ever happened and start over with someone new.
   c. set aside time to grieve and find ways to make amends with Tom as well as with herself.
   d. vow to remain alone so as to avoid being hurt in the future.

40. Three decades have passed since the decision was made to no longer consider homosexuality
   a. a cultural tradition.
   b. a worldwide trend.
   c. a form of psychopathology.
   d. a lifestyle choice.

41. In the therapeutic groups that they facilitate, the Coreys hope that participants
   a. will continue to meet on their own as a group long after the therapeutic group officially ends.
   b. will confront people in their personal lives after they symbolically address their issues with those individuals in the group.
   c. will be able to translate what they learned about creating intimacy into their outside relationships.
   d. will be inspired to join other therapeutic groups for years to come.

42. Darcie has been experiencing problems in her relationship with Joe for most of their marriage. She finds herself getting into shouting matches with her husband whenever he wants to watch sports on TV because she thinks he should be more focused on her needs. As a first step to improve her situation, Darcie should
   a. divorce Joe to find someone more compatible.
   b. make changes in herself so that she is not dependent on Joe to entertain her so much of the time.
   c. try other tactics to change Joe.
   d. insist that Joe go to therapy.

43. If sexual partners experience different degrees of intensity in an ongoing relationship, they
    a. can continue to create a climate of romance and closeness.
    b. should give up on the relationship and find partners who experience the same level of intensity as them.
    c. will inevitably lose interest in each other.
    d. need to seek couples therapy.

44. The absence of conflict in a relationship
    a. should be the ultimate goal of couples.
    b. is not as important as being able to deal with conflict constructively.
    c. possible if both partners agree upfront to be honest with each other.
    d. a and c

45. _____ characteristics are often attributed to those who are physically attractive
    a. Unfavorable; if they are shy.
    b. Desirable; regardless of their true nature.
    c. Desirable; only if they have pleasant personalities.
    d. Unfavorable; if they are personality disordered.

46. In looking for intimate relationships, women tend to place a premium on finding partners
    a. who are exceptionally attractive
    b. who are adventurous and unpredictable
    c. with promising financial prospects and a good career
    d. a and b

47. Forgiveness is
    a. an emotion-focused coping strategy
    b. associated with enhanced personal adjustment and well-being
    c. not a one-time event
    d. all of the above

48. Common factors underlie all forms of intimate relationships except for
    a. heterosexual relationships
    b. homosexual relationships
    c. bisexual relationships
    d. none of the above

49. The term _____ refers to the gender or genders that a person is attracted to physically, emotionally, sexually, and romantically.
    a. sexual orientation
    b. homophobia
    c. heterosexism
    d. gender identity

ANSWER KEY FOR CHAPTER 7
RELATIONSHIPS

1.	a	p.194
2.	c	p. 194-195
3.	d	p. 194-195
4.	a	p. 194
5.	b	p. 197-200
6.	b	p. 197
7.	b	p. 197-198
8.	a	p. 198-199
9.	d	p. 199
10.	a	p. 213
11.	c	p. 199
12.	c	p. 207
13.	e	p. 207
14.	c	p. 208
15.	e	p. 213
16.	d	p. 217
17.	d	p. 209
18.	b	p. 209
19.	c	p. 209
20.	c	p. 203
21.	c	p. 210
22.	d	p. 211
23.	d	p. 211
24.	a	p. 212
25.	b	p. 213

26.	b	p. 212
27.	d	p. 213
28.	a	p. 211
29.	b	p. 213
30.	c	p. 216-217
31.	d	p. 217
32.	a	p. 218
33.	c	p. 219
34.	d	p. 219
35.	e	p. 219
36.	a	p. 219
37.	b	p. 220
38.	a	p. 221
39.	c	p. 221
40.	c	p. 211
41.	c	p. 194
42.	b	p. 194-195
43.	a	p. 199
44.	b	p. 199-200
45.	b	
46.	c	p. 201
47.	d	p. 205
48.	d	p. 210-211
49.	a	p. 211

Activities and Exercises for Classroom Participation for Chapter 7

1. As you work through the questions for reflection, bring into your group any of these questions you'd like to explore. Select the ones most concerned with your own struggles or conflicts about your relationship with a partner.

2. In your group or in smaller subgroups, explore the following:
a. Describe the best relationship you have ever seen. What qualities make it the best relationship you know of? Discuss in your group the qualities you regard as most essential in a successful relationship.
b. Now each describe the worst relationship you have ever seen. What factors make this arrangement destructive? Discuss in your group the elements you feel are least conducive to a successful couples relationship.

3. For each person in the group who is involved in an intimate relationship, try this exercise as a go-around. One person begins by saying "If only my partner were not ____ , then I ____ ." The intent of this exercise is to help us see how we often blame another person for our own inability to change our part in a relationship.

4. Ask students what they consider to be effective communication. When do they feel heard and understood? What difficulties do they have communicating and understanding others? Suggest that students role-play positive and negative ways of communicating. What effect does their style of communicating have on others?

5. As a class discussion topic, explore the common communication blocks. How do stereotypes serve as barriers to interpersonal communication?

6. Have students devote some time in a small group to exploring effective and healthy ways to deal with anger and conflict in relationships. Ask them to discuss their reactions to this section in the chapter. What are their thoughts about the guidelines presented for dealing with conflict in an effective manner?

7. As a lecture you may want to address gay and lesbian relationships. Ask your students what their reactions are to the discussion of this topic in this chapter. To what degree do your students think there is prejudice and discrimination against lesbians and gay men? What personal reactions do they have to Ann and Berit's story.

8. A useful topic for small group discussion is learning when and how to terminate a significant relationship. Ask students to share their personal reactions to this section on when to terminate a relationship. What do they think about the suggesting listed for dealing effectively with the ending of a meaningful relationship?

9. What are some arguments for and against the proposal that a couple should obtain a license before they have children? Assume that they would have to demonstrate their competence to rear children in a caring climate. What criteria would you use to determine their competence?

CHAPTER 8: BECOMING THE WOMAN OR MAN YOU WANT TO BE

Outline

Where Am I Now?
Male Roles
    The Value of Men's Groups
    Roles that Alienate Men
    Stereotypical View of Males
    African American Masculinity
    Masculinity and Latino Cultures
    Asian American Masculinity
    The Price Men Pay for Remaining in Traditional Roles
    Challenging Traditional Male Roles
Female Roles
    Traditional Roles for Women
    Challenging Traditional Female Roles
    Women and Work Choices
    Women in Dual-Career Families
Alternatives to Rigid Gender-Role Expectations
    Androgyny as an Alternative
    Gender-Role Transcendence
Chapter Summary
Where Can I Go From Here?
Website Resources

Chapter Objectives

- to realize the role of socialization in defining gender-role identity

- to critically evaluate traditional notions of being a male or female

- to challenge stereotypes and appreciate the role of choice in defining oneself

- to consider alternative gender-role models

- to become aware of how gender-roles impact relationships

Questions for Thought, Class Discussion, and Evaluation

1. What is your reaction to Kevin, who was discussed at the beginning of this chapter? To what degree do you think he is the product of his social and cultural conditioning? How did crisis in his life act as a catalyst to change his view of himself as a man and what he wanted in life?

2. Along the same lines as above, what are your reactions to the case of Leroy? To what extent can you identify with him, whether you are a man or a woman? If you are a man, how would you like Leroy as your closest friend? If you are a woman, what do you imagine it would be like to live with him?

3. What are your reactions to the concept of the traditional male, as portrayed in the chapter? What price do you see men as paying for living by such roles? To what degree do you see evidence that men are challenging traditional roles?

4. The chapter describes the trend of women challenging traditional gender roles. What evidence, if any, do you find for this? To what degree do you think that women have an increase in options concerning lifestyles?

5. How can developing more flexible views of gender-role expectations be liberating for both women and men? How does this apply to you?

6. What are your thoughts about androgyny as an alternative to rigid gender roles? What are the characteristics of both sexes that you'd like to incorporate into your personality?

7. Can you trace a few significant influences on your own gender-role identity development? How was your image as a woman or a man shaped?

8. What are some of the stereotypic traits typically assigned to being feminine and to being masculine?

9. Given the fact that there are definite cultural pressures toward adopting given gender roles, where does choice enter into this picture? Are we hopelessly cemented into a rigid way of being, or are we able to choose our own concept of what kind of woman or man we want to be?

Glossary of Key Terms

Gender-role socialization is the process of learning those behaviors (norms and roles) that are expected of people in a particular society.

Gender is the state of being female or male.

Gender roles are the cultural expectations about what is appropriate behavior for each gender.

Gender-role identity is the ability to clearly classify oneself as male or female.

Gender stereotypes pertain to the commonly shared beliefs about males' and females' abilities, personality traits, and behaviors.

Gender-role strain is the condition of striving to live up to unrealistic societal expectations that often result in a variety of psychological problems.

Sexism is a bias against people on the basis of their gender.

Agency is a concern with one's own self-interests, such as competition and independence.

Communion is a concern for one's relationship with other people.

Androgeny is the blending of typical male and female personality traits and behaviors in the same person.

Gender-role transcendence is the notion that to be fully human, people need to move beyond gender roles as a way of organizing the world and of perceiving themselves and others.

TEST ITEMS FOR CHAPTER 8
BECOMING THE WOMAN OR MAN YOU WANT TO BE

1. According to the Coreys, the traditional male role is
   a. increasing in popularity among most men.
   b. increasingly being challenged by many men.
   c. something that men must tolerate, since cultural conditioning is so strong.
   d. best considered a myth.

2. The one characteristic that is *not* listed as part of the all-American male image is
   a. he doesn't recognize bodily cues that may signal danger.
   b. he tends to have many close male friends.
   c. he does not disclose himself to women.
   d. he feels he must be continually active, aggressive, assertive, and striving.

3. A man tends to show his affection by being
   a. emotionally available.
   b. vulnerable.
   c. androgynous.
   d. a "good provider."

4. Because a man would find the range of feelings to be terrifying, he has unconsciously sealed off most of his feelings in an attempt to
   a. protect his inner self.
   b. be vulnerable.
   c. avoid human contact.
   d. avoid "feminine" qualities.

5. The theme of men hiding their true nature
   a. relates only to the "macho male. "
   b. is characteristic of many men, regardless of their racial, ethnic, and cultural background.
   c. relates only to males who are driven to succeed.
   d. is due to a lack of bodily self-awareness.

6. The price men pay for living by stereotypical standards is (are)
   a. that they lose a sense of themselves by doing what is expected of them.
   b. striving for perfectionism in most aspects of life.
   c. hiding their loneliness, anxiety, and hunger for affection, which makes it difficult for anyone to love them as they really are.
   d. all of the above.

7. According to the Coreys, traditional male roles
   a. are completely unhealthy for both men and women.
   b. are a part of the social fabric that will never change.
   c. may be satisfying for some men and may not need to be changed.
   d. must be discarded if men hope to be healthy and happy.

8. Below is a principal cost to men of remaining tied to gender roles:
   a. excessive pressure to succeed.
   b. inability to express emotions.
   c. sexual difficulties.
   d. all of the above.

9. According to Robert Bly, because boys were emotionally cut off from their fathers, it is important for them as men to
   a. get in touch with their primal rage and vent this rage.
   b. express the deep source of grief over the longing for bonding with their father.
   c. experience psychological healing from a nurturing mother figure.
   d. identify themselves with traditional male roles as a way to protect themselves from emotional pain.

10. According to Bly, author of *Iron John*, men suffer from
    a. fear of intimacy.
    b. lack of bodily self-awareness.
    c. "father hunger."
    d. emotional stagnation.

11. Traditional gender roles
    a. are in a state of transition and will likely remain that way for some time to come.
    b. are next to impossible to change in this society.
    c. are simply a myth, since gender roles are merely stereotypes.
    d. affect women but not men in this society.

12. Concerning men, all of the following are true statements *except*:
    a. There is an increase of male consciousness that involves a lessening of rigid defensiveness.
    b. There is an increased interest in men's consciousness-raising workshops.
    c. There is a trend for men to cling more steadfastly to traditional male roles.
    d. More men are exploring the impact of their relationship with their father on their current behavior.

13. Typically, if women do strive toward career aspirations, they
    a. also carry the responsibilities of parent and spouse.
    b. do not feel pressure to carry out family responsibilities.
    c. decide not to marry or to have a family.
    d. are able to hire household help so they can devote the time they need to be successful in their career.

14. Which of the following is a typical feminine stereotype?
    a. possessing an aggressive and independent spirit
    b. tendency to be rational rather than emotional
    c. decisiveness and tactfulness
    d. passivity and submissiveness

15. Joan is unhappy in her role as a housewife although she is indecisive about making a change in her life. When challenged by her husband regarding her unwillingness to explore her options, she becomes emotional and resorts to tears. Joan's situation is an example of
    a. a traditional, feminine gender-role stereotype.
    b. androgyny.
    c. the self-fulfilling prophecy.
    d. the animus.

16. The changing structure of gender relations has
    a. altered what women expect of men and the role that men play in women's lives.
    b. made it possible to use previous generations as a model.
    c. led to the conclusion that the traditional division of labor between the sexes is natural and inevitable.
    d. all of the above.

17. Concerning women and work, which of the following statements is *false*?
    a. The number of women looking to an occupation outside of the home as a major source of their identity is decreasing.
    b. Occupational options for women are increasing.
    c. Many women work not only out of choice but also out of necessity.
    d. Women are starting new businesses twice as fast as men do.

18. Women who make the choice to find their fulfillment primarily through the roles of wife, mother, and homemaker do so mainly because they
    a. feel that they cannot enter the world of work.
    b. want to devote most of their time to their family.
    c. are fearful of balancing both a career and family.
    d. have no sense of identity outside of their homes.

19. Ideally, a successful and independent woman
    a. doesn't need anyone and can make it entirely on her own.
    b. knows she can achieve independence, exhibit strength, and succeed while at times being dependent and in need of nurturing.
    c. will hear "inner voices" that will guide her towards total autonomy.
    d. will forfeit marriage and children until her career is on the decline.

20. Women who have followed traditional roles for many years and successfully shed them by defining new roles for themselves may struggle with the following theme:
    a. dependence vs. independence.
    b. fear of success.
    c. looking outside oneself for support and direction.
    d. expecting to be taken care of.
    e. all of the above.

21. Traditional gender stereotypes categorize women as having all the traits except for being
    a. nurturing.
    b. emotional and intuitive.
    c. independent.
    d. unaccomplished.

22. The alternative to living according to a stereotype is to
    a. accept the roles and expectations that have been imposed on us as children.
    b. become totally independent without relying on others for support.
    c. realize that we can actively define our own standards of what we want to be like as women or as men.
    d. acquire all the characteristics of the opposite sex.

23. George is able to exhibit high levels of characteristics generally associated with both males and females. This is an example of
    a. synergy.
    b. androgyny.
    c. undifferentiation.
    d. dichotomy.

24. Androgyny refers to
    a. a reversal of roles.
    b. a person's flexibility in gender-role behaviors.
    c. one's sexual orientation.
    d. people who are low in both stereotypical masculine and feminine traits.

25. According to Jung, the notion that accounts for the masculine dimension of a woman's personality is the
    a. persona.
    b. shadow.
    c. anima.
    d. animus.

26. Jung developed the notions of the animus and the anima, which refer to
    a. the masculine and feminine aspects within us that are usually hidden.
    b. achieving individuation.
    c. the dark side of personality, which is thought to contain the basic and primitive instincts.
    d. the collective unconscious.

27. Monica McGoldrick maintains that traditional gender roles will not change until
    a. men are willing to become more feminine.
    b. men move toward an androgynous model for living.
    c. we have worked out a new structure in relationships that is not based on the patriarchal family hierarchy.
    d. women become more assertive in refusing to act as they have been socialized.

28. In writing about women and work choices, Monica McGoldrick notes that
    a. paid work increases stress and has negative effects on the health of women.
    b. women who work outside the home tend to show more symptoms of psychological and physical distress.
    c. women can easily choose their roles in meeting the demands they face.
    d. there are many social pressures against women feeling good about working outside the home.

29. The gender-role transcendence model implies that
    a. gender is an efficient means of characterizing traits.
    b. gender is a function of social approval or disapproval.
    c. personality traits should be divorced from the individual's biological sex.
    d. gender-role identity is biological, therefore difficult to change.

30. Which of the following aspects of therapy do men often have difficulty with?
    a. disclosing oneself to an authority figure
    b. revealing failures and insecurities
    c. revealing family and personal matters
    d. all of the above

31. Therapy is often viewed by men as
    a. something that is foreign to the male psyche.
    b. a welcome opportunity for personal growth and self-exploration.
    c. an experience that is reminiscent of their early socialization.
    d. b and c

32. Which of the following statements is/are *not* true with regard to men's groups?
    a. Men's groups can counteract the negative side of male gender-role socialization.
    b. Men's groups can help members become more stoic in the face of pain.
    c. Men's groups can help men to modify some of the ways in which they feel they must live.
    d. Men's groups can help members restructure some of the beliefs they have long held.

33. Which of the following themes or topics are often discussed in men's groups?
    a. How men's bodies carry the weight of their unexpressed emotions and desires.
    b. How men's inner judges keep them from being satisfied with their lives.
    c. How the fear of abandonment keeps men from taking risks.
    d. All of the above.

34. _____ are widely accepted beliefs about females' and males' abilities, personality traits, and behavior patterns.
    a. Sexual values
    b. Sexual discrimination practices
    c. Gender stereotypes
    d. Gender preferences

35. _____ are considered to be higher in _____, which suggests they are concerned with self-interests such as competition and independence.
    a. Women; agency
    b. Men; agency
    c. Women; communion
    d. Men; communion

36. _____ are considered to be higher in _____, which suggests they are concerned about relationships with other people.
    a. Women; agency
    b. Men; agency
    c. Women; communion
    d. Men; communion

37. General beliefs about gender have
    a. remained fairly consistent throughout recent decades.
    b. fluctuated moderately over the past two decades.
    c. not changed at all over the past few decades.
    d. changed radically over the past decade.

38. Men are frequently shut off from their emotional selves because
    a. their partners/ spouses drive them to shut down.
    b. they see the subjective world of feelings as being essentially feminine.
    c. they resent their mothers.
    d. they are incapable of accessing their emotions at a deep level.

39. In order to define who they want to be for themselves, men
    a. may need to conform to or reject traditional gender roles.
    b. will need to embrace traditional gender roles.
    c. will need to reject traditional gender roles.
    d. should not think about gender roles at all and leave the factor of gender out of the equation.

40. Age-old gender-roles stemmed from
    a. the biological need of men to feel a sense of entitlement.
    b   fairy tales.
    c. a need for a division of labor in society.
    d. women's innermost desires to stay at home.

ANSWER KEY FOR CHAPTER 8
BECOMING THE WOMAN OR MAN YOU WANT TO BE

1.	b	p. 228
2.	b	p. 233
3.	d	p. 232
4.	a	p. 232
5.	b	p. 234
6.	d	p. 236
7.	c	p. 239
8.	d	p. 236
9.	b	p. 238
10.	c	p. 238
11.	a	p. 237
12.	c	p. 237
13.	a	p. 241
14.	d	p. 241
15.	a	p. 242
16.	a	p. 242
17.	a	p. 244
18.	b	p. 245
19.	b	p. 248
20.	e	p. 249
21.	c	p. 241

22.	c	p. 250
23.	b	p. 251
24.	b	p. 251
25.	d	p. 251
26.	a	p. 251
27.	c	p. 251
28.	d	p. 244
29.	c	p. 252
30.	d	p.229
31.	a	p. 229
32.	b	p. 230
33.	d	p. 230
34.	c	p. 231
35.	b	p. 232
36.	c	p. 232
37.	a	p. 232
38.	b	p. 233
39.	a	p. 239
40.	c	p. 237

Activities and Exercises for Classroom Participation for Chapter 8

One of the main goals in discussing gender-role identity is to free students up so they can express some of their concerns in class. We think it's valuable for men and women to share with one another what they think about their own gender-role conditionings. We have found that many students feel less isolated if they feel the trust to share their own concerns, doubts, and questions. To facilitate this sharing, you might consider trying any of the following exercises.

1. Have a group of students read a book on the subject of the chapters and then form a panel. Examples of suggested readings are found at the end of each chapter. The panel shares with the class some key ideas found in the book.

2. In small groups, discuss traditional views pertaining to gender-role identity for both men and women. Are there some ways you'd like to challenge the traditional roles?

3. In your groups, discuss the concepts of male roles and female roles, especially as these roles relate to relationships. What kinds of gender roles may interfere with your relationships?

4. Ask students to examine how their culture has influenced their view of appropriate role behavior. What messages did they receive in growing up from their culture? How do these cultural messages either help or hinder them in developing relationships? How has it affected students' view of themselves?

5. There are common myths and misconceptions associated with being a woman and being a man. Take the following inventory by writing an "A" in the blank on the left if you agree more than you disagree with the statement, or a "D" in the blank if you disagree more than you agree. Then, in the next space, answer the statement in the way you think most of your friends and associates of the same sex as you would be likely to respond.

Statements about men:

a. Men are often defined by what they achieve.

b. Men should have more social freedom than women.

c. Men should display courage and be strong.

d. Men are more concerned about the world of work than about relationships.

e. Men are more competitive than women.

Statements about women:

a. Women by nature have a need to have and take care of children

b. Women define themselves by giving to others.

c. Women should make a primary commitment to the home.

d. Women should not have a career if it jeopardizes their family life.

e. Women, by nature, are more emotional than logical.

Now, compare your responses with those of others in your class, both men and women. Are there many differences? You could discuss the degree to which your attitudes concerning gender roles might have been influenced by your environment. A lively discussion could be geared around determining which of the above statements are perceived as myths and misconceptions, and which are seen as "facts of life."

6.   Are there genuine sex differences between women and men? Below are some popular stereotypes. As you did in the above inventory, decide whether you are more in agreement (A) or disagreement (D) with each statement.

a.   Women are more susceptible to persuasion than men.

b.   Women react with more emotion to stressful events than do men.

c.   Women are more passive than men.

d.   Women are more interested in people, whereas men are more interested in things.

e.   Women are more dependent on love relationships than men.

f.   Women are more sensitive to the feelings of others than are men.

g.   Women are more accurate than men in understanding nonverbal signals.

h.   Women are less interested in sex than are men.

i.   Women are more nurturant than men.

j.   Women tend to be less aggressive than men.

In reviewing research evidence on the above popular stereotypes, Wayne Weiten found that there was some research evidence to sup-port statements "c," "f," "g," and "j;" research evidence did not support statements "a," "b," "d," "e," "h," and "i." In general, according to Weiten, the stereotypes had little relation to reality. He concluded that the similarities between women and men greatly outweighed the differences. Gender-role stereotypes lead to errors in social perception, and this inaccurate perception is often harmful to one's psychological health and interferes with social relationships.

CHAPTER 9: SEXUALITY

Outline

Where Am I Now?
Learning to Talk Openly about Sexual Issues
Developing Your Sexual Values
      Sexual Abstinence as an Option
      Formulating Your Sexual Values and Ethics
Misconceptions about Sexuality
Sex and Guilt
      Guilt Over Sexual Feelings
      Guilt Over Sexual Experiences
Learning to Enjoy Sensuality and Sexuality
      Listening to Our Bodies
      Asking for What We Want
Sex and Intimacy
AIDS: A Contemporary Crisis
      Basic Facts About AIDS
Other Sexually Transmitted Infections
Chapter Summary
Where Can I Go From Here?
Website Resources

Chapter Objectives

- to become aware of the sources of our sexual values

- to appreciate the relationship of sexuality in intimate relationships

- to see ways that love and sex are related

- to understand common sexually transmitted infections

- to understand basic facts about HIV/AIDS

Questions for Thought, Class Discussion, and Evaluation

1. How have you developed your attitudes and values regarding sex? What factors have influenced your attitudes? Have you tried to form your own standards?

2. What are your thoughts about the discussion in this chapter on developing your own sexual values?

3. What are your thoughts about celibacy as an option? What importance do you place on being able to cultivate emotional intimacy without physical intimacy?

4. Is there a double standard of morality of "acceptable" sexual behavior for women and men? If so, how do you feel about it? Is there any reason for a double standard?

5. Review the misconceptions about sexuality that are listed in this chapter. List and discuss several of the misconceptions about sex and sexuality that you find interesting. Are there any misconceptions that you had about sex that you have had to challenge?

6. What are some of your concerns regarding sexual attitudes or sexual behavior?

7. Discuss the father/daughter relationship as the foundation for a woman's relationship with other men in her life. Does she seek men to give her what her father never gave her? Is a woman's capacity to receive from a man, and her ability to give to a man, directly related to her relationship with her father?

8. Evaluate the impact of the mother/son relationship as a determinant of how a man relates to other women. Does a man look to women to give him what his mother did not? Is he looking for a mother? Are a man's capacity to receive from a woman and his ability to give to a woman directly related to his relationship with his mother?

9. What do you consider to be normal and abnormal in sexual relationships, behavior, and attitudes? How have you developed your concepts of what is normal and what is abnormal? What norms, standards, and guides do you use? Are standards of sexual normality simply products of social and cultural conditioning?

10. What kinds of sexual ethics would you like your children to develop? Do you want them to have your sexual values? If not, why not? In what ways do you hope they might be different?

11. If you believe in sex outside of a committed relationship, what kind of responsibility do you think should be involved?

12. In your discussion group, spend some time clarifying your value system as it relates to sexual concerns. Consider some of these issues:
    a. What are your views on abortion?
    b. What are your views on birth control?
    c. How do you feel about sex outside of marriage or a committed relationship?
    d. How do you decide with whom you will be sexually intimate?
    e. How do you decide what your sexual ethics are?
    f. What are some unresolved questions you have about your sexual values?

13. Differentiate between sensuality and sexuality. What do the two have in common? How are they different?

14. How has the AIDS crisis revolutionized sexual practices in this country?

15. Be able to explain in a few words some of the basic facts about AIDS. Be able to address questions such as: What causes AIDS? How is the AIDS virus transmitted? Who are the people at most risk of contracting AIDS? Why is there a stigma attached to this disease? How can AIDS be best prevented?

Glossary of Key Terms

Abstinence refers to refraining from intercourse and often other forms of sexual contact.

Sexual abstinence implies refraining from sexual intercourse until entering a committed, long-term, monogamous relationship.

Masturbation refers to self-stimulation of one's genitals for sexual pleasure.

Sensuality pertains to enjoying all of one's senses.

Orgasm is a series of muscular contractions of the pelvic muscles occurring at the peak of sexual arousal.

Erectile dysfunction (ED), sometimes referred to as impotence, is the consistent inability to achieve and maintain a penile erection required for adequate sexual relations.

Sexual dysfunctions are impairments in sexual functioning that cause distress.

Mutual empathy is the awareness that each partner in a relationship cares for the other and knows that this care is reciprocated.

Intimacy is a close emotional relationship characterized by a deep level of caring for another person, which is a basic component of all loving relationships.

Acquired immunodeficiency syndrome (AIDS) is the last stage of a disease caused by the human immunodeficiency virus (HIV), which attacks and weakens the body's natural immune system.

Human immunodeficiency virus (HIV) is an immune-system destroying virus that causes AIDS.

Sexually transmitted infections (STIs) are transmitted by sexual contact.

Condom is a sheath that fits over the penis and is used for protection against unwanted pregnancy and sexually transmitted infections.

TEST ITEMS FOR CHAPTER 9
SEXUALITY

1. The media has given increased attention to all aspects of sexual behavior, which has resulted in people
   a. talking more freely about their own sexual concerns.
   b. having increased knowledge about sexuality but still hesitant to talk openly about sexual matters.
   c. communicating their sexual wants to their partners.
   d. being less anxious about sexual matters.

2. According to the Coreys, the following is a misconception about sex:
   a. I am responsible for the level of my sexual satisfaction.
   b. Being sexually free means acting without any guilt or restrictions.
   c. I have the ability to overcome any negative conditioning I received about sex as I was growing up.
   d. Sexual relationships can remain exciting, even with the passage of time.

3. In the mid-18th century, masturbation was erroneously believed to cause
   a. blindness
   b. mental illness
   c. acts of homicide
   d. all of the above
   e. a and b

4. The following is a typical concern about sexuality:
   a. fear of getting AIDS or other sexually transmitted infections.
   b. doubt about capacity as a lover.
   c. worry about performance standards.
   d. all of the above.

5. Which of the following is *false* concerning celibacy?
   a. Choosing celibacy is a viable option.
   b. Some choose celibacy out of moral or cultural convictions.
   c. Some choose celibacy because of various fears about sex.
   d. Fear is always a bad reason to choose celibacy.

6. The following is true concerning guilt over sexual matters:
   a. All guilt over sexual matters is unhealthy and irrational.
   b. Guilt keeps us in control over our sexual impulses.
   c. There is real value in learning to challenge sexual guilt feelings and rid ourselves of those that are unrealistic.
   d. Sexual guilt is often the result of an ambiguous moral upbringing.

7. The World Health Organization claims that _____ account(s) for three percent of HIV transmissions.
   a. homosexual intercourse
   b. heterosexual intercourse
   c. breast feeding and blood transfusions
   d. intravenous drug use

8. According to the Coreys, guilt over sexual feelings
   a. should be examined to determine whether we are needlessly burdening ourselves.
   b. are always unhealthy.
   c. are irrational responses that need to be uprooted.
   d. typically result in sexually acting-out behavior.

9. Perhaps the best way to free ourselves from guilt over sexual feelings is
   a. to discard one's values and do what one wants.
   b. to become aware of early verbal and nonverbal messages about sexuality and work to modify them.
   c. to accept our sexual feelings and act on our impulses.
   d. to eliminate all guilt feelings since they keep us from having a satisfying sex life.

10. The following is true about sensuality:
    a. Sensuality is the same as sexuality.
    b. Sensuality necessarily leads to sexual experiences.
    c. Sensual experiences involve the enjoyment of all of our senses and can be enjoyed separately from sexual experiences.
    d. Performance standards and expectations has nothing to do with sensual and sexual pleasure.

11. The following can get in the way of sensual and sexual pleasure, especially for men:
    a. unrealistic expectations.
    b. overemphasis on orgasm.
    c. fear of being unable to perform.
    d. all of the above.

12. Goldberg maintains that impotence is
    a. a lifesaving and life-giving response.
    b. related to feelings of guilt, hostility, resentment, or anxiety about personal adequacy, or low self-esteem.
    c. an authentic response to anxiety over not performing.
    d. all of the above

13. One of the major sources of sexual dysfunction is
    a. seeking too much pleasure for oneself.
    b. being overly involved in the sensual experience.
    c. attempting to live up to unrealistically high performance standards.
    d. not having the technical mastery needed to satisfy one's partner.

14. _____ is a major factor that can interfere with being in a frame of mind that will allow a woman's body to respond.
    a. Stress
    b. Negative conditioning
    c. Sensual deprivation
    d. Mechanical lovemaking

15. _____ can be conceived of as a close emotional relationship characterized by a deep level of caring for another person.
    a. Sexuality
    b. Sensuality
    c. Intimacy
    d. Enmeshment

16. Fear-arousing campaigns have been _____ in getting young sexually active people to use condoms with regularity and engage in safer sex practices.
    a. extremely effective
    b. somewhat effective
    c. ineffective
    d intermittently successful

17. The last stage of a disease caused by the human immunodeficiency virus, which attacks and weakens the body's natural immune system, is
    a. HIV.
    b. AIDS.
    c. STIs.
    d. HPV.

18. People who have AIDS are vulnerable to serious illnesses that would not be a threat to anyone whose immune system was functioning normally. These illnesses are referred to as
    a. "opportunistic."
    b. HIV-positive.
    c. immunodeficiency syndrome.
    d. invasive agents.

19. AIDS is best described as a(n)
    a. pandemic
    b. epidemic
    c. outbreak
    d. national threat

20. AIDS has been called an "equal opportunity disease," although it appears that the largest growth in HIV infection is occurring among
    a. bisexual and homosexual men.
    b. blood transfusion recipients.
    c. intravenous drug users.
    d. women.

21. A positive HIV antibody test result
    a. means that the person will get AIDS.
    b. can indicate whether the individual will eventually develop signs of illness related to the viral infection.
    c. will give precise indication of how serious the illness will be.
    d. indicates that the person has been infected by the virus and could transmit it to others.

22. Below are all common reactions of people who test HIV positive, *except*:
    a. They may feel they have been given a death sentence.
    b. It is quite common to experience a gamut of emotional reactions from shock, to anger, to fear and anxiety.
    c. They may experience grief over the loss of their previous sexual freedom and over their uncertain future.
    d. They are likely to have a sense of freedom since they are no longer governed by their sex drive.

23. There is stigma attached to AIDS because
    a. it will ultimately lead to death.
    b. when the disease was first discovered, those who contracted AIDS belonged primarily to the sexually active homosexual or bisexual male population or were present or past abusers of intravenous drugs.
    c. family members will disown the person with AIDS out of fear.
    d. it is a sexually transmitted disease.

24. Regarding the treatment of AIDS, which of the following statements contains the *most* truth?
    a. No drug currently available will completely destroy HIV.
    b. There are some herbs that show positive results in the treatment of AIDS.
    c. AZT has been effective in curing most AIDS patients.
    d. Doctors are unable to treat the various acute illnesses affecting those with AIDS.

25. As a measure to prevent the spread of AIDS, the following is *not* true:
    a. Consistent use of condoms and spermicidal barriers is 100% effective in preventing HIV or other STDs.
    b. Engage in sexual activities that do not involve vaginal, anal, or oral intercourse.
    c. Avoid having sex with multiple partners and have intercourse only with one uninfected partner.
    d. Avoid the use of intravenous drugs or having sex with a partner who uses them.

26. Which of the following is considered to be "safer" behavior when attempting to protect yourself against contracting AIDS?
    a. choosing to be sexually active with multiple partners.
    b. restricting sex to just one mutually faithful, uninfected partner.
    c. having sex only with partners who look fine and feel well.
    d. if you use intravenous drugs, sharing needles only with those who are not infected with the AIDS virus.

27. All of the following are common sexually transmitted infections *except* for
    a. herpes.
    b. delirium tremins.
    c. Chlamydial infection.
    d. genital warts.

28. Designing a personal and meaningful set of sexual ethics
    a. leads to irrational guilt based on giving behavioral expression to sexual desires.
    b. means assuming responsibility for yourself, taking into consideration how others are affected by your choice.
    c. allows us to act out sexual desires without guilt.
    d. is an easy task that can be accomplished through a process of honest questioning.

29. When condoms are used reliably, they
    a. prevent pregnancy up to 98% of the time.
    b. provide a high degree of protection against a variety of sexually transmitted infections.
    c. reduce the chances of HIV infection.
    d. all of the above.

30. Which of the following statements is true regarding safer sex practices?
    a. Any form of unprotected sex is risky.
    b. People who carry the HIV virus often feel sick; thus, they are aware that they are infected.
    c. Using latex condoms and spermicidal barriers will eliminate the possibility of transmitting HIV.
    d. If you are intoxicated and have unprotected sex, you are at no greater risk of being infected with HIV than if you have unprotected sex when you are sober.

31. If saying "No" to sex ends a relationship
    a. this is a sign that the relationship was troubled from the start.
    b. you should consider changing your mind.
    c. you may have come across as overly harsh.
    d. b and c

32. Which of the following statements is *not* true about sexuality?
    a. Sexuality can contribute to your physical and psychological well-being.
    b. Sex can be used to hurt others and can lead to guilt, shame, anxiety, and inhibition.
    c. Sexual coercion is one way sex can be misused to exploit and harm others.
    d. Increased media saturation on the topic of sexuality has resulted in more people talking more freely about their own sexual delights and concerns.

33. According to Crooks and Baur (2008), what is the basis for effective sexual communication?
    a. nonverbal cues
    b. mutual empathy
    c. a spirit of adventure
    d. cultural conditioning

34. _____ refers to refraining from intercourse and often other forms of sexual contact.
   a. Abstinence
   b. Avoidance
   c. Menopause
   d. Sexual dysfunction

35. The largest growth in HIV infection is occurring among
   a. heterosexual men
   b. gay men
   c. heterosexual women
   d. lesbians

36. According to the Centers for Disease Control and Prevention (CDC), about _____ of those infected with HIV are unaware of their status.
   a. 10%
   b. 25%
   c. 55%
   d. 70%

1.	b	p. 258		19.	a	p. 273
2.	b	p. 263		20.	d	p. 273
3.	e	p. 264		21.	d	p. 272
4.	d	p. 259		22.	d	p. 273
5.	d	p. 260		23.	b	p. 273
6.	c	p. 265		24.	a	p. 273
7.	c	p. 273		25.	a	p. 274
8.	a	p. 265		26.	b	p. 274
9.	b	p. 265		27.	b	p. 275
10.	c	p. 266		28.	b	p. 261
11.	d	p. 266		29.	d	p. 274
12.	d	p. 267-268		30.	a	p. 274
13.	c	p. 266-268		31.	a	p. 262
14.	a	p. 268		32.	d	p. 258
15.	c	p. 269		33.	b	p. 258
16.	c	p. 275-276		34.	a	p. 260
17.	b	p. 271		35.	c	p. 273
18.	a	p. 272		36.	b	p. 273

Activities and Exercises for Classroom Participation for Chapter 9

1. **A questionnaire.** Have the class compose its own questionnaire on sexual attitudes and behavior. Ask class members to write several questions they'd like to explore in class. All the questions will be turned in to one person for typing and mimeographing. When everyone has responded to the questionnaire, a tally of responses can be made and reported to the class, and the results can be used as a basis for discussion. Some of the questions that we've received when we've used this exercise include:

a. What do you most like about men (women)?
b. What do you least like about men (women)?
c. Do you think that there are basic psychological differences between men and women?
d. Have you ever initiated a sexual relationship?
e. How would you rate yourself sexually?
f. Have you engaged in premarital sexual intercourse?
g. Have you gotten tired of having sex with the same person?
h. Have you ever used fantasy in obtaining an orgasm during intercourse?
i. Do you feel comfortable communicating your sexual feelings and needs to your partner?
j. Do you feel threatened by aggressive women (men)?
k. Do you like an aggressive sex partner?
l. Do you sometimes think of sex as "dirty"?
m. Would you date a married person?
n. Do you have a difficult time touching women (men)?
o. Do you feel accepting of your body?
p. If you are sexually active, would you engage in unprotected sex?
q. If married, would you consider a sexual relationship with another person?
r. Have you ever had an extramarital love affair?
s. Are you knowledgeable about safer-sex practices?
t. Do you presently use masturbation as a sexual outlet?
u. Do you enjoy sex?
v. Have you ever had a homosexual experience?
w. Have you ever fantasized a homosexual encounter or experience?
x. Do you feel that you must perform in sex?
y. Are you bound by social expectations in terms of your sex-role identity?
z. Have you changed your views about masculinity and femininity?

2. **Writing Questions on Sex.** Each person writes down a question that he or she would most like to hear the women or the men in the class respond to. Some questions can be directed to both men and women, while others can be directed to men or women only. The students do not put their names on these slips of paper, but they might put down their sex. Then the men can sit on one side of the room and the women on the other, while they respond to the questions. Alternatively, the students can react to the questions in small groups.

3. **Working with the Questions in Small Groups.** Depending on the size of the class, the structure of the class, and the general trust level, I have often had students write down their questions and share and respond to them in small groups. After an hour or so, all the groups meet as a class, and we have the basis for a fruitful discussion on some of the topics and themes that were explored in each group. The opportunity to discuss their concerns in small groups gives more people a chance to participate, while reconvening as a class allows for a general sharing and pooling of results.

4. **Misconceptions About Sexuality.** Review the section on misconceptions about sexuality. Ask for reactions to each of the misconceptions. What are the sources of these misconceptions? Do the students agree or disagree with each misconception?

5. **Developing Your Own Sexual Values**. Review the section on developing your own sexual values. In small groups invite students to discuss where their values came from and to raise questions they would like to explore in the larger class.

6. **Guest Speakers**. It is a good idea to invite experts on family planning, STD's, and safer sex to speak to the class. A guest speaker might develop the topic that knowledge can lead to safer sex practices. It would be helpful to emphasize that there are degrees of risk in engaging in sex. Knowledge and responsible choices make *safer* sex possible.

A Group Exercise in Learning How to Discuss Sex

This group exercise consists of several stages: (1) A guided fantasy can be presented to the entire group or class to help each person to get in clearer focus regarding his or her sexuality. (2) Men then form an inner circle and share some of their concerns or questions briefly, and during this time the women are in the outer circle as silent observers. (3) Then the women form an inner circle, while the men become the observers in the outer circle. The women can briefly raise issues they would like to explore, questions they would like answered, things they might like to know about men or about other women, and so forth. (4) Now, two separate subgroups are formed: the "women's only" group, and the "men's only" group. Their discussions can last for an hour or more. (5) Then the entire group or class reconvenes. The subgroups can again assume the inner/outer circle format. They can begin by briefly sharing some of the highlights of things they discussed in their separate groups, or the members can spontaneously engage in dialogue regarding the issues they've just pursued. The purpose is to get an open dialogue going between the men and the women. This sharing process is often characterized by a high degree of openness, trust, and willingness to share in a mixed group feelings that are usually kept hidden.

CAUTION: We'd like to emphasize the importance of respecting *students' rights to privacy*. We hope instructors make a point of emphasizing to their students that they make only those disclosures they are *willing* to make. At times, students need to be protected from undue pressure to be totally honest and open. We know of some teachers who probe students to reveal their innermost secrets. We think there is a critical difference between *inappropriate* disclosure and *appropriate* sharing of personal experiences. Although it may be helpful for people to be encouraged to talk more openly about sexual concerns, they should not be pushed to disclose personal sexual thoughts, fantasies, and experiences. Students can be taught that it is *not* important that they reveal details. Instead, the point is that students can share their concerns and discover that they are not alone. There is a delicate line between being sexually repressed and being indiscriminately open about our sexual lives.

145

CHAPTER 10: WORK AND RECREATION

Outline

Chapter Objectives

- to see the relationship between college education and one's work

- to examine the factors in choosing a career

- to develop an understanding of the process of deciding on a career

- to explore available choices at work

- to identify challenges of changing careers in midlife

- to present a context for the meaning of retirement

- to appreciate how work and recreation are related

Questions for Thought, Class Discussion, and Evaluation

1. Discuss the concept that work itself does not give meaning in life, but that a person gives meaning to his or her occupation.

2. What options do you think people have who feel that they're caught in dead-end jobs that give little satisfaction? What would you say if they claim that they can't quit and that there are no other jobs available to them?

3. Do you see choosing a career as a developmental process, or do you see it as making a choice and sticking by it?

4. What meaning have you found in the work you've done so far? Has work been a means of self-expression for you?

5. Do you agree or disagree with the position that your adjustment to work affects all the other areas of your life? Discuss.

6. Some people feel that they have to play a role in order to keep their jobs, which may necessitate being untrue to themselves. Do you feel this way? Is it possible to be honest and at the same time keep your job?

7. How important do you think it is for you to feel a sense of pride in the work you do? Have you felt valued in your work?

8. Discuss what you get or expect to get from work. What might your life be like if you weren't able to work? How do you imagine life would be if you were retired?

9. Do you see any way to incorporate your interests and hobbies into your career or vocation?

10. Do you think that you've been pressured to choose a vocation too soon? Where have these pressures come from? Discuss some of the dangers of choosing an occupation too soon.

11. In choosing a job, which would be more important to you: security or the opportunity for self-expression?

12. What factors would you consider most in selecting your occupation? Mention the top three, and explain why you picked these three factors.

13. Some experts claim that most people will change their jobs five times during their working years. What implication does this trend have for you personally?

14. Do you believe that you can choose your attitude toward work and thus change the meaning it has for you?

15. Do you regard most people as trapped in meaningless work, or do you think they have a choice and can change their work situations?

16. What are some of the parallels between attending college and working at a career? What are some of your behavioral styles in college that might carry over to your eventual career?

17. Discuss vocational choice as a process, rather than an event. Mention the main factors that should be carefully considered in vocational decision-making.

18. How is self-concept related to satisfaction in a career?

19. What role do values play in the career decision process?

20. Explain the meaning of being active in career planning.

21. What are some of the main dangers of selecting a career too soon?

22. What are some of the ways that work and leisure are related?

23. Discuss the dynamics of discontent in work as a factor within the individual rather than external factors creating dissatisfaction.

24. What are some ways people can create meaning in their work?

25. Discuss briefly the increasing choices women have in the world of work. Mention some of the basic problems women experience who are involved in a dual-career family.

26. How is satisfaction in one's career important with respect to the other facets of one's existence?

27. What can you do to prepare for retirement? How can you continue living and feeling a sense of productivity even though you may eventually retire?

28. Discuss the concept of your college education as your work. To what degree do you think your level of satisfaction of your work will parallel your level of satisfaction as a student? Do you think that the kind of student you are will also have some influence on the kind of worker you are likely to become?

29. Holland developed an approach to occupational theory that identifies worker personality types. As you review the six personality types, which are the types that you think are most characteristic of you? Compare your ratings of yourself on these six personality types with someone who knows you well. Is your assessment of yourself close to the assessment that others make of you? What practical value do you find in using these personality types as a guide for selecting a career?

30. The process of selecting a career involves more than simply matching information about the world of work with your personal characteristics. What are the specific steps that you would take in the process of selecting a career for yourself?

Glossary of Key Terms

Work is an activity that produces value for ourselves and others.

Recreation means to restore, to refresh, to put new life into, and to create anew; it involves leisure time and what we do away from work.

Leisure is the free time that we control and can use for ourselves; it involves unpaid activities we choose to engage in because we enjoy them and they are personally meaningful.

Career refers to one's life's work.

Occupation refers to one's vocation, profession, business, or trade.

Job refers to one's position of employment within an occupation.

Ability refers to one's competence in an activity.

Aptitude tests measure specific skills or the ability to acquire certain proficiencies.

Interests pertain to one's experiences or ideas pertaining to work-related activities that one likes or dislikes.

Occupational interest inventories are tests that measure one's interests as they relate to various jobs or careers; they are assessment tools that are used to compare one's interests with those of others who have found job satisfaction in a given area.

Self-concept refers to a pattern of beliefs about one's unique qualities and typical behavior.

Values pertain to what is important to us and what we want from life.

Work values pertain to what we hope to accomplish through our role in an occupation.

Personality types, within the context of Holland's typology, refer to certain values and particular personality traits which can be helpful in choosing a career. The six types are Realistic, Investigative, Artistic, Social, Enterprising, and Conventional.

Personal agency refers to certain attitudinal and behavioral characteristics such as a belief that one's career develops through effort, initiative, and self-development.

TEST ITEMS FOR CHAPTER 10
WORK AND RECREATION

1. Which of the following statements is *false*?
   a. Externally, the working world is constantly changing.
   b. Internally, a person's needs, motivations, values, and interests may change.
   c. Deciding on a career involves integrating the realities of the above two worlds.
   d. Choosing an occupation is a relatively simple process.

2. Deciding on a career involves
   a. surrendering some of your autonomy in order to fit into the work world.
   b. making a commitment to a life-time occupation.
   c. integrating the constantly changing work world with internal changes, such as expectations, needs, motivation, values, and interests.
   d. all of the above.

3. Your career can be thought of as
   a. your life's work spanning a period of time and involving one or several job changes.
   b. what you do to earn money to survive and to do the things you'd like to do.
   c. your best source of self-fulfillment.
   d. your profession, vocation, business, or trade.

4. Your vocation, profession, business, or trade is your
   a. career.
   b. job.
   c. occupation.
   d. life's work.

5. John went to college right out of high school because he wasn't certain what he wanted to do with his life and hoped that he could clarify his thoughts. When he graduated, he still wasn't certain what he should do, so he decided to get a graduate degree. According to research, his category of motivation for going to college is the
   a. self-fulfiller.
   b. careerist.
   c. avoider.
   d. procrastinator.

6. If you typically do more than is required as a college student, you are likely to do the following on your job:
   a. go beyond doing what is expected of you.
   b. feel utter frustration and exhaustion because of your need to prove yourself.
   c. take on too many tasks, which will lead to burnout.
   d. get behind in your work due to poor planning.

7. Holland believes that the choice of an occupation reflects the person's
   a. interests and skills.
   b. motivation, knowledge, personality, and ability.
   c. intellectual functioning.
   d. vocational awareness.

8. The following factors have been shown to be important in determining a person's occupational decision-making process:
   a. self-concept, motivation, achievement.
   b. occupational attitudes, abilities, interests, values.
   c. temperament and personality styles.
   d. all of the above.

9. All of the following are true concerning the relationship of self-concept to vocational decision-making *except*:
   a. negative self-attitude has little influence on making appropriate vocational decisions.
   b. people with poor self-concepts tend to keep their aspirations low, usually resulting in low achievements.
   c. people with poor self-concepts may select and remain in a job they do not enjoy or derive satisfaction from, based on their conviction that such a job is all they are worthy of.
   d. low self-esteem can result in limiting one's career choice.

10. People with poor self-concept
    a. generally do well in the world of work.
    b. tend to see themselves as having a meaningful job.
    c. identify themselves with their work.
    d. are not likely to envision themselves in a meaningful job.

11. Motivation is an important factor in career decision making because
    a. your abilities are related to your aptitude.
    b. your need to achieve is related to your self-concept.
    c. if you have career goals but do not have the persistence to pursue them, then your goals will not materialize.
    d. realistic career choice depends on your interest in earning money.

12. A person's aptitude refers to his or her
    a. ability to learn.
    b. motivation to achieve goals.
    c. interest in work-related activities.
    d. occupational choice.

13. In terms of occupational attitudes,
    a. it is difficult for people to feel positive about themselves if they have to accept an occupation they perceive as low in status.
    b. typical first-graders are already highly aware of the differential status of occupations.
    c. as students advance to higher grades, more and more occupations become acceptable to them.
    d. children move from ranking occupations in a manner similar to that of adults to ranking them according to their own interests.

14. When children are asked what they want to be when they grow up, the implication is that
    a. they will not be grown up until they decide on a career.
    b. those who ask the question are completely inappropriate and are violating boundaries by pressuring the children.
    c. they are destined to become eminent in their fields one day.
    d. none of the above

15. Research has shown a significant relationship between
    a. interests and abilities.
    b. self-concept and motivation.
    c. abilities and aptitude.
    d. occupational attitudes and success.

16. Helping others, influencing people, finding meaning, prestige, status, friendships, creativity, recognition, adventure, and challenge are examples of
    a. work values.
    b. interpersonal values.
    c. spiritual values.
    d. occupational attitudes.

17. Holland's theory is based on the assumption that
    a. there is a relationship between interests and attitudes towards work.
    b. people can be classified as having one of six types of personal orientations to life that are relevant to the career decision-making process.
    c. a person's self-concept is the best single predictor of vocational success.
    d. academic aptitude is directly linked to occupational choice.

18. A person who fits into the realistic type would have the following characteristics:
    a. has strong interpersonal and verbal skills.
    b. has a theoretical, analytic outlook.
    c. likes to work with things, objects, and animals rather than with ideas, data, and people.
    d. tends to be emotional and complicated.

19. A person who fits into the investigative type would have the following characteristics:
    a. scholarly and scientific, having a need to understand, explain, and predict what goes on around them.
    b. tends to have good leadership and persuasive skills.
    c. likes to be different and strive to stand out from the crowd.
    d. thrives in highly structured situations with externally imposed rules.

20. What personality type tends to be theoretical and analytic in outlook and tends to be naturally curious about the world?
    a. social type
    b. investigative type
    c. scientific type
    d. realistic type

21. Theresa is getting a degree in fine arts. She is a non-conformist, dressing to suit her personality, and expresses her personality by writing poetry and taking drama classes at the local community theater. According to Holland, Theresa has the following type of personality:
    a. artistic type.
    b. social type.
    c. enterprising type.
    d. abstract type.

22. Which personality type tends to be creative, expressive, original, intuitive, individualistic, and strives to stand out from the crowd?
    a. social type
    b. realistic type
    c. enterprising type
    d. artistic type

23. Roger is a friendly, enthusiastic, outgoing individual. People seek him out with their problems because they perceive Roger to be understanding, supportive and caring. In fact, he often takes on the role of counselor when dealing with others. According to Holland, Roger has the following type of personality:
    a. social type.
    b. counselor type.
    c. interpersonal type.
    d. facilitating type.

24. According to Holland, social types of personality dislike
    a. being in the company of other people when they have problems.
    b. being the center of attention.
    c. working with machines or data and at highly organized, routine, and repetitive tasks.
    d. expressing their emotions.

25. Which personality type tends to be the most understanding and insightful concerning the feelings and problems of others and likes to be helpful by serving in facilitative roles?
    a. investigative type
    b. social type
    c. counselor type
    d. interpersonal type

26. Which personality type likes to organize, direct, and control the activities of groups, places a high value on status, power, money, and material possessions, and also sees themself as popular and having leadership abilities?
    a. supervisory type
    b. enterprising type
    c. social type
    d. enterprising type

27. Shannon enjoys working in clerical and computational activities. She works as an administrative assistant and is appreciated by her supervisor for being dependable, efficient, and conscientious. According to Holland, Shannon has the following type of personality:
    a. social type.
    b. enterprising type.
    c. realistic type.
    d. conventional type.

28. Each of Holland's personality types can best be understood through the following diagram:
    a. hexagon.
    b. circle.
    c. bar graph.
    d. cube.

For nos. 29–33, match the personality type with the possible occupations associated with each type below.
29. Realistic
30. Investigative
31. Social
32. Enterprising
33. Conventional

a. accounting, travel agency management, banking and finance, business administration, fashion merchandising
b. carpenter, electronics engineer, industrial design, wildlife conservation management, diesel mechanics
c. computer and data processing, bookkeeping, secretarial science, office machine technology, personnel clerk
d. education, social work, nursing, psychology, school administration, physical therapy, labor relations
e. economics, marketing, biology, linguistics, optometry, medicine, biochemistry, veterinary medicine, chemistry

34. Which personality type is well-organized, persistent, and practical; enjoys clerical and computational activities that follow set procedures; enjoys the security of belonging to groups and organizations; and makes a good team member although does not usually aspire to high positions of leadership?
    a. enterprising type
    b. conventional type
    c. realistic type
    d. organizational type

35. It is important to remember that career decision
    a. is an ongoing process, rather than a step to be completed.
    b. is a process by which we make one choice that we stay with permanently.
    c. involves implementing your career decision without fear.
    d. is simply a matter of matching information about the world of work with your personality type.

36. The following is an internal factor associated with job dissatisfaction:
    a. low morale among fellow workers.
    b. authoritarian supervisors who make it difficult for you to feel any sense of freedom on the job.
    c. organizational blocks to your creativity.
    d. feeling stuck in a job that offers little opportunity for growth.

37. The following is an *ineffective* way to deal with the issue of meaninglessness and dissatisfaction in work:
    a. look at how you really spend your time and consider what activities are draining you, and which are energizing.
    b. focus on factors within your job that you *can* change.
    c. find ways of advancing within your present job, making new contacts or acquiring skills necessary to move on.
    d. adopt a passive position and dwell on those things that cannot be changed.

38. Lisa decided to return to college after her children reached high school age. She looks forward to starting a career after many years of working in the home. This is an example of
    a. midlife change.
    b. self-identity.
    c. housewife burnout.
    d. the work ethic.

39. When people no longer work at a job, they can become involved by
    a. going back to school to take classes simply for interest or to prepare for a new career.
    b. taking time for more physical activity.
    c. cultivating hobbies that they have neglected.
    d. all of the above.

40. Bob made a decision that he must remain in a job that allows little scope for personal effort and satisfaction. It would be best if he
    a. recognizes the fact that if he only had a job that he liked, then he would be fulfilled.
    b. acknowledges that he feels trapped in an unfulfilling job.
    c. finds something outside the job that fulfills his need for recognition, significance, productivity, and excitement.
    d. knows that job dissatisfaction always leads to physical or psychological illness.

41. The most appropriate description of leisure time is
    a. "free time," the time that we control and can use for ourselves.
    b. time planned that requires a certain degree of perseverance and drive.
    c. compulsively planning leisure time so that we can accomplish all that is required to relax.
    d. planned spontaneity.

42. When making career decisions, it generally is wise to
    a. match your personal characteristics with occupational information and trends in the world of work.
    b. base your decision on your childhood dreams.
    c. take the first path that comes to mind since it probably is the right path for you.
    d. not dwell on how your values might influence your choice.

43. Which of the following should be *avoided* when exploring one's career options?
    a. Using the resources at your college or university
    b. Using online resources
    c. Talking to other people about their job satisfaction
    d. none of the above

44. Interest inventories are designed to
    a. predict job success.
    b. give some indication of job satisfaction.
    c. predict the job market.
    d. assess your work values.

45. Belinda completed an interest inventory designed by Holland and discovered that her three most prominent areas were Artistic, Social, and Enterprising (ASE). Which of the following behaviors/attitudes/qualities would Belinda be *least* inclined to demonstrate based on her Holland profile?
    a. She would enjoy social gatherings and like to associate with well-known and influential people.
    b. She would be creative, expressive, original, intuitive, unconventional, and individualistic.
    c. She would engage in scholarly and scientific endeavors and be pessimistic and critical about nonscientific, simplistic, or supernatural explanations.
    d. She would behave in a friendly, warm, trusting, generous, enthusiastic, outgoing, and cooperative manner.

46. The jobs of court reporter, editorial assistant, website editor, or investment analyst would be aligned with which of the following personality types according to Holland?
    a. Investigative Type
    b. Conventional Type
    c. Artistic Type
    d. Realistic Type

47. Due to the great emphasis that is placed on career in this society, the transition to retirement
    a. can be a period of upheaval.
    b. can be a positive experience with many benefits.
    c. is almost always devastating for the retiree.
    d. a and b

48. Which of the following statements is *not* true about leisure activities?
    a. Leisure can become a substitute for work and provide opportunities to try out new activities and find meaning apart from our work.
    b. Contrary to a widely held belief, leisure does not give us a respite from the responsibilities of work and relieve work stress because it tends to take too much time.
    c. Pursuit of leisure activities is associated with improved physical and cognitive functioning, increased happiness, and greater longevity.
    d. Leisure time activities can satisfy self-expressive needs.

ANSWER KEY FOR CHAPTER 10
WORK AND RECREATION

1.	d	p. 282	25.	b	p. 290
2.	c	p. 282	26.	d	p. 290-291
3.	a	p. 282	27.	d	p. 291
4.	c	p. 282	28.	a	p. 291
5.	c	p. 283	29.	b	p. 293
6.	a	p. 283-284	30.	e	p. 294
7.	b	p. 284	31.	d	p. 294
8.	d	p. 285	32.	a	p. 294
9.	a	p. 287-288	33.	c	p. 294
10.	d	p. 287	34.	b	p. 291
11.	c	p. 285	35.	a	p. 295
12.	a	p. 286-287	36.	d	p. 298
13.	a	p. 286	37.	d	p. 298-299
14.	a	p. 285	38.	a	p. 301
15.	a	p. 287	39.	d	p. 303-304
16.	a	p. 287	40.	c	p. 301
17.	b	p. 288	41.	a	p. 306
18.	c	p. 288	42.	a	p. 282
19.	a	p. 289	43.	d	p. 283
20.	b	p. 289	44.	b	p. 287
21.	a	p. 289	45.	c	p. 289-291
22.	d	p. 289	46.	b	p. 294
23.	a	p. 290	47.	d	p. 304
24.	c	p. 290	48.	b	p. 306

Activities and Exercises for Classroom Participation for Chapter 10

1. A group can form a panel and interview some people they know to determine what work means in their lives. Some questions can result from this type of panel, particularly if the people interviewed represent a varied and interesting population.

2. People from various occupations can be invited to class as guest speakers. They can talk about the meaning work has for them, what they like and don't like about their work, and other questions that the students might raise. Students can be given the responsibility to recruit some speakers, and a group of students can work on this project together to increase the pool of potential speakers.

3. In small groups, students can discuss how they have related to work so far in their lives. Have they made any major decisions?

4. In discussion groups, pursue the topic of your values and work. Look at your values related to security, money, status, achievement, helping others, finding meaning, personal growth, and so on. How do your values relate to your career selection?

5. Students might consider making a trip to the Counseling Center/Career Development Center on campus to investigate the possibilities of taking a series of tests and inventories that were described in Chapter 10. After the tests are scored and interpreted, these students can discuss what they learned about themselves and their choice of a vocation through this process.

6. If students make an appointment at the career development center, suggest that they explore the following questions:

- What are my interests?

- Do my interests match the careers I am thinking about pursuing?

- Do I have the knowledge I need to make a career choice? If not, what kind of knowledge do I need to get?

- Do I have the aptitude and skills for the career I have in mind?

- What are the current prospects and future possibilities in the career areas I have in mind?

- Where can I go for further exploration?

    Once your students have completed this investigation, have them write a paper on what they learned from this activity and what they will do with the knowledge they now have about their occupational interests.

7. Several students might read *What Color Is Your Parachute?* and give a report on some section of this book. Students can create an imaginative oral presentation designed to involve the entire class in the discussion of practical ways of finding a job and changing careers.

8. Some students might form a panel and present various facets on the topic of job burnout, and ways to stay alive on one's job.

9. Encourage students to follow up on the Take Time to Reflect sections within the chapter and the end of the chapter exercises as well. Encourage them to become active in choosing their career. Stress that making a career decision is an ongoing process. Consider sharing the process that brought you to a teaching position. If you have had several career changes, students may profit from hearing what motivated you to make changes.

10. On most college campuses a career day is scheduled. If such an event is held on your campus, attendance could be a required assignment that is written into your class syllabus. It is an excellent way for students to meet potential employers, graduate school representatives, and alumni. They often feature

mini-workshops on volunteer opportunities, internships, successful resume writing, preparing for an interview, and occupational trends. This assignment can be one of the options on your list if you require students to attend a certain number of campus activities as a part of the course.

11. After students complete the Holland personality inventory, create small groups based on the students' types. Ask students to bring the results of their ratings on the Holland inventory into a small group. Students can share their types with one another and discuss their similarities and differences as they pertain to career interests and plans. Students could explore what kinds of jobs might fit with their types. This might result in insights that similar types do look toward similar occupations or that similar types still have individual differences in goals and passions. Other questions that you can suggest your students explore in their small group include:

- As you review the six personality types, which types do you think are most characteristic of you?

- Compare your ratings of yourself on these six personality types with someone who knows you well. Is your assessment of yourself close to the assessment that others make of you?

- What practical value do these personality types provide as guide for selecting a major or a career?

- What kinds of jobs would fit with these types

12. Ask students to review the Holland types and rank the three types that resemble them most closely. Then ask students to review the occupations associated with each type and ask themselves these questions:

- What does the occupation require?

- What are the main rewards of the occupation?

- What values or personal styles does this occupation express?

- What does the occupation involve?

- What are some sample jobs within the occupation?

13. As a class discussion topic, ask students to identify some of their recreational pursuits. How do your students view the importance of recreation? What kind of balance do they have between the demands of work and school with making time for recreation?

14. Ask students what they envision when they retire. Ask: What are your thoughts about the kind of retirement you want to have? What can you do, if anything, to prepare for a meaningful retirement?

CHAPTER 11: LONELINESS AND SOLITUDE

Outline

Chapter Objectives

- to come to appreciate the value of loneliness and solitude

- to encourage readers to explore their fear of loneliness

- to understand the meaning of shyness

- to provide an overview of loneliness at various life stages

- to appreciate the importance of time alone as a source of creativity

Questions for Thought, Discussion, and Evaluation

1. Is it true that, ultimately, we are alone? How do you cope with your aloneness?

2. What are some ways of encountering loneliness? How can you discover your resources through loneliness?

3. What are some specific ways through which you escape loneliness, being alone, and experiencing solitude? What is the price of this escape?

4. Think of relationships you have that are special to you. Do you often feel alone even when you are with these special people?

5. Recall and try to re-experience some moments of loneliness. How did you feel, and how did you deal with these experiences?

6. What do you actually do to get time alone? When you're alone, how do you usually feel? What do you do with this time?

7. Have you experienced being lonely in a crowd? What is this feeling like? In what ways have you attempted to deny your loneliness through interaction with others?

8. For you, what are the benefits of being alone?

9. Can you tolerate being alone, or do you find all sorts of ways of escaping encountering yourself? If you can't enjoy yourself, do you think anyone else can?

10. How do some people create their own loneliness through shyness? What is shyness? How common a problem is it?

11. Is shyness a problem in your life? If so, how have you attempted to cope with it?

12. How is loneliness related to the following life stages: childhood? adolescence? young adulthood? middle age? the later years?

13. What are a few of the main points Anne Morrow Lindbergh makes in her book *Gift from the Sea*? How do some of these points apply to your life or to people that you know?

14. How can solitude be an avenue toward personal growth? How can solitude provide us with the opportunity to gain a perspective on our lives?

15. Can the group be a refuge from facing yourself alone? Do you ever feel that you use your group to avoid the anxiety of standing alone? Do we place so much stress upon encountering others because we fear encountering ourselves?

16. Think of a time in your life when you were particularly lonely. What was this like for you?

17. Discuss the idea that loneliness and solitude can be paths to personal growth. List and discuss a few of the values of solitude.

18. Do you attempt to escape from your loneliness? If so, make a list of some of the escapes you sometimes use. How do you think using these devices affects you?

19. Did you experience loneliness as a child or an adolescent? If so, describe briefly what it was like for you, and mention how it may have an impact on you now.

20. What kind of experience do you have as you walk around your campus? Do you feel that it's a friendly place? Do you feel close to others? Do you feel isolated and left out? Do you experience your college campus as an impersonal place? Mention some things that *you* can choose to do to feel more connected to others.

Glossary of Key Terms

Loneliness is an experience that arises when our network of social relationships is lacking or when there are strains on these relationships; an emotional state that occurs when we have fewer social relationships than we want or when our relationships are not satisfying.

Solitude is a state that we choose for ourselves that allows us to make time to be with ourselves, to discover who we are, and to renew ourselves.

Transient loneliness involves brief feelings of loneliness that occurs when people have had satisfactory social relationships in the past, but experience some disruption in their social network, such as the breakup of a relationship.

Chronic loneliness is a condition that involves the inability to establish meaningful interpersonal relationships over a relatively long period of time.

Everyday loneliness involves the pain of being isolated from other people.

Existential loneliness, or sometimes referred to as existential isolation, is a profound sense of an unbridgeable gap that separates us from others.

Shyness refers to anxiety, discomfort, inhibition, and excessive caution in interpersonal relationships.

TEST ITEMS FOR CHAPTER 11
LONELINESS AND SOLITUDE

1. Loneliness is often the result of
   a. failing to listen to ourselves and our own feelings.
   b. feeling apart from others.
   c. the death of someone we love.
   d. all of the above.

2. According to the Coreys, solitude can be considered as
   a. basically the same thing as loneliness.
   b. something that happens to us when we experience a loss.
   c. a choice we make when we take time to be with ourselves, discover who we are, and renew ourselves.
   d. something that needs to be avoided at all costs.

3. The Coreys distinguish between loneliness and
   a. intimate relationships.
   b. solitude.
   c. shyness.
   d. separation anxiety.

4. Loneliness is *not* something that
   a. generally results from certain events in our life.
   b. can occur when we feel set apart in some way from everyone around us.
   c. we choose to experience.
   d. can indicate we have failed to listen to ourselves and our own feelings.

5. In her book *Gift from the Sea,* Anne Morrow Lindbergh describes her own need to
   a. get away by herself in order to find her center, simplify life, and nourish herself so she can give to others again.
   b. quit her hectic job because of its many and conflicting demands.
   c. see loneliness as a choice she made as a means of finding spirituality by the sea.
   d. allow herself to be an introvert.

6. Through solitude, Anne Morrow Lindbergh found
   a. replenishment and became reacquainted with herself.
   b. that she was overwhelmingly lonely.
   c. that she could avoid her busy life with its conflicting demands.
   d. that she enjoyed collecting seashells.

7. Laurie is being honored for her outstanding work achievements by her boss at a social function attended by many attractive and accomplished people in her field. Others can't seem to find her because she keeps leaving the function to take cigarette breaks whenever her name is mentioned. Laurie's behavior may be
   a. an indication that she cares neither about the honor nor the respect of her boss or colleagues.
   b. a sign that she has a severe tobacco addiction.
   c. indicative of shyness.
   d. a sign that she doesn't deserve the honor.

8. Many of us fail to experience solitude because we
   a. allow our lives to become more and more frantic and complicated because we enjoy being busy.
   b. may fear that we will alienate others if we ask for private time.
   c. don't know how to make up good excuses when we want to decline invitations to be with friends.
   d. are social beings with a need to belong.

9. Many people fear loneliness because they may associate the lonely periods of their lives with
   a. pain and struggle, a condition to avoided at all costs.
   b. rejection of self and being cut off from others.
   c. abandonment and isolation.
   d. all of the above.

10. Paradoxically, out of fear of rejection and loneliness, we may
    a. make ourselves needlessly lonely by refusing to reach out to others.
    b. share ourselves fully in our intimate relationships.
    c. compensate for our loneliness by working harder to form new relationships.
    d. all of the above.

11. We can escape from facing and coping with our loneliness by
    a. scheduling every moment and overstructure our lives.
    b. surrounding ourselves with people and becoming absorbed in social functions.
    c. trying to numb ourselves with self-destructive compulsive behavior.
    d. all of the above.

12. Edward Arlington Robinson's poem "Richard Cory" best illustrates the
    a. image of a man who is justifiably envied by everyone he knows.
    b. murder of a wealthy man.
    c. quiet desperation that occurs when we pretend to others that we are not who we really are.
    d. loneliness we feel when we fail to have an intimate relationship.

13. If we want to get back into contact with ourselves, we can begin to examine how we have learned to escape being lonely by
    a. evaluating the values of our society and questioning whether they are contributing to our sense of isolation.
    b. asking whether the activities that fill our time actually satisfy us or leave us discontented and lonely.
    c. strengthening our awareness of ourselves as the true center of meaning and direction in our life.
    d. spending more time being alone.
    e. all of the above.

14. According to Phil Zimbardo, shyness is an experience that is
    a. a universal experience.
    b. almost nonexistent in today's society.
    c. due to separation anxiety.
    d. an attempt to get some solitude.

15. Zimbardo's research on shyness indicates that shyness does *not*
    a. exist on a continuum.
    b. result in feelings of depression, anxiety, and loneliness.
    c. prevent people from expressing their views and speaking up for their rights.
    d. mean that the shy individual has a disease that needs to be cured.

16. Jeff is quite shy and has difficulty meeting new people, making friends, and getting involved in many social activities. The Coreys would *not* suggest that
    a. he put himself in situations where he would be forced to make social contact, even though he feels intimidated.
    b. he try to pinpoint the reasons or combination of factors underlying his shyness.
    c. since his shyness is totally negative, he needs to become an extroverted personality.
    d. he challenge the personal fears that keep him from being comfortable in social situations.

17. According to Zimbardo, there is a constellation of factors explaining shyness. Each of the following would apply *except*:
    a. being oblivious to negative feedback from others.
    b. fearing rejection.
    c. lacking self-confidence and specific social skills.
    d. being frightened of intimacy.

18. Below is an example of negative "self-talk" that can set the shy person up for failure in social situations:
    a. "I'd better try something new, because it doesn't matter if I look like a fool."
    b. "If people only knew what I was like, they would really like me."
    c. "I have nothing to fear by trying to approach a person I'd like to get to know."
    d. "Others constantly evaluate and judge me, and I'm sure I won't measure up to what they expect."

19. Reliving some of our childhood experiences of loneliness can
    a. bring on pain and should be avoided at all costs.
    b. be a futile attempt to rewrite the past.
    c. help us come to grips with present fears about being alone or lonely.
    d. only be done with the help of a counselor.

20. As we try to relive lonely experiences from early childhood, we should remember that
    a. children live in a logical, well-ordered world and our memories are certain to be accurate.
    b. our childhood fears were greatly exaggerated so we are unlikely to carry them over into adulthood.
    c. strategies we adopted as children may remain with us into adulthood, even if they are no longer appropriate.
    d. all of the above.

21. _____ often feel that they are all alone in their world, that they are the first ones to have had the feelings they do, and that they are separated from others by some abnormality.
    a. Children
    b. Adolescents
    c. Young adults
    d. The elderly

22. Adolescents often feel lonely because
    a. their bodily changes and impulses alone are enough to bring about a sense of perplexity and loneliness.
    b. they are developing a sense of identity.
    c. they want to be accepted and liked, but they fear rejection, ridicule, or expulsion by their peers.
    d. all of the above.

23. Ethnic minority adolescents often face unique challenges in terms of feeling connected to others because
    a. they have learned that loneliness results from being alone.
    b. of an inadequate resolution of the intimacy vs. isolation psychosocial crisis.
    c. they have bought into stereotypes that contribute to feeling alone and different.
    d. they haven't developed an ego identity.

24. The question of what to do with our lives, what intimate relationships we want to establish, and how we will chart our future most likely occurs during
    a. adolescence.
    b. young adulthood.
    c. middle adulthood.
    d. a major crisis in our lives.

25. Bill realizes that he paid a terrible price in lost relationships for the success he has obtained. He finds himself surrounded by material possessions, yet overwhelmingly lonely. Bill is in a crisis associated with
    a. young adulthood.
    b. middle age.
    c. old age.
    d. adolescence.

26. The following is a change or crisis that is *not* likely to occur during middle age:
    a. Our significant other may grow tired of living with us and decide to leave.
    b. Our life may not have turned out the way we had planned.
    c. Our children may leave home, and with this change we may experience emptiness and a sense of loss.
    d. We may struggle with role confusion.

27. Those who find themselves having to cope with feelings of isolation and abandonment after a divorce may
    a. feel panic and retreat from people.
    b. quickly run into a new relationship to avoid the pain of separation.
    c. be controlled by their fear of being left alone for the rest of their lives if they don't confront their fears and pain.
    d. all of the above.

28. Loneliness and hopelessness are experienced by anyone who feels there is little to look forward to or that he or she has no vital place in society, and such feelings are particularly common among
    a. young adults.
    b. adolescents.
    c. middle-aged individuals.
    d. older adults.

29. What is the relationship between shyness and loneliness?
    a. People who have difficulty dealing with shyness often withdraw socially, and social withdrawal generally exacerbates matters and can lead to loneliness.
    b. People who are shy tend to gravitate towards other people who are shy, which creates a communication barrier, and ultimately, loneliness.
    c. Shy people typically move far away from their families and end up with poor social networks, exacerbating their loneliness.
    d. There is no relationship between shyness and loneliness.

30. Frankl noted that many inmates in the Nazi concentration camp where he was imprisoned kept themselves alive by looking forward to the prospect of being released and reunited with their families. He refers to this as the
    a. "hope fantasy."
    b. "will to meaning."
    c. "denial syndrome."
    d. "collective unconscious."

31. Ellen is an 85-year-old widow who spends most of her days watching television and doing crossword puzzles. She has few friends and only has occasional contact with her family because she doesn't want to be a burden to them. Ellen complains that she is lonely and is unable to recognize that she
    a. is a prisoner of her loneliness because she fails to realize how much others could benefit from her company.
    b. is unable to change her pattern because she is set in her ways.
    c. needs to stop complaining so people will want to be with her.
    d. is feeling sorry for herself.

32. According to counselors who work with children, many of them suffer from stress and have "overstuffed" lives. These children tend to do all of the following *except*
    a. become impatient with lack of stimulation
    b. feel bored without activity
    c. enjoy their quiet time relaxing
    d. a and b

33. Taking time to be alone gives us the opportunity to
    a. think, plan, imagine, and dream.
    b. listen to ourselves and become sensitive to what we are experiencing.
    c. appreciate anew both our separateness from and our relatedness to important people and projects in our lives.
    d. all of the above.

34. Which of the following statements is *not* true about loneliness?
    a. We often experience loneliness when our network of social relationships is lacking, when there are strains on these relationships, or when these relationships are not satisfying to us.
    b. Loneliness can occur when we feel set apart in some way from everyone, which can have its roots in the lack of attachment in early childhood.
    c. Loneliness generally happens to us rather than being chosen by us.
    d. We should not allow ourselves to fully experience our loneliness because the pain can become unbearable and it is not productive.

35. _____ involves brief feelings of loneliness that occur when people have had satisfactory social relationships in the past but experience some disruption in their social network.
    a. Transient loneliness
    b. Chronic loneliness
    c. Temporary despair
    d. Profound loneliness

36. _____ exists when people are unable to establish meaningful interpersonal relationships over a relatively long period of time.
    a. Transient loneliness
    b. Chronic loneliness
    c. Psychosis
    d. Severe loneliness

37. Yalom (2008) writes about two kinds of loneliness:
    a. everyday and existential loneliness.
    b. transient and chronic loneliness.
    c. aloneness and meaninglessness.
    d. neurotic and psychotic loneliness.

38. Sarah's loneliness seems to stem from her fear of intimacy and feelings of shame, rejection, and of being unlovable. Her loneliness is best described as
    a. transient loneliness
    b. chronic loneliness
    c. everyday loneliness
    d. existential loneliness

39. As people age and move closer to death, they tend to become increasingly aware that their world will disappear and that others cannot accompany them to their final destiny. This experience is best described as
    a. transient loneliness
    b. chronic loneliness
    c. everyday loneliness
    d. existential loneliness

40. Jerilyn recently ended a lengthy relationship and seems to be filling all of her free time going on dates and attending parties. She also seems to be eating more than usual for emotional reasons. These behaviors could be indicative of
    a. Jerilyn's changing metabolism
    b. Jerilyn's fear of loneliness
    c. Jerilyn's need for excitement
    d. Jerilyn's inability to reflect on her life

ANSWER KEY FOR CHAPTER 11
LONELINESS AND SOLITUDE

1. d p. 316
2. c p. 316
3. b p. 316
4. c p. 316
5. a p. 316
6. a p. 316
7. c p. 321
8. b p. 317
9. d p. 318
10. a p. 318
11. d p. 319
12. c p. 320
13. e p. 321
14. a p. 322
15. d p. 323
16. c p. 324
17. a p. 323
18. d p. 323
19. c p. 326
20. c p. 326
21. b p. 327

22. d p. 328
23. c p. 329
24. b p. 329
25. b p. 331
26. d p. 331
27. d p. 332
28. d p. 332
29. a p. 324
30. b p. 334
31. a p. 318
32. c p. 317
33. d p.335
34. d p. 317-318
35. a p. 318
36. b p. 318
37. a p. 318
38. c p. 318
39. d p. 318
40. b p. 319

Activities and Exercises for Classroom Participation for Chapter 11

1.   Is there anyone in your life (either past or present) who stirs up feelings of loneliness in you? If so, write a letter telling this person(s) what he or she means to you now. Express the things you've never said to this person but perhaps wanted him or her to know. Then go one step further: allow yourself to become that person and respond to your letter. In this letter, have that special person say all the things you imagine he or she thinks and feels about you now. The crucial part of this exercise is actually writing your letter. However, do not mail the letter.

2.   Explore this theme in your group: Do you sometimes feel alienated, separated, alone, or lonely in your group? If so, how do you deal with these feelings? Do you express them in your group?

3.   Compose a personal poem, song, or short story that describes in depth your experience with loneliness or being alone. Consider bringing your writing to your class or group and sharing it with others.

4.   Select a poem, an excerpt from a book, or a picture that captures the loneliness you have felt at some time in your life. Bring this to your group and share it with the rest of the members.

5.   Select a song that says something about a time in your life when you were particularly lonely. Bring in this song to your group, and then tell the others how you identify with this song.

6.   Go to a place, such as a city park, where you can observe people. What do you notice? Consider talking with some of the people you see. When you return home, write down your reactions.

7.   Look for a song, a poem, a poster, a photograph, or some other representation of peaceful solitude. Bring it to your class or group and share it with the others. Let them know how it reminds you of a pleasant and solitary experience.

8.   Decide whether or not you want to take more time for being alone, even for only short periods each day. If you decide you'd like more solitude, write down some of the things you might want to experience more. Bring your list to class and share some of the things you'd like to experience more often by yourself.

9.   Consider picking a friend and sharing with him or her some times that you have felt loneliness in your life.

10. Ask students to review the section on shyness in this chapter. Explore how shyness might be a problem in class discussions and in getting to know others. Encourage students to challenge their fears and find ways to express their ideas in this class.

11. Invite students to explore the sources of their shyness. Ask them to pay attention to possible negative self-talk that prevents them from interacting with others or speaking out in class.

12. Talk with your students about strategies for successfully dealing with times they may inhibit themselves from participating in class discussions. Spend some time teaching students about the importance of taking small steps to overcome inhibitions. Although some students may be shy, it is possible for them to participate in class activities by taking steps to gradually let others know them. Encourage students to talk in dyads or small groups, giving them practice is talking with others.

CHAPTER 12: DEATH AND LOSS

Outline

Chapter Objectives

- to learn about our fears of death

- to see how death influences the meaning of life

- to explore the impact of suicide

- to learn about the stages of death and loss

- to appreciate the value of grief work

- to determine how fully we are living

Questions for Thought, Discussion, and Evaluation

1. How often do you devote time to reflecting upon the meaning of your death? Do you allow yourself to think of yourself as being finite?

2. In what ways do you attempt to deny the inevitability of death for both yourself and those you love?

3. If you were dying now, and you could review your life to date (what you have been, what you have become, and so on), how would you view your life? What would you want to complete before your death?

4. Respond to the personal meanings these statements have for you:

   • "Unless you take death seriously, life has little meaning."

   • "Everyone knows they are going to die, but nobody believes it. If we did, we would do things differently."

   • "Facing death is often the catalyst that enable people to reach out for what they want."

   • "The truth is, once you learn how to die, you learn how to live."

   • "Contemplate death if you would learn how to live."

   • "It is only in the face of death that man's self is born."

5. Do you believe in life after death? How does your belief or non-belief in life after death relate to how you live your life now?

6. What does immortality mean to you? In what ways might you be immortal? Do you seek immortality through having children, through work, through religion?

7. How might your life be different if at times you were to reflect upon your own death and dying? What is the meaning and importance for you of dying with dignity?

8. If you knew you were going to die within a limited time span (say one week or one year), in what ways would you live your life differently from the way you're living it now? What would you want to be doing that you're not doing now? What things would you be giving up? What would you be seeking most?

9. How does your belief or disbelief in religion relate to your acceptance or fear of dying?

10. What are some ways that you can be "dead" without actually having experienced death? What parts of you are dead? What parts of you are not fully alive?

11. When are you most alive? When do you experience life the most fully? What happens to blunt this feeling of aliveness?

12. In what ways are your fears of death manifest? What have you done to become more fully aware of your death, without being in dread of it? Mention some of the fears of death that people commonly hold.

13. Briefly describe the essence of the hospice movement.

14. What is your reaction to the question "Is suicide an ultimate choice or an ultimate cop-out?"

15. How might you live your life differently if you knew you had only a short time to live? What does your answer tell you about the way you are living now?

16. The existentialists contend that the awareness of death gives meaning to life, for it forces us to recognize that we are finite and jolts us into taking the present seriously. Is this contention valid for you? Explain why or why not.

17. List and briefly describe the five stages of death and dying as developed by Dr. Elisabeth Kübler-Ross.

18. Compare the stages of death (according to Kübler-Ross) to any type of significant loss in your life.

19. Do you believe that our society denies the reality of death? If so, cite some examples of denial that you've observed.

20. Discuss the importance of allowing yourself to grieve and mourn over your losses. What are some of the problems that can arise if you aren't able to grieve fully?

21. Why is it essential to express grief if one hopes to work through some of the pain of a loss? What are some of the effects of refusing to express and explore feelings of sorrow, anger, guilt, and grief over losses?

22. Discuss this statement: "Finding meaning is perhaps the most difficult task we come to grips with, especially within the context of accepting our mortality." How is the reality of your death a catalyst for finding the meaning of your life and how well you are living?

23. What are some ways that facing the reality of death can give meaning to what is left of life for those who are terminally ill?

24. Discuss some of the common reactions to a suicide. What kind of unfinished business do those who are left behind often experience?

25. What are the specific tasks associated with the task-based model of coping with dying? Compare Kubler-Ross's stage-based model with the task-based approach to understand the dying process.

Glossary of Key Terms

Death anxiety pertains to fears about one's own death and dying.

Suicide is the taking of one's own life.

Rational suicide refers to one's decision-making process without coercion from others to end one's life because of extreme suffering involved with a terminal illness.

Assisted suicide involves providing lethal means to cause a person's death, with the person performing the act that ends his or her own life.

Hastened death involves speeding up the dying process, which can entail withholding or withdrawing life support.

Advance directives pertain to decisions people make about end-of-life care that is designed to protect their self-determination when they reach a point in their lives when they are no longer able to make decisions on their own about their care.

Living will is a formal, written statement that specifies a person's preferences for end-of-life care.

Five stages of dying personal to the phases in the dying process that terminally ill people often experience: denial, anger, bargaining, depression, and acceptance.

Task-based model for coping with dying pertains to specific physical, psychological, social, and spiritual tasks in dealing with dying.

Physical tasks pertain to bodily needs and physical conditions such as coping with pain.

Psychological tasks are associated with autonomy, security, and richness in living.

Social tasks pertain to sustaining and enhancing the interpersonal attachments valued by the dying person.

Spiritual tasks pertain to common themes such as meaningfulness, connectedness, transcendence, and fostering hope.

Hospice programs are designed to offer care for those who are in the final stages of the journey of life.

Grief involves a psychologically necessary and natural process of expressing and exploring thoughts and feelings over a significant loss.

Grief work refers to the exploration of feelings of sorrow, anger, and guilt over the experience of a significant loss.

Bereavement is the process of expressing and exploring those feelings associated with a significant loss.

Mourning pertains to the formal practices of an individual or community in response to a death or significant loss.

The relational model is an alternative way of thinking about death, dying, and the grieving process. It emphasizes that people are born into networks of relationships and remain woven into those networks long after they die.

Re-membering is about continuing to foster the memory of a person's life even after he or she dies by involving the person in our daily lives, in our conversations, in the choices we make, and in our resources for living.

TEST ITEMS FOR CHAPTER 12
DEATH AND LOSS

1. The awareness of death
   a. tends to paralyze us in terms of taking action.
   b. can act as a catalyst in the search for meaning in life.
   c. inevitably leads to a chronic state of depression.
   d. is considered to be unhealthy by most psychologists.

2. In the five stages of dying that Kübler-Ross has delineated, many people tend to experience them in a(n) _____ fashion.
   a. linear
   b. nonlinear
   c. orderly
   d. identical

3. Death is feared because
   a. it seems to condemn us to total loneliness and to loss of our identity.
   b. it entails leaving behind those we love.
   c. of the uncertainty we have of what, if anything, exists after death.
   d. all of the above.

4. The ancient Greeks had an attitude toward death that is best summed up in the dictum:
   a. "Eat, drink, and be merry, for tomorrow you may die."
   b. "Live each moment to the fullest and forget about dying."
   c. "Contemplate death if you would learn how to live."
   d. "Be willing to die for those things we believe in."

5. Psychiatrist Irvin Yalom's work in group therapy with cancer patients demonstrated that
   a. they felt utter hopelessness about changing their lives.
   b. they had the capacity to view their life crisis as away to change their lives.
   c. most of them denied they had cancer.
   d. there was a move on their part to cut off communications with their loved ones.

6. The meaning of our life depends on the fact that we
   a. are finite beings and our time is invaluable precisely because it is limited.
   b. can choose to become all that we are capable of becoming or we can let life slip by us.
   c. can settle for letting events happen to us or we can actively choose and create the kind of life we want.
   d. all of the above.

7. In Corr's (1992) task-based model for coping with dying,
   a. it is never possible to finish all of the tasks facing an individual.
   b. it is expected that individuals will finish all of the tasks facing them.
   c. finishing even one particular task is important..
   d. a and c

8. People who attempt suicide
   a. see life as unbearable.
   b. are unaware that there are options for living differently.
   c. tend to give up too quickly without exploring other possibilities.
   d. all of the above.

9. Jane feels unappreciated and is contemplating suicide with the idea that people would talk about her and feel sorry for the way they treated her. The hidden meaning for her thoughts about suicide is an
   a. act of hostility.
   b. attempt to control and exert power over people.
   c. attempt to be noticed.
   d. escape from a difficult or impossible situation.

10. Jerry is dying a slow, painful death from cancer and has thought about ending his life by suicide. His desire to die is most likely based on his need to
    a. end the pain.
    b. get relief from hopelessness.
    c. escape from a difficult or impossible situation.
    d. plead for euthanasia.

11. A task-based model for coping with dying involves
    a. addressing the whole human being.
    b. specifying stages that all people experience in the dying process.
    c. meeting physical, psychological, social, and spiritual tasks.
    d. considering all who are involved with the dying person.

12. _____ involves providing lethal means to cause a person's death, with the individual performing the act that ends his or her own life.
    a. Irrational suicide
    b. Impulsive suicide
    c. Assisted suicide
    d. Letting nature take its course

13. Which of the following statements is *false*?
    a. Only ten states have enacted legislation allowing doctor-assisted suicide.
    b. Rational suicide is sometimes argued to be morally and ethically appropriate when people are in severe pain and there is no hope of recovery.
    c. Many people oppose interventions that unnecessarily prolong life by artificial and unusual means.
    d. There is a difference between suicide and allowing nature to take its course.

14. When a family member commits suicide, the immediate reaction is generally
    a. shock and distress.
    b. fear that another family member may repeat the act.
    c. a sense of shame because of the stigma of suicide.
    d. anger toward the deceased.

15. Joe's parents are seeking counseling after their 16-year-old son committed suicide. It is the role of the counselor to help them deal with
    a. the nature of unfinished business.
    b. their feelings of abandonment, loneliness, and isolation.
    c. correcting distortions they may hold.
    d. helping them let go of regrets and blame and give expression to their anger.
    e. all of the above.

16. The process of dying involves
    a. choice concerning the losses we suffer in dying.
    b. a gradual diminishing of the choices available to us although we still have choices about how we handle it.
    c. an inability to choose our attitude toward our death and the way we relate to it.
    d. methodically going through the 5 stages of dying.

17. The typical sequence in the stages of dying, according to Kübler-Ross, is
    a. anger, denial, bargaining, despair, acceptance.
    b. denial, anger, bargaining, depression, acceptance.
    c. shock, questioning, denial, bargaining, acceptance.
    d. anxiety, depression, anger, hope, joy.

18. Kübler-Ross emphasizes that the stages of dying
    a. are neat, compartmentalized stages and every person passes through them in an orderly fashion.
    b. do not apply to those who are dying of AIDS.
    c. are a standard by which to judge whether a dying person's behavior is normal or right.
    d. are fluid, and a person may experience a combination of stages, skip one or more stages, or go back to earlier stages.

19. When Bill first found out he had cancer and only about a year to live, his first reaction was in keeping with Kübler-Ross's first stage of dying, which is
    a. anger.
    b. depression.
    c. denial.
    d. shock.

20. Ann had cancer and was given one year to live. She tried every type of available treatment so she could live long enough to graduate from college before she died. When it became evident that the treatments were no longer working, she became
    a. frustrated.
    b. angry.
    c. depressed.
    d. suicidal.

21. The third stage of dying as theorized by Kübler-Ross, basically an attempt to postpone the inevitable end, is
    a. pleading.
    b. bargaining.
    c. praying.
    d. negotiating.

22. The following tactic would be helpful to use when dealing with a dying person who is depressed:
    a. trying to cheer them up.
    b. helping them avoid the reality of the situation.
    c. encouraging them to talk about their feelings and make final plans.
    d. teaching them how to overcome the irrational "self-talk" that is keeping them stuck in their depression.

23. In regard to the acceptance stage of dying,
    a. it is a happy stage because the person is no longer struggling with a desire to live.
    b. all people achieve acceptance before dying.
    c. it is almost devoid of feelings, the struggle is over, and it is a time for "the final rest before the long journey."
    d. it is one of surrender and despair because of the realization it is futile to fight any longer.

24. The trend toward more direct involvement in the care for the dying of significant others is exemplified in the
    a. hospice movement.
    b. "right to live" movement.
    c. "right to die" movement.
    d. "assisted suicide" movement.

25. The hospice movement came about in response to what many people perceived to be
    a. inadequate care for the dying in conventional hospitals.
    b. insurance companies taking charge of what treatments are available to a dying person.
    c. doctor's unwillingness to take drastic measures to save the dying person's life.
    d. all of the above.

26. Emily is dying, and her family has placed her in a homelike environment where she will be allowed to die with dignity. Emily is in a
    a. hospital.
    b. hospice.
    c. nursing home.
    d. transitional home.

27. _____ refers to the exploration of feelings of sorrow, anger, and guilt over the experience of a significant loss.
    a. Grief work
    b. Primal therapy
    c. Catharsis
    d. Dream work

28. In American society, there appears to be a cultural norm about grief that fosters an expectation
    a. of rituals signifying that the period of mourning is over.
    b. that the grieving person will be "back to normal" in a short period of time.
    c. of years of counseling in order to fully process the grief.
    d. of a prolonged period of mourning.

29. A chronic stage of depression and a restricted range of feelings suffered by some grieving persons are often attributed to
    a. a hesitant move toward resolution.
    b. operating on an intellectual level.
    c. being stuck in the bargaining stage.
    d. some unresolved reaction to a significant loss.

30. In learning to resolve grief, regardless of its source, people need to
    a. be able to talk about what they are telling themselves internally and what they are feeling.
    b. understand that their feelings over the lack of fairness about their situation are irrational.
    c. face up to the fact that there is a rational reason that will explain their loss.
    d. change their negative thoughts and feelings to positive ones.

31. Roger and Becky are divorcing. Even after the decision is made they try to convince themselves that the state of their marriage isn't all that bad, that nobody is perfect, and that things would be worse if they separate. According to Kübler-Ross, they are in the following stage of grief:
    a. numbness and shock.
    b. rationalization.
    c. denial.
    d. reaction formation.

32. Once people accept the reality that they are divorcing, they frequently experience anger and rage. If they keep it bottled up inside, it is likely to
    a. go away over time.
    b. turn into passive/aggressive behavior.
    c. be turned against themselves and may take the form of depression.
    d. become overwhelming and explode.

33. In the case of divorce, once the two persons have finished their grieving, they can begin to
    a. make a life for themselves without the other person and let go of resentments that hold them back from doing that.
    b. look for another spouse.
    c. recycle into the five stages of grief at a deeper level.
    d. reevaluate whether it's worth the effort to risk being intimate again.

34. When our roles begin to deaden us, we can ask if
    a. we've taken on a function or identity that others have defined, instead of listening to our own inner promptings.
    b. we are alive to our senses and our body.
    c. we can be spontaneous and playful.
    d. we are alive to our thoughts and feelings.

35. Wolfert's (2003) model of understanding grief includes 10 _____ that can be used to navigate through the process of grief and bereavement.
    a. touchstones
    b. trail markers
    c. wisdom teachings
    d. all of the above

36. Corey and Corey suggest a way of taking stock of your life by
    a. writing a list of what you value and who you resent.
    b. exaggerating your accomplishments and ignoring your failures.
    c. imagining your own death, including the details of the funeral and the things people might say about you.
    d. rewriting your past in an autobiography.

37. Which of the following theorists made this comment: "Life has inevitable suffering as well as pleasure. By realistically thinking, feeling, and acting to enjoy what you can, and unangrily and unwhiningly accepting painful aspects that cannot be changed—you open yourself to much joy"?
    a. Albert Bandura
    b. Albert Ellis
    c. Arnold Lazarus
    d. Aaron Beck

38. Which of the following statements is *not* true about the concept of death anxiety?
    a. Yalom believes that for most clients, it is not an issue of major concern.
    b. The wish to survive and the dread of annihilation are always present.
    c. It can teach us as much about living as dying.
    d. None of the above

39. Which theorist made the following statement about death anxiety? "It's not easy to live every moment wholly aware of death. It's like trying to stare at the sun in the face: you can stand only so much of it. Because we cannot live frozen in fear, we generate methods to soften death's terror."
    a. Albert Bandura
    b. Albert Ellis
    c. Irvin Yalom
    d. William Glasser

40. What do experiences such as school and college reunions, estate planning and making a will, and significant birthdays and anniversaries have in common?
    a. They are milestones that can evoke a range of feelings in us about how fast life is going by and can encourage us to reflect on the choices we want to make for the rest of our life.
    b. They have nothing in common.
    c. They tend to be positive and productive.
    d. They provide people with an opportunity to reconnect with people.

41. Yalom asserts that a belief in God
    a. softens the pain of mortality through a vision of an afterlife.
    b. provides a clear blueprint for living a meaningful life.
    c. is helpful for neurotic people, but not for psychotic people who might develop delusions of grandeur and believe they are carrying out actions for God.
    d. a and b

42. Which of the following signs may indicate that an individual is at risk for suicide?
    a. Absence of a sense of purpose in life
    b. Giving away prized possessions
    c. Increased substance use
    d. all of the above
    e. a and b

43. Which of the following statements is/are *not* true about the prevention of suicide?
    a. It is possible to prevent all suicides.
    b. Preventive measures can reduce the number of suicides.
    c. When someone displays suicidal signs, it is crucial to provide empathy and sup|
    d. Suicide prevention centers with 24-hour-a-day telephone support are available in , ost cities.

44. Gabrielle's older sister recently committed suicide. She doesn't believe that she needs counseling to work through her pain. If you were Gabrielle's friend, which of the following benefits of counseling would be important for you to emphasize to convince your friend to seek counseling?
    a. Counseling can help people to correct distortions they may hold, prepare for their future, learn to let go of regrets and blame, and give expression to their anger.
    b. Survivors are encouraged to talk about the things they may be rehearsing over and over in their heads, and it can help them to talk about their thoughts and feelings with one another.
    c. Survivors can be helped to remember aspects of a person's life that were not defined by the way the person died.
    d. all of the above

45. Which of the following statements is true regarding hospice?
    a. Much hospice home care replaces more expensive and impersonal treatment options including multiple hospitalizations.
    b. Hospice home care is more expensive than most other treatment options.
    c. The hospice movement was developed to give caregivers of sick relatives the hope that their loved ones can make full recoveries.
    d. The hospice movement was developed to give caregivers of sick relatives the hope that their loved ones can make partial recoveries.

46. Which model of coping with grief and bereavement posits that people are born into networks of relationships and remain woven into those networks long after they die?
    a. The relational model
    b. Kübler-Ross' five stage model
    c. Corr's task-based model
    d. The hospice movement

47. _____ is about continuing to foster the memory of a person's life even after he or she dies by involving the person in our daily lives, in our conversations, in the choices we make, and in our resources for living.
    a. Denial
    b. Delusional thinking
    c. Re-membering
    d. Post-Death Remembrance Syndrome

ANSWER KEY FOR CHAPTER 12
DEATH AND LOSS

1. b   p. 340
2. b   p. 358-359
3. d   p. 341
4. c   p. 343
5. b   p. 343
6. d   p. 343
7. d   p. 359
8. d   p. 348
9. c   p. 349
10. a   p. 349
11. c   p. 359
12. c   p. 350-351
13. a   p. 351
14. a   p. 349
15. e   p. 350
16. b   p. 351
17. b   p. 357
18. d   p. 357
19. c   p. 357
20. c   p. 357
21. b   p. 357
22. c   p. 358
23. c   p. 358
24. a   p. 354

25. a   p. 355
26. b   p. 355
27. a   p. 360
28. b   p. 361
29. d   p. 362
30. a   p. 360-361
31. c   p. 357
32. c   p. 357
33. a   p. 364
34. a   p. 365-366
35. d   p. 360
36. c   p. 369
37. b   p. 340
38. a   p. 341
39. c   p. 344
40. a   p. 344
41. d   p. 344
42. d   p. 348
43. a   p. 348
44. d   p. 350
45. a   p. 354-355
46. a   p. 364
47. c   p. 364

Activities and Exercises for Classroom Participation for Chapter 12

1. Has anyone you've been close to died? If so, think about what his or her dying was like for you. What did you experience? What did you learn? You might share some of your reactions with other members in your class.

2. What do you think the significant people in your life would write on your tombstone? What would you like them to say? Bring your own tombstone inscription to class. What have you said about yourself on your stone?

3. Write the eulogy you'd like delivered at your funeral and memorial service. Bring it to class and share it with the members of your group.

4. Assume that you know you are going to die within 24 hours. What would you do during these last hours? What does this tell you about what you value? Write this without censoring it, and share it in your group.

5. Tell the other members of your group what you would most like to accomplish before you die. What is some unfinished business that you'd like to take care of?

6. Have you experienced a loss in your life that was significant to you? Have you allowed yourself to grieve over your loss? What did you want from others when you went through this loss?

7. After reading the story of Jim Morelock in this chapter, what are your thoughts, feelings, and reactions? Would you like a friend such as Jim? Why or why not? Is there any lesson you can learn from Jim that you can apply to your life?

8. Discuss any other stories in this chapter that held special meaning for you.

9. In a small group, explore topics such as the following: your fears of death; how the reality of death might give your life increased meaning; ways you can live more fully. Discuss how death and the meaning of life are interrelated notions.

10. Explore the value of grieving over death, separation, and other loses. Why is grief a necessary and natural process after a significant loss? What are some of the consequences of failing to grieve a loss?

CHAPTER 13: MEANING AND VALUES

Outline

Chapter Objectives

- to understand what is involved in the search for meaning

- to examine the foundations of meaning

- to provide a framework for understanding religion and spirituality

- to examine the context of diversity in society

- to come to a deeper appreciation of the value of diversity

- to see the role of choice in relating to diversity`

- to become aware of our prejudices and to challenge them

Questions for Thought, Discussion, and Evaluation

1. What are some specific things you most value in your life? What would your life be like without them?

2. What are the most important elements in your life that give you a sense of purposefulness?

3. Do you experience an "existential vacuum?" Is your life without substance or depth, empty and devoid of meaning? If you do experience this sense of life without purpose, what is this like for you? What are you doing about it? Are you trying to escape these feelings of emptiness?

4. Describe the concept of searching for meaning. What implications do you find in this concept that can assist you in finding meaning and purpose in your own life?

5. What do we need to do to keep ourselves from spiritually dying?

6. Psychiatrist Irvin Yalom described the results common to a number of empirical studies of meaning in life. What did he find? Also, what did he learn from his work in group therapy with cancer patients about death and the meaning in life?

7. Describe the relationship that exists between death and meaning in life. In what ways can the concept of death be a catalyst for creating meaning in our lives?

8. Be familiar with the European psychiatrist Viktor Frankl's ideas on the search for meaning. What is the essence of his therapeutic approach known as *logotherapy*? What are his thoughts on meaninglessness?

9. How is religion a pathway to finding meaning and purpose? What are some current trends that might explain an increased interest in religion and values?

10. What are your thoughts on religion? Is religion a part of your life? What does religion mean to you?

11. How did you acquire the religious beliefs you now have? Have you really questioned and challenged your beliefs?

12. Can you be religious without a religion? What does being a religious person mean to you? What differences, if any, do you see in spirituality and religion?

13. How does having or not having a set of religious convictions help or hinder you in constructing a philosophy of life?

14. What major factors have influenced your core beliefs and attitudes toward life? Do you ever question these influences?

15. What people in your life have had the most influence on the formation of your values? Do you want to be like these people?

16. Is work a source of deriving meaning for living? Is it the only source of finding meaning? What would life be like if you were not doing the work you're now doing?

17. Assume that you are creating a new religion. What would be the main virtues you would want people to acquire? What kind of person would you like to see emerge from your religion? What would you hope your religion could be for the person? What would be your list of sins? Would you have any sins? What commandments would be a part of your religion? How would you define sin?

18. What are the sources of guilt in your life? When do you feel guilty? What feelings do you experience that produce guilt? What behavior produces guilt? Is this guilt realistic? How did you learn to feel guilty about certain things?

19. Are you an inner-directed person who acts out of values you've examined and made your own? Do you find yourself simply reflecting what others expect of you? Are you living your life by becoming what others expect you to become? Are your values merely your reflection of others' values?

20. What kinds of values would you like to see your children incorporate into their lives? What kind of moral code do you hope they acquire? What standards of conduct would you want for them? What religious attitudes and beliefs do you want them to be exposed to? In what ways would you like them to be like you, and in what ways different from you?

21. How is your philosophy of death related to your philosophy of life? Can you separate the two?

22. Do you truly like the kind of person you are becoming? When you look at what you were like five years ago, how have you changed? In what ways have your attitudes about life been modified during the past five years?

23. What are some of the major struggles you are now experiencing in regard to making sense out of life? What value struggles do you now have?

24. Do you set aside even a few minutes each day to reflect upon the meaning and quality of your life and to examine the direction you're taking? Do you experience solitude so that you are able to reexamine the values that give your life meaning? Do you ask yourself what you most want from life? Do you ask yourself what you are doing, or not doing, to get what you want from life?

25. How would you define the phrase "philosophy of life"? What does this entail? How does one develop such a personal philosophy?

26. What does the phrase "embracing diversity" mean to you? How is this concept different from the phrase "tolerance for diversity?"

27. How is embracing diversity related to finding meaning in one's life? How do you interpret this statement: "Meaning in life can be found by paying attention to the common ground we all share and by becoming aware of universal themes that unite us in spite of our differences."

28. How are stereotypes barriers to understanding others? How are stereotypes related to prejudice and discrimination? How might you challenge stereotypes that you may hold?

29. What is implied by the phrase "unintentional racism?" In what ways can we become aware of our own unintentional racism and also challenge these attitudes?

30. What is your thinking about the concept of White privilege? How does White privilege put Whites at an advantage and at the same time people of color at a disadvantage?

31. What are some specific ways that you can think of for breaking down the barriers that separate you from those who are different from you? What are some advantages of doing so, both for yourself and for others?

32. To what degree do you understand and accept your cultural background? How is understanding your own cultural heritage important if you hope to develop a better appreciate of the cultures of others?

33. Why is it important that we understand and build connections with diverse cultures?

34. What is your understanding of the phrase "ethnocentric bias?" If you hold such a bias, how might this get in the way of understanding those who differ from you?

35. In what ways can you augment the meaning of your life by making connections with others and striving to make a significant difference? How can you change the world in small ways by touching the lives of others through your acts of kindness and generosity?

Glossary of Key Terms

Values are core beliefs that influence how we act.

Crisis of meaninglessness pertains to addressing the question, "How do we find meaning in a universe that has no meaning?"

Logotherapy means "therapy through meaning" or "healing through meaning."

Philosophy of life constitutes our fundamental beliefs, attitudes, and values that govern our behavior.

Spirituality refers to a set of beliefs and practices that can result in a life-changing path that gives greater meaning, purpose, and fulfillment to a person's life.

Basic spiritual values include qualities of goodness, kindness, love, compassion, tolerance, forgiveness, warmth, and caring.

Compassion involves caring about another's suffering and doing something about it.

Ethnocentric bias refers to using our own culture or country as a standard of what is right and good and judging other cultures or countries by our own frame of reference.

Encapsulated world pertains to seeking support from others who think and value as we do, and as well, having negative attitudes toward those who are different from us.

Stereotype is a judgmental generalization applied to an individual without regard to his or own uniqueness.

Prejudice is a preconceived notion or opinion about someone or some group of people.

Discrimination refers to biased behavior toward a particular group of people.

Unintentional racism consists of assuming that one is free of any traces of prejudicial attitudes or racism.

White privilege refers to the unearned advantages and benefits of White people that puts them at an advantage to people of color.

Diversity involves understanding and appreciating differences among people based upon such variables as age, gender, culture, disability, educational level, residential location, socio-economic situation, race, ethnicity, language, sexual orientation, and spiritual/religious beliefs.

Culture pertains to the knowledge, language, values, and customs that are passed from person to person and from one generation to the next generation.

TEST ITEMS FOR CHAPTER 13
MEANING AND VALUES

1. Bellah and his associates assert that the core problem with our society is that
   a. we have put our own good, as individuals and as groups, ahead of the common group.
   b. there is growing interest in finding meaning through acquisition of material possessions.
   c. we place more emphasis on the common good than on our individual needs.
   d. the increased use of alcohol and drugs is an attempt to enjoy life in a meaningless society.

2. Achieving identity means
   a. stubbornly clinging to a certain way of thinking or behaving.
   b. something we achieve for all time.
   c. being continually willing to reexamine our patterns, our priorities, our habits, and our relationships.
   d. successfully transcending role diffusion.

3. Our search for identity involves asking the following key existential questions, none of which has an easy or definite answer:
   a. "Who am I?" "Where am I going?" "Why?"
   b. "What is the matter with me?" "How can I find happiness?"
   c. "Where can I go from here?" "Who is there to help me?"
   d. "When will I feel complete?" "What is my life all about?"

4. The following existential question relates to the issue of our lifetime plans and the means we expect to use in attaining our goals:
   a. "Who am I?"
   b. "Where am I going?"
   c. "How can I find happiness?"
   d. "What is my life all about?"

5. The existential question "Why?" implies that we are
   a. attempting to set our life goals.
   b. actively searching for meaning, trying to make sense of the world in which we find ourselves.
   c. into self-pity because we believe that life is unfair.
   d. reluctant to take responsibility for our own actions.

6. Awareness of our mortality can
   a. create anxiety.
   b. be a catalyst for making major life decisions.
   c. only lead to negative consequences.
   d. a and b

7. Although we may not be responsible for systemic racism, we are responsible for
   a. how we respond to racism in our own lives.
   b. how others we know respond to racism in their lives.
   c. the feelings of oppressed minorities when others discriminate against them.
   d. erasing all of the past hurts and pain that the majority culture has caused.

8. Logotherapy is an approach to psychotherapy that involves healing through
   a. catharsis.
   b. religion.
   c. meditation.
   d. meaning.

9. The European psychiatrist who dedicated his professional life to the study of meaning in life is
   a. Victor Frankl.
   b. Dalai Lama.
   c. Irvin Yalom.
   d. Maya Angelou

10. According to Frankl, what distinguishes us as humans is our
    a. awareness of death.
    b. self-awareness.
    c. search for meaning.
    d. cognitive ability.

11. Drawing on his experiences in the death camp at Auschwitz, Frankl asserts that the inmates who had a much greater chance of surviving were those who
    a. had a vision of some goal, purpose, or task in life.
    b. were able to concentrate on their own survival.
    c. had the ability to get their needs met.
    d. were able to accept their fate.

12. Even in the most dire situations, it is possible to give a new meaning to such circumstances by
    a. ignoring what is happening.
    b. escaping through fantasy.
    c. our choice of attitudes.
    d. effective use of our defense mechanisms.

13. A philosophy of life is made up of
    a. religious beliefs that we were raised with.
    b. early childhood messages.
    c. accepting the ambiguity of life.
    d. the fundamental beliefs, attitudes, and values that govern a person's behavior.

14. We begin to develop an implicit philosophy of life when we
    a. first began, as children, to wonder about life and death, love and hate, joy and fear, and the nature of the universe.
    b. were adolescents, seeking our own identity and questioning the meaning of life.
    c. are faced with a crisis and forced to face the fact that the meaning of life is the result of our own choosing.
    d. enter adulthood and formulate a clear sense of meaning and purpose in life.

15. During the adolescent years, the process of developing a philosophy usually assumes new dimensions through the struggle with the following question:
    a. Are the values that I've believed in before those I want to continue to live by?
    b. Is there a God?
    c. What explains the inhumanity I see in our world?
    d. What do I base my ethical and moral decisions on?
    e. all of the above.

16. When you are attempting to develop a philosophy of life, the Coreys suggest that you
    a. frequently create time to be of benefit to others.
    b. make significant contact with others who reinforce your belief system.
    c. consider what meaning the fact of your eventual death has for those who are important in your life.
    d. adopt an accepting attitude toward those whose belief systems differ from yours.

17. In regard to religion, it appears that, at the present time,
    a. there is a decrease of interest in religion in our society.
    b. more people are deciding that some sort of religious faith is necessary if they are to find meaning and purpose in life.
    c. an increasing number of people are rejecting any form of religion as a form of superstition.
    d. people are going to 12-step groups in place of religious services.

18. The Coreys suggest that you might consider reflecting on whether or not your religion is a constructive force in your life by asking this question:
    a. Does my religion provide me with a set of values that is congruent with the way I live my life?
    b. Does my religion encourage me to exercise my freedom and assume responsibility for the direction of my life?
    c. Is my religious faith something that I actively choose or that I passively accept?
    d. all of the above.

19. According to the Coreys, which statement is *not* true concerning your values?
    a. Your values influence what you do.
    b. Your daily behavior is an expression of your basic values.
    c. Your values have a significant impact on your relationships with others.
    d. It is appropriate to strive to convert others to adopt your perspective on life.

20. In his book *God's Love Song,* Sam Maier teaches that
    a. once you have found meaning in life, it is important to influence others to embrace your thinking.
    b. diversity of cultures, religions, and world views implies an attempt to tolerate differences even though you don't accept them.
    c. sharing diversity fosters understanding, caring, and the creation of community.
    d. all of the above.

21. The following is *not* true about prejudice:
    a. Prejudice is a preconceived notion or opinion about someone.
    b. Prejudice can function as a defense mechanism, protecting individuals from facing undesirable aspects of themselves by projecting them onto others.
    c. Prejudice is the same as discrimination.
    d. At the root of prejudice is fear, low self-esteem, ignorance, and feelings of inferiority.

22. The Coreys state that when attempting to break down barriers that keep people separate, one would *not*
    a. seek universal themes that unite us with others.
    b. be willing to test, adapt, and change our perceptions.
    c. attempt to learn about cultures that differ from our own.
    d. challenge our prejudices by looking for data that supports our preconceived biases.

23. If you recognize that you are culturally encapsulated, it will help if you
    a. blame the media for giving wrong messages about culturally diverse populations.
    b. recognize that your lack of cultural awareness is a product of early childhood messages that cannot be changed.
    c. give yourself credit for acknowledging your limitations and work toward enriching your life with diversity.
    d. repress your judgmental attitude towards those who differ from you.

24. The search for meaning and purpose in life is *not*
    a. the result of your active thinking and choosing.
    b. accompanied by a degree of anxiety.
    c. automatically bestowed on you.
    d. one that lasts a lifetime.

25. Being secure about your values implies that you
    a. will change your values without giving the matter considerable thought.
    b. will be able to respect values of others that may differ from your own.
    c. need to impose your values on other people.
    d. avoid interacting with people whose values differ from yours.

26. At its worst, living without meaning and values can
    a. result in suicide.
    b. cause moderate distress.
    c. lead to boredom and stagnation.
    d. reduce one's productivity at work.

27. In order to heal relationships with significant people in your life and to improve your life in every way, which of the following should you do?
    a. Be impeccable with your word.
    b. Don't take anything personally.
    c. Don't make assumptions.
    d. Always do your best.
    e. All of the above

28. *The Four Agreements Companion Book* (Ruiz, 2000) described in the text outlines a
    a. code of conduct for attaining personal freedom and happiness.
    b. philosophy of life.
    c. legal document in laymen's terms about divorce and child custody.
    d. a and b

29. Spirituality is often viewed as
    a. a journey
    b. an odyssey
    c. a pilgrimage
    d. an expedition into the meaning of life.
    e. all of the above

30. _____ is at the foundation of healing in Twelve Step programs for people struggling with addictions to alcohol and mood-altering substances.
    a. Medication
    b. Tough love
    c. Spirituality
    d. Solitude

31. Alcoholics Anonymous and other 12-Step Programs endorse relying on _____ as a source of strength and support.
    a. God
    b. Allah
    c. a Higher Power
    d. Jesus Christ

32. The Coreys _____with the Dalai Lama's position that religious teachings should be evaluated by the degree to which the faithful act more loving toward others.
    a. agree
    b. fundamentally disagree
    c. find certain flaws
    d. neither agree nor disagree

For numbers 33-37 match the sacred text to the appropriate religion below.

33. *The Torah*

34. *The Bible*

35. *Dharma*

36. *Qur'an*

37. *The Vedas*

    a. Christianity
    b. Buddhism
    c. Hinduism
    d. Islam
    e. Judaism

38. Yan, a middle-aged woman who immigrated to the U.S. from China, and Tracy, a white young woman in her mid twenties, share an office at a university, where they work together as research assistants. Tracy seems to keep her distance from Yan (and vice versa) outside of work-related tasks because they appear to have vastly different world views. Their boss should
    a. challenge them to learn to embrace and appreciate each other's worldview rather than be threatened by it.
    b. fire one or both of them if they refuse to become friendly with each other.
    c. reassign them to different offices so they will be with coworkers who are similar to them.
    d. ignore the tension as long as they are completing their tasks.

39. Dismantling racism will benefit
    a. only racial minorities who have been oppressed.
    b. only people of color who are socioeconomically disadvantaged.
    c. us all individually and will support a better society and nation collectively.
    d. a and b

40. The first step in protecting our planet is to
    a. recognize that we are indeed in the midst of a growing global crisis.
    b. recognize that each of us can and must assume personal responsibility to bring about changes.
    c. realize we are helpless in the face of global warming.
    d. purchase a fuel-efficient hybrid vehicle if we don't already have one.

ANSWER KEY FOR CHAPTER 13
MEANING AND VALUES

1.	a	p. 379		21.	c	p. 393
2.	c	p. 374		22.	d	p. 395-396
3.	a	p. 374		23.	c	p. 393, 396
4.	b	p. 374		24.	c	p. 376
5.	b	p. 374		25.	b	p. 387
6.	d	p. 374		26.	a	p. 376
7.	a	p. 393		27.	e	p. 380-381
8.	d	p. 377		28.	d	p. 380
9.	a	p. 377		29.	e	p. 383
10.	c	p. 377		30.	c	p. 383
11.	a	p. 377		31.	c	p. 383
12.	c	p. 377		32.	a	p. 383
13.	d	p. 380		33.	e	p. 385
14.	a	p. 381		34.	a	p. 385
15.	e	p. 381		35.	b	p. 385
16.	d	p. 382		36.	d	p. 385
17.	b	p. 383		37.	c	p. 385
18.	d	p. 385		38.	a	p. 389
19.	d	p. 387		39.	c	p. 393
20.	c	p. 388		40.	a	p. 398

Activities and Exercises for Classroom Participation for Chapter 13

There are some things you can do that may help you come more to terms with the meaning in your life, the personal values you live by, and your personal identity. Many of these exercises can be done on your own before coming to your group or class. Add some of your own suggestions for group exercises.

1. Make a list of the major accomplishments in your life. What have you actually done for yourself and for others that has made your life worthwhile? Share a few of the accomplishments with other members of your group.

2. In your group, let yourself imagine a typical day in your life five years ago. What was it like, and what were you like then? How do you see yourself and your life differently now that five years have passed? What factors have contributed to any changes you're aware of? Share with your group some of the most significant changes you've made over this five-year period.

3. Project yourself five years into the future. Ask yourself: What will I be like five years from now? What do I hope I might become by then? What do I want in my life then? What do I most fear I or my life might be like at this future time? What am I doing now to make a reality out of what I would like to be and what I want from life?

4. Go around your group and tell each person (or just the persons to whom this applies) what he or she has that you want for yourself. In what ways would like to be more like them?

5. As a variation of the preceding exercise, try this exercise in your group. The group members tell one another one thing about themselves that they would be willing to trade for a trait in the other person.

6. What are some specific things you do for others that show you care? Make a list, and then share some of these things in your group.

7. This is a valuable group exercise that can be done toward the end of the group's time together. Each member writes down some wish he or she has for every other member. In composing this major wish for each person, the members should think of what they see each person struggling with and what each person says he or she would most like to change. The participants then collect the wishes the other members have for them and read them in a group session, exploring what the other members are telling them. This is a useful form of feedback, one that can help us clarify the specific kind of identities we wish for ourselves.

8. In this group exercise, each person shares one crucial turning point in his or her life. You decide which crucial turning point it might be—a decision you made, a struggle you were involved in, or some other significant experience. What might be different in your life now if you hadn't had this experience or if you'd made a different decision?

9. Construct a personal-identity road map. On this road map, indicate some critical incidents in your own struggle toward autonomy. Consider some of these questions as you construct your map:
    a. Who am I? What made me this way?
    b. What are some of my earliest recollections?
    c. What are some key decisions I made at various points?
    d. What choices did I make? What choices did others make for me?
    e. How has my life now been shaped by past actions, influences, people, incidents, and so on?

For this personal-identity road map, we suggest that you think about these questions and add some of your own as well. As a second part of the activity, have someone close to you answer these questions for you, as they see you and experience you. This will allow you to compare your own perceptions of your personal identity with another person's perception of you.

10. Brainstorm for a time in your group with this issue: If you were to develop a way of helping children and adolescents cope with discovering meaning, creating an identity, and searching for values to guide their daily behavior, how would you go about it? Can this be done in school? How? What kind of assignments and activities might be useful?

11. Review the section on the foundations of meaning, with particular attention to the variety of quotes to the question – What is the meaning of life? Which of these quotes has the most personal meaning for you?

12. Review the personal stories in this chapter. Are there any personal stories that particularly catch your attention?

13. Embracing diversity is a part of this chapter. It might well be that the students in your class are diverse. Why not use this as a basis for discussion to help students appreciate differences? At the same time, with the actual racial and ethnic makeup of your class in mind, you will have to use some careful judgment about which topics or exercises to introduce. It is good to keep in mind that some students may have cultural biases and may be relatively closed to exploring the value of diversity, let alone embracing diversity. Do not pressure students to disclose all of their attitudes about cultural differences; simply getting them to think of how they have been influenced by their own socialization and by their cultural background is a significant step.

14. In your lectures on cultural diversity, strive to help students realize that diversity is not something to be feared, but to be welcomed. Stress that part of becoming an educated person implies understanding diverse ways of viewing the world.

15. Ask students if they have encountered any sort of discrimination on campus. What kinds of suggestions can the students come up with to lessen discrimination?

16. Ask students to look up resources on the Internet pertaining to preserving and protecting our planet.

17. Ask students to spend a few minutes in class writing a paragraph on the kind of world they want their children, grandchildren, and great grandchildren to inherit.

18. In small groups, have students review the list of specific suggestions that they are able and willing to take as a way of adopting a more Earth-friendly lifestyle. The results of the small groups can be shared with the entire class.

19. Review the section dealing with developing a philosophy of life in this chapter. How can you use the ideas here to write some of your thoughts on this topic in your journal? **For Instructors:** Consider as one of the requirements of your course a "Writing Your Philosophy of Life" assignment, which is one of the detailed exercises given at the end of the chapter. Some instructors make a philosophy of life paper the central requirement for the course. Sections of this paper can be initiated early in the course, and various topics can be written each week as new topics are introduced.

20. The *Quick Discrimination Index*
For instructors --- You may want to reproduce this self-assessment and use it as an exercise in your class.
The Quick Discrimination Index can help you assess your attitudes toward cultural diversity. Even if you think you are free of prejudice toward others, you may discover some subtle biases. Once you are aware of them, you can begin working toward tolerance and acceptance.

<qt>The Quick Discrimination Index
<qx>We hope you will take and score this social-attitude survey, which is designed to assess sensitivity, awareness, and receptivity to cultural diversity and gender equity. This is a self-assessment inventory, and

it is essential that you strive to respond to each item as honestly as possible. This inventory is not designed to assess how you should think about cultural diversity and gender equity issues; rather, its aim is to assess subtle racial and gender bias. You can use this inventory to become more aware of your attitudes and beliefs pertaining to these issues.

<qdd>DIRECTIONS: Remember there are no right or wrong answers. Please circle the appropriate number to the right.

<qsn>The *Quick Discrimination Index* (QDI) is copyrighted by Joseph G. Ponterotto, Ph.D. No further reproduction or xeroxing of this instrument is permitted without the written permission of Dr. Ponterotto. If you are interested in using this instrument for any purpose, write to Joseph G. Ponterotto, Ph.D. (at the Division of Psychological and Educational Services, Fordham University at Lincoln Center, Room 1008, 113 West 60th Street, New York, NY 10023-7478) and request the "User Permission Form," the QDI itself, and the latest reliability and validity information.

<qtch>	Strongly disagree	Disagree	Not sure	Agree	Strongly agree
<qtb>1. I do think it is more appropriate for the mother of a newborn baby, rather than the father, to stay home with the baby (not work) during the first year.	1	2	3	4	5
2. It is as easy for women to succeed in business as it is for men.	1	2	3	4	5
3. I really think affirmative-action programs on college campuses constitute reverse discrimination.	1	2	3	4	5
4. I feel I could develop an intimate relationship with someone from a different race.	1	2	3	4	5
5. All Americans should learn to speak two languages.	1	2	3	4	5
6. It upsets (or angers) me that a woman has never been president of the United States.	1	2	3	4	5
7. Generally speaking, men work harder than women.	1	2	3	4	5
8. My friendship network is very racially mixed.	1	2	3	4	5
9. I am against affirmative-action programs in business.	1	2	3	4	5
10. Generally, men seem less concerned with building relationships than women.	1	2	3	4	5
11. I would feel OK about my son or daughter dating someone from a different race.	1	2	3	4	5
12. It upsets (or angers) me that a racial minority person has never been president of the United States.	1	2	3	4	5
13. In the past few years, too much attention has been directed toward multicultural or minority issues in education.	1	2	3	4	5

14. I think feminist perspectives should be an integral part of the higher education curriculum.	1	2	3	4	5
15. Most of my close friends are from my own racial group.	1	2	3	4	5
16. I feel somewhat more secure that a man rather than a woman is currently president of the United States.	1	2	3	4	5
17. I think that it is (or would be) important for my children to attend schools that are racially mixed.	1	2	3	4	5
18. In the past few years too much attention has been directed toward multicultural or minority issues in business.	1	2	3	4	5
19. Overall, I think racial minorities in America complain too much about racial discrimination.	1	2	3	4	5
20. I feel (or would feel) very comfortable having a woman as my primary physician.	1	2	3	4	5
21. I think the president of the United States should make a concerted effort to appoint more women and racial minorities to the country's Supreme Court.	1	2	3	4	5
22. I think white people's racism toward racial-minority groups still constitutes a major problem in America.	1	2	3	4	5
23. I think the school system, from elementary school through college, should encourage minority and immigrant children to learn and fully adopt traditional American values.	1	2	3	4	5
24. If I were to adopt a child, I would be happy to adopt a child of any race.	1	2	3	4	5
25. I think there is as much female physical violence toward men as there is male physical violence toward women.	1	2	3	4	5
26. I think the school system, from elementary school through college, should promote values representative of diverse cultures.	1	2	3	4	5
27. I believe that reading the autobiography of Malcolm X would be of value.	1	2	3	4	5
28. I would enjoy living in a neighborhood consisting of a racially diverse population (Asians, blacks, Latinos, whites).	1	2	3	4	5
29. I think it is better if people marry within their own race.	1	2	3	4	5
30. Women make too big a deal out of sexual-harassment issues in the workplace.	1	2	3	4	5

<qx>The total score measures overall sensitivity, awareness, and receptivity to cultural diversity and gender equality. Of the 30 items on the QDI, 15 are worded and scored in a positive direction (high scores indicate high sensitivity to multicultural/gender issues), and 15 are worded and scored in a negative direction (where low scores are indicative of high sensitivity). Naturally, when tallying the total score response, these latter 15 items need to be *reverse-scored.* Reverse scoring simply means that if a respondent circles a "1" they should get five points; a "2" four points, a "3" three points, a "4" two points, and a "5" one point.

The following QDI items need to be *reverse-scored:* 1, 2, 3, 7, 9, 10, 13, 15, 16, 18, 19, 23, 25, 29, 30.

Score range = 30 to 150, with high scores indicating more awareness, sensitivity, and receptivity to racial diversity and gender equality.

CHAPTER 14: PATHWAYS TO PERSONAL GROWTH

Outline

Pathways for Continued Self-Exploration
      Developing a Reading Program
      Continuing Your Writing Program
      Practice Ongoing Self-Assessment
      Contemplate Self-Directed Behavior Change
      Take Advantage of Support Groups
Counseling as a Path to Self-Understanding
Dreams as a Path to Self-Understanding
      Exploring the Meaning of Dreams
      Dare to Dream
Concluding Comments
Where Can I Go From Here?
Website Resources

Chapter Objectives

- to identify ways of furthering personal growth

- to understand how counseling can be a resource for change

- to appreciate the value of dreams as a path to self-understanding

- to review significant learnings based on this book

Questions for Thought, Discussion, and Evaluation

1. Mention and briefly discuss some pathways for continued self-exploration and personal growth.

2. In what specific ways can counseling be viewed as a path to self-understanding? When might you consider seeking counseling for yourself?

3. What are some specific signs indicating a need to consider seeking personal counseling?

4. In what sense are counselors mentors? What are the main functions of a counselor?

5. What are some ways to best select a counselor?

6. How can counseling be preventive in nature? Do you see any comparison between consulting with a counselor for psychological health in much the same way as you might consult with a physician for physical health?

7. What are some specific functions that professional counselors serve? What are some things they do to help people move toward empowerment?

8. What are some attitudes people hold that sometimes make it difficult for them to seek professional counseling, even if they are struggling with personal problems?

9. How are dreams an avenue to self-understanding? How does dreaming allow people to think creatively about coping with their problems? How can dreams reveal clues to events that have meaning to us?

10. What is the connection between remembering your dreams and your readiness to deal with problems and internal conflicts?

11. Fritz Perls viewed dreams as "the royal road to integration." Explain how the Gestalt therapy approach to dream work can illuminate existential messages.

12. Discuss the following concepts: If you can listen to your dreams, you will learn something more about yourself. You can use this knowledge to make better choices and to live your life more fully.

Glossary of Key Terms

Self-directed behavior change pertains to a program you design to modify specific behavioral patterns (such as exercising, eating habits, and practicing relaxation methods).

Support groups provide help for individuals who want to change and maintain certain behaviors; the group experience of others with similar concerns helps individuals appreciate that they are not alone in their struggles.

Counseling consists of professional assistance in identifying and effectively dealing with thoughts, feelings, and behaviors one may be interested in changing; counselors can be considered as mentors who guide people in making full use of their inner resources.

Dreams are our inner creation during sleep states that can help us to better understand what is going on in our life.

TEST ITEMS FOR CHAPTER 14
PATHWAYS TO PERSONAL GROWTH

1. The Coreys list all of the following as pathways for continued self-exploration *except* for:
    a. paying attention to your astrological sign.
    b. developing a reading and writing program.
    c. practicing ongoing self-assessment.
    d. contemplating self-directed behavior change.

2. The following is true in regard to counseling:
    a. Effective counseling must involve a major revamping of your personality.
    b. It's important to wait until you are unable to cope or function before reaching out for help.
    c. You can benefit from counseling without being psychologically impaired.
    d. You need to be in crisis in order to benefit from either individual or group counseling.

3. Ineffective professional counselors
    a. are psychological educators, teaching you ways to get the most from living.
    b. may attempt to solve your problems for you.
    c. are like mentors in that they guide you to make use of your inner resources.
    d. will ask what you want from counseling and explore your expectations about the kind of help you can expect to get.

4. Therapeutic work can be difficult for those who seek counseling because
    a. self-honesty isn't easy.
    b. confronting and dealing with your problems can be painful.
    c. self-exploration requires discipline, patience, and persistence.
    d. all of the above.

5. Which of the following statements is *false*?
    a. Counseling is a process of self-discovery aimed at empowerment.
    b. If counseling is successful, you will mainly learn how to solve a specific problem.
    c. Counseling enables you to effectively cope with future blocks that you are likely to encounter.
    d. Counseling can equip you to make your own choices about how you want to live.

6. According to the Coreys, dreams
    a. contribute significantly to our health and well-being, as well as to being useful for self-understanding.
    b. can reveal significant clues to events that have meaning for us.
    c. can be healing if we learn to pay attention to the wisdom of our unconscious.
    d. can shed light on our past, present, and future dynamics and on our attempt to identify meaning.
    e. all of the above.

7. One of the best ways to keep track of your dreams is to:
   a. simply try to remember them later on during the week.
   b. record them in your journal.
   c. ignore them, since focusing on a dream will be self-defeating.
   d. none of the above.

8. Which approach to working with dreams asks the dreamer to consider that all the images manifested in their dreams are some dimension of themselves?
   a. Gestalt therapy approach
   b. cognitive, problem-solving view
   c. psychoanalytic
   d. none of the above

9. In Gestalt dream work, the dreamer
   a. brings the dream back to life and relives it in the present.
   b. engages in a dialogue between opposing sides.
   c. finds his or her own meaning for the dream.
   d. all of the above.

10. Perls' Gestalt approach to dreams is based on the belief that
    a. every dream contains an existential message of oneself and one's current struggle.
    b. we can be taught to change the plots of our dreams towards happier endings.
    c. dream symbols have an apparent universality, having the same meaning across all humanity.
    d. recurrent childhood dreams are more important to the therapeutic process than recent dreams.

11. If you decide to join a support group, you should
    a. ask yourself if this is the right group for you at this time in your life.
    b. join the first one you can find before you lose your nerve.
    c. hold off in joining for at least six months to make sure you've made the right choice.
    d. try to get as many of your friends to join with you to increase your comfort.

12. Personal growth is a
    a. quick and painless process if you are competent.
    b. life-long process.
    c. magic bullet for life's problems.
    d. gimmick that doesn't really work.

13. When people are physically ill, they generally seek a physician's help. When people are not psychologically well, they often
    a. hesitate to ask for help.
    b. don't hesitate to ask for help.
    c. wait so long to seek help that they develop psychosis.
    d. end up being mandated by the courts to receive counseling.

14. Participating in counseling is a sign of
    a. weakness.
    b. character deficits.
    c. strength.
    d. cowardice.

15. "God, grant me the serenity to accept the things I cannot change, courage to change the things I can, and wisdom to know the difference." These words are widely known as
    a. a personal mission statement
    b. The Serenity Prayer
    c. a poem
    d. a Hallmark greetings card message
    e. a campaign slogan

ANSWER KEY FOR CHAPTER 14
PATHWAYS TO PERSONAL GROWTH

1. a   p. 408-410
2. c   p. 410-411
3. b   p. 412
4. d   p. 412
5. b   p. 413
6. e   p. 413
7. b   p. 414
8. a   p. 414-415
9. d   p. 415
10. a   p. 415
11. a   p. 410
12. b   p. 410
13. a   p. 411
14. c   p. 411
15. b   p. 412

Activities and Exercises for Classroom Participation for Chapter 14

1. **One year hence exercise**. In small subgroups, discuss the changes you hope to have made in your life one year from today. Assume that your class and the subgroup you're in now will have a reunion next year. Now tell the other members the things you'd *most* like to be able to say about your life then. What changes have you made? What decisions have you made? How is your life different? You might want to write down contracts and keep them in a sealed envelope. A year from now you could look at your contracts to see whether you've made any progress.

2. **Assessment of your personal growth.** In your groups, discuss all the things you did for yourself while you were reading this book and taking this course that related in some way to your personal growth. You might discuss some of the following questions:

(1) What risks have you taken during the past few months?

(2) Are you glad that you took these risks?

(3) What are some things that you wanted to do for yourself, but did not do? What stopped you?

(4) What are a few specific things that you'd like to do in the near future that might lead to continued growth?

3. **Closure exercises.** In this manual (see Part 7) are some very detailed suggestions for a wrap-up and integration of the course. Part 7 will provide you with specific guidelines for assisting students in consolidating their learning and for helping them to apply what they learned in the class to daily life.

Reviewing what students have learned during the course is certainly useful, especially with the focus being on their personal learning and how they can apply what they have learned to their educational and life goals. Students will have hopefully experienced a lot of intellectual, emotional, and spiritual growth and taken a lot of personal risks, which should be honored and acknowledged. Here are a few suggestions for helping students bring closure to their experience in the course:

- Students could give a five-minute oral presentation on the most important things they learned in the course and where they see themselves going from here.

- Some kind of celebration can be planned for the final session.

- Consider giving some memento to mark the completion of the course. An inspirational quote might be good to hand out.

- In small groups, students can share some of the personal highlights of the course. They can each identify some of the most significant things they learned about themselves, along with how they plan to continue implementing what they learned once this course has ended. After the small group session, a spokesperson for each group can give a brief summary of what the group came up with pertaining to highlights of the experience of the course.

- Let students know how they can connect with you in the future and encourage them to maintain contact with you at various points in their education and after they graduate. You might ask some of your former students to return to your class as guest speakers. The chances are that your students have formed a significant bond with you and they will need to feel free to continue seeing you as a source of support as future challenges arise. This sense of availability of ongoing sources of support is a crucial factor in promoting students' successes.

4. **Dare to dream.** Ask students to carefully read the short section, Dare to Dream. Invite students in class to write even a paragraph or a page on pursuing their passion in life. Ask students: What is the kind of life you would most want for yourself? What are some dreams that you hope will become reality?

Do you have the courage to follow your passions? Once students have written about their personal vision, they might share their hopes for their future in small groups. How has the course encouraged them to dream and become more open to options?

5. **Review of Self-Assessments**. Toward the end of the course is a good time for allocating at least a class period for students to review and discuss what they learned about themselves from taking these interactive sections throughout the book:

- Where Am I Now?

- Take Time to Reflect Exercises

- Where Can I Go From Here?

What themes do they see in their responses? What commitments are they willing to make to continue their personal growth?

6. **Review of Journals**. Suggest to your students that they review their journal entries toward the end of the term. What can they learn about their personal journey during this term based on reading and reflecting on their journal entries? Are they willing to make a commitment to continue writing in their journals?

7. **Student evaluation of the course**. Most colleges require some form of anonymous student evaluation of the course during the last week of the term. Even if such a procedure is not required, it is a good idea to make time for students to anonymously react to the course, stating what they found most valuable and least valuable. In this manual, Part 8 deals with approaches to evaluate the personal-growth course. In Part 8 you will find a wide range of question to select from in constructing your own set of questions aimed at assessing the course.

PART 7

Guidelines for the Wrap-Up
and Integration of the Course

Suggestions for Some Wrap-Up Exercises

In talking with many instructors who teach this course, I (Jerry Corey) have found that many of them devote at least a part of the class to some type of experiential group work. In my own classes, I meet with each class once a week for a three-hour period. The first half of the session is devoted to lectures, class presentations, guest speakers, panels, and demonstrations, as well as whole-class activities and discussions. During the second half of the period, the students form subgroups (about 8 people to a group) and talk in more personal ways about how the topic applies to them. So at least half of my class is a group experience. During the last couple of weeks of the course, I like to focus on what the course has meant to them, what they have learned about themselves and others as a result of their group work, and where they want to go from here.

If you'd like a further discussion of how to close a group or a personal-growth class, we'd like to recommend our book, *Groups: Process and Practice* (8th ed.) by Marianne Schneider Corey, Gerald Corey, and Cindy Corey (Belmont, CA: Brooks/Cole, Cengage Learning, 2010). Chapter 8 (the final stages of a group) gives many details on guidelines for the ending stages of a group. The book may also be helpful as a reference if you do incorporate aspects of a group experience in your class.

Here we'd like to describe a few techniques that we frequently use during the closing sessions. You may want to adapt some of these questions or exercises to your own teaching style and classroom setup. In the material that follows, we've addressed the student directly. This is a sample of the major themes that we focus on during the final stages of a group or during the ending of an experiential class. We are particularly concerned with helping students integrate and apply their learnings from the class to their everyday lives. What follows gives a flavor of how we attempt to encourage this consolidation of learning.

Terminating the Life History of a Group

Eventually you will stop being a member of a particular group/class, or the group will come to a predetermined end. Learning to deal with your feelings of separation and loss, and expressing these feelings and working them through in group, are central tasks of groups during the final stages of their existence. We now explore what you might expect during the termination phase of your group.

There is the danger of avoiding any discussion of your inevitable end as an intact group. Yet on some level, you all recognize this, and there may be a resistance to opening up any new material. You may begin to experience distance with each other and not speak about this.

Another danger consists of discounting the importance of the relationships you've formed with people during the life of your group because you realize it won't be ongoing. You could conclude that because your group will end, it is not really worthwhile to form close bonds because soon they will be broken. You could conclude, too, that it's exciting to get to know strangers by sharing yourself with them. You can also find out that emotional closeness is possible and that you can *make* this happen in other groups and in situations separate from groups.

You could make the false assumption that achieving closeness is possible only in a group such as yours. Hopefully, you've learned that a group or class situation can teach you the way to get close with whomever you decide and that you won't rely on the group as an exclusive way to meet your needs for closeness.

You can find ways to build bridges between the group and the world outside. With *selected* others, you can make what occurred in your group occur outside of it. In doing so, beware of the dangers of trying to be open and close with everyone. Some may not be ready, or may not want the closeness you expect.

Realize that you can really change no one but yourself. If you make a project out of attempting to change another, you may very well end up feeling powerless. If you concentrate on a plan for self-directed change, you have a much better chance of feeling a sense of power. Don't underestimate your capacity to influence others through the changes you make in your life apart from group. If others in your life sense that you are liking yourself more, they may begin to think of what they, too, can do to make some of the changes you've made.

Consolidating Your Learnings

During the final session, we generally ask members to give a brief report on how they've perceived themselves in the group, what the group has meant to them, what they have learned about their behavior, what decisions they have made, and the specific things they are willing to continue doing to extend their learning, now that the group is coming to an end.

Our experience has taught us that this review on the part of every member is critical if actual changes in out-of-group behavior are expected. We ask members questions geared to help them tie together in a meaningful way what they most want to remember from their group experience. We encourage you to answer the following questions for yourself:

1. What is the *most* important thing about yourself that you've learned? _____

    _____

    _____

    _____

2. *As a group,* what changes have you noticed from the initial session to this last session? _____

    _____

    _____

    _____

3. *Who* and *what* brought the above changes about? _____

    _____

    _____

    _____

4. What has this group taught you about interpersonal relationships? _____

    _____

    _____

    _____

5. How might you discount what you've experienced in this group as time passes? How do you think you might forget some significant learnings?_____

_____

_____

_____

6. What steps can you take to remember those things you deem most significant? _____

_____

_____

_____

7. What are some specific contracts you are willing to make now that your group has come to an end?

_____

_____

_____

Giving and Receiving Feedback

One of the best ways of consolidating your gains from a group experience is to exchange feedback during the final sessions. Hopefully, at this stage members will give honest and direct feedback; one function of a group is to learn how others experience us. Assuming that you receive honest feedback, you can benefit from it by getting a sample of how people in your everyday life view you. In your daily interactions, most people will not share their honest impressions with you. They may not want to extend themselves and risk your disapproval. This makes the quality of feedback you give and get in a group all the more valuable. Of course, you have been giving and receiving feedback during each session, for members do respond to one another and share their impressions. However, the feedback during the final session is aimed particularly at providing members with reactions they can use to continue working on when the group terminates. At the ending stage of a group, the feedback needs to be constructive in that a person has some way of dealing with these reactions when he or she leaves the group. For example, if you consistently felt bored around a group member and never shared this with the person before, it could be seen as a "hit-and-run" for you now to tell him that you were bored with him all semester. You aren't really giving him any opportunity to examine that behavior in relation to you.

A suggestion for focusing feedback to each person is to ask yourself, "What is the *one* thing I most want to say to each person that I hope he or she remembers and considers seriously?" We urge that when you give others feedback, you do so in a concrete manner so that they have a clear idea of what you perceive as their strengths and weaknesses. Thus, we tell members to avoid limiting themselves exclusively to saying only favorable things, and to avoid statements that are so vague that they are meaningless. For example, saying "I really like you" or "I really think you are quite a person" leaves members with nothing tangible. Instead of being so general, you can tell members *what* you like about them and *how* you see them as being unique or special for you. We also ask members to express to the other members what their fears and concerns are for them. In that way you can share how you see each person blocking their strengths, what you are concerned they might do to discount what they've experienced in the group, and issues you hope they'll seriously consider. We have used the structure of asking members to complete sentences such as the following for each individual in the group:

- My fear for you is . . .

- My hope for you is . . .

- The one thing I most hope you'll consider is . . .

- One of your traits that I most respect is . . .

- A way I see you as blocking your strength is . . .

- One more thing I want to tell you is . . .

Applying Group Learnings to Daily Life

As you reach the final stages of your group, the pivotal questions are: How can you translate your in-group learning to the way you are in the outside world? If you achieved closeness and trust in the group, can you learn to achieve them outside the group? Is the group setting the only safe place to risk intimacy? If you convince yourself that only in group can you experience honest and intense interactions, then what becomes of you when you leave it?

It is our conviction that group members *can* transfer what they learn as participants to the real situations they encounter outside the group. The more this application to daily life is made, the more real your group becomes. Throughout this book, our basic assumption has been that groups are places to experiment with changes you would like to consider making in your everyday living.

Your group may have been characterized by a shared journey of uncertainty, love, trust, hesitation, resistance, pain, anger, tenderness, joy, and so forth. Hopefully a therapeutic community was formed. In this setting you most likely have learned that you are capable of risking, trusting, demanding, and caring. Perhaps it has been a significant breakthrough for you to learn that you can be emotionally close to others and that you *do* have something to offer to others.

To make the transition to your outside life, it is helpful to talk about what you've learned in your group and how it can be applied outside. It's foolish to open yourself indiscriminately to everyone, saying, in effect, "Here I am, ready and willing to form loving bonds with everyone." As we have already mentioned, you need to choose the people with whom you desire more intimacy and then work toward this goal. There are no guarantees that you're reaching out will always be reciprocated, but you may learn that you can have more acceptance than you imagined. Hopefully, your group experience taught you it is up to you to initiate contacts instead of waiting for others to come to you. You can continue in your everyday life to ask for what you want and actively practice many of the new behaviors and skills you acquired in your group. In this way, you are building bridges from your group to the outside world.

Throughout this course we have discussed the skills that are necessary for group participation. These same skills are necessary for effective living. We hope you will not settle for feeling alive only in a group and that you will consolidate your gains and make decisions on how you'll modify your life beyond the group.

Problems in Translating Your Group Behavior to Your Everyday Life

Learn to recognize how your in-group behavior is a sample of your out-of-group behavior. If you see each of these as separate and distinct worlds, you probably will encounter problems in carrying your changes over to your everyday behavior.

A problem exists when you make the group an end in itself. When you seek *in-group* friendship, acceptance, security, and understanding but do *not* seek these same things outside, you then begin to set up an artificial dichotomy. You also lessen your chances of finding what you seek apart from your group because you don't believe it is possible to find this situation outside it.

Groups are a place to learn about yourself and others. Groups provide safety for exploring. In them you can learn what it means to take charge of your life; get clarity on issues that were foggy to you; start out fresh and create a new identity for yourself; and change the way you are with others. The key point we want to stress is that you can take this power and clarity with you by applying it to your daily life. A problem exists if you fail to make plans for ways to apply what you've learned in your group to your daily life.

You need to realize that although you may have made changes, other persons in your life may resist your changes. They may have an investment in keeping you in old and familiar ways. Your changes might be a threat to them, for now *they* must change in relation to you.

A lack of sensitivity on your part may impede your becoming different out of group over a period of time. You need to be sensitive toward those who were not in group. Sometimes you can badly alienate others by forcing yourself on them. Further, you may want to be fully open with others and tell them what you *really* think about them, when they really *don't* want to know this. If you make the mistake of forcing honesty upon everyone you work with, for example, you might conclude that indeed it is not possible to build bridges between what you can experience in group and what you can experience in everyday life.

You can set yourself up for failure by expecting too much too soon. Remember that in your group, others responded to you in new ways in large measure because you showed different facets of yourself. They saw you differently because you behaved differently. When you go back to familiar surroundings, others may expect you to be as you were, and you may revert to predictable patterns of behavior. You can also set yourself up for failure by expecting your relationships to be a certain way, and when these situations don't match your fantasies, you could become deflated.

A problem can occur by demanding perfection from yourself—and right now. Sometimes after a group is over, people expect that they will progress forward from this time on. Recognize that setbacks will occur at times and that this doesn't mean you didn't make any *real* changes. This does mean that your changes need some reinforcement if they are to last. If you are not reinforced in your environment, it becomes particularly crucial that you discover some kind of support group so that you can continue to develop along the lines you desire. Also, learning to reinforce your own changes, or liking what *you* are becoming, is essential so that your changing does not depend upon external confirmation exclusively.

Perhaps the major obstacle to making and maintaining actual changes in your everyday life involves a lack of belief and hope that this is possible. Changing is hard work, and while it may have seemed easy to be different in your group, you may face real difficulty in maintaining these changes when others do not appreciate your new values. Remember that in the group you had support and were rewarded for some of the very behavior that will be frowned upon apart from the group. Courage and hope, coupled with hard work, can offset the discouragement that occurs when you find it difficult to recreate the atmosphere of acceptance you experienced in your group.

PART 8
Evaluation of the
Personal-Growth Course

Evaluation of the Group/Class Experience

To assist students in reviewing the highlights of the course and to help them focus on some of the things they have learned about themselves and others, I (Jerry Corey) generally give them a handout with many of the questions listed below. I ask them to write a final paper describing what the experience of the class was like for them and what they would like to do now to build on what they've ned. I suggest that they use these questions as guides only and that they don't necessarily have to address every question. Then during the last couple of sessions I give students the chance to reflect and talk in small subgroups about the meaning of the class for them.

1. What general effect has this class had on your life?

2. What were the highlights of the class experience for you? What were some of its most meaningful aspects for you?

3. What were some specific things that you became aware of about yourself, in terms of your lifestyle, attitudes, and relationships with others?

4. What are some changes you've made that you can attribute at least partly to the class?

5. Now that you are leaving this class, what kind of personal questions do you have that you'd like to answer? What questions about yourself? About others?

6. Did this class experience have any negative effects on you? If so, what were they?

7. If a close friend were to ask you today to tell in a sentence or two what the class meant to you, how would you respond?

8. Have you talked with other people about what you learned in this class? Have you asked others to read your book, and have you discussed with others some of the topics and issues of the course?

9. What do you intend to do to continue your personal growth, now that the course is coming to an end?

10. What is the one most valuable lesson you learned about yourself as a result of this course?

Student Evaluations and Assessments of the Course During the Semester

I like the idea of giving some type of written questionnaire to be filled out anonymously by the students around the fifth week, again at the end of the tenth week, and finally at completion of the course. Sometimes I give out evaluation forms at the midterm and again at the end of a course, depending upon the course or how I think a particular class is going. The earlier evaluations give students a chance to contribute their input before it is too late to change anything. Generally, the assessment is on a page or two, with short spaces to reply to such questions as the following:

1. How is the class going for you so far? Mention some things that you either *most* like or *least* like.

2. How interesting and valuable are the lectures and presentations? Any suggestions for change?

3. How interesting and valuable are the small-group discussions? Any suggestions for change?

4. Generally, are you keeping up with the readings and other assignments?

5. What are your reactions to the required readings? Are you doing much extra reading?

6. Do you have any suggestions for guest speakers? What has been your reaction to the speakers we've had so far?

7. What is your reaction to the topics we've covered so far? Are they topics that you can relate to? What ideas do you have for other topics that we might add to the course before the end of the semester?

8. How much trust do you feel when you come to this class? Do you trust your fellow students? Your teacher? Yourself?

9. Is your instructor available to you for outside consultation? Do you feel free enough to come in during office hours and talk about yourself and your reactions to the class?

10. Are you noticing any changes in yourself as a result of the course so far? For example, are you speaking out more in other classes? Are you thinking about your life outside of the class sessions? Are you talking in more direct and honest ways with those you're close to in your life? Are you making new decisions? Are you becoming more the person *you* want to become?

11. Are you having any particular problems with the class? If so, what are they? Any suggestions on how your instructors might be of more help to you?

12. Mention any comments at all you'd care to make at this relatively early period in the course that you think could improve the course or make it more meaningful to you.

After I've read all the evaluations, I make a general tally summarizing the trends in how the students experience the course; then I bring this summary to class, and we talk about the results. Finally, I give an evaluation form to the students at the end of the course so that they can assess the course as a whole.

PART 9

On-Line Quiz Items

TEST ITEMS FOR CHAPTER 1
INVITATION TO PERSONAL LEARNING AND GROWTH

1. Maslow's theory stresses
   a. the concept of the "fully functioning person."
   b. a hierarchy of needs with a central theme of self-actualization.
   c. acceptance of the dark side of our nature.
   d. a deterministic view of human behavior.

2. Adlerian psychologists contend that humans are
   a. the victims of fate.
   b. choice-making beings whose every action has purpose and meaning.
   c. driven by primitive impulses such as selfishness and greed.
   d. by nature irrational and destructive unless they are socialized to identify and have empathy with others.

3. Joan has highly developed auditory skills, enjoys reading and writing, likes to play Scrabble, likes to tell stories, and has a good memory for names, dates, and places. Her primary intelligence is
   a. musical-rhythmic.
   b. visual-spatial.
   c. logical-mathematical.
   d. verbal-linguistic.

4. Robert likes to explore patterns and relationships. He enjoys doing activities in sequential order and learns best by classifying information, engaging in abstract thinking, and looking for common basic principles. His primary intelligence is
   a. visual-spatial.
   b. logical-mathematical.
   c. verbal-linguistic.
   d. complex and multidimensional.

5. What is the acronym for the key procedures used by Dr. Robert Wubbolding in reality therapist?
   a. WDEP
   b. RTCT
   c. REBT
   d. CHOICE

TEST ITEMS FOR CHAPTER 2
REVIEWING YOUR CHILDHOOD AND ADOLESCENCE

6. Jason was born to a single mother who is preoccupied with her problems. She went back to work soon after Jason was born and changed childcare quite often. Since she is exhausted after coming home from work, she seldom gives the attention that Jason needs. According to Erikson, Jason would likely to be stuck in the following core struggle:
   a. a general sense of mistrust toward human relationships.
   b. shame over his mother's stressful life.
   c. doubt over his ability to make another person happy.
   d. inability to form a positive self-concept.

7. According to Erikson, the conflict that characterizes early childhood is
   a. initiative vs. guilt.
   b. autonomy vs. shame and doubt.
   c. industry vs. inferiority.
   d. trust vs. mistrust.

8. From the self-in-context view, _____ is a time for becoming aware of "otherness" in terms of gender, race, and disability.
   a. adolescence
   b. early childhood
   c. middle childhood
   d. early adulthood

9. Helen refused to allow her teachers or parents to help her with schoolwork even though she was having trouble. Accepting offers of help would have indicated she really was incapable. She is using the following defense mechanism:
   a. reaction formation.
   b. projection.
   c. denial.
   d. displacement.

10. According to Erikson, the conflict that characterizes adolescence is
    a. identity vs. role confusion.
    b. autonomy vs. shame and doubt.
    c. generativity vs. despair.
    d. industry vs. inadequacy.

TEST ITEMS FOR CHAPTER 3
ADULTHOOD AND AUTONOMY
11. According to the theory of transactional analysis, early decisions are
    a. made by children for the purpose of psychological survival.
    b. influential in later adult behavior.
    c. able to be changed through a process of redecision.
    d. all of the above.

12. _____ is a lethal message often given nonverbally by the way parents hold (or don't hold) the child. The basic message is "I wish you hadn't been born."
   a. "Don't be close"
   b. "Don't be a child"
   c. "Don't be"
   d. "Don't be you"

13. Sally's date didn't show up, and she felt depressed, rejected, and unlovable. According to Ellis, the cause of these feelings is
   a. the activating event.
   b. her belief system.
   c. the emotional consequence.
   d. all of the above.

14. A characteristic of the inner critic is
   a. allowing you to feel free enough to make mistakes.
   b. freeing you from the judgments of others.
   c. preventing you from taking risks.
   d. expanding your ability to be creative.

15. According to Erikson, the period of early adulthood is characterized by the core struggle of
   a. identity vs. role confusion.
   b. generativity vs. stagnation.
   c. integrity vs. despair.
   d. intimacy vs. isolation.

TEST ITEMS FOR CHAPTER 4
YOUR BODY AND WELLNESS

16. The concept of wellness fits into all of the following *except*
   a. a holistic view of health.
   b. traditional medicine.
   c. considering the relationships among physical, psychological, social, and spiritual dimensions.
   d. emphasizing positive health rather than disabling symptoms.

17. Traditional medicine focuses on
   a. identifying symptoms of illness and curing disease.
   b. every facet of human functioning.
   c. herbal and naturalistic means of healing.
   d. the intimate relationship between mind and body.

18. Wellness is
   a. a choice, a decision you make to move toward optimal health.
   b. a way of life, a lifestyle you design to achieve your highest potential for well-being.
   c. a process, a developing awareness that there is no end point; health and happiness are possible in the here and now.
   d. the loving acceptance of yourself.
   e. all of the above.

19. Psychologically oriented physicians emphasize
    a. the role of choice and responsibility as critical determinants of our physical and psychological well-being.
    b. medication to alleviate the symptoms of what they see as problematic lifestyles.
    c. psychotherapy as a means of getting in touch with the reason their patient acquired the disease.
    d. taking surveys at regular intervals to monitor patients' health practices.

20. Being physically fit includes all of the following benefits *except*
    a. improved bone density
    b. lower risk of Type 2 diabetes
    c. prevention of hypertension
    d. none of the above

TEST ITEMS FOR CHAPTER 5
MANAGING STRESS
21. According to the text, the two major sources of stress are
    a. environmental and personal.
    b. daily hassles and major life changes.
    c. psychosocial conflicts and significant relationships.
    d. physiological and psychological.

22. _____ is a source of stress that occurs when two or more incompatible motivations or behavioral impulses compete for expression.
    a. Frustration
    b. Conflict
    c. Pressure
    d. Change

23. John has been unemployed for six months and has gone through all of his savings while attempting to find a job. He has finally been offered a position in a job that he finds unattractive since the pay and benefits are less than desirable and there is little room for advancement. In attempting to make a decision, he is struggling with the following type of conflict:
    a. approach/avoidance conflict.
    b. approach/approach conflict.
    c. multiple approach/avoidance conflict.
    d. avoidance/avoidance conflict.

24. _____ takes place when a woman is forced to have unwanted sex with someone she knows, such as a friend, co-worker, neighbor, or relative.
    a. Date rape
    b. Acquaintance rape
    c. Incest
    d. Sexual harassment

25. Which of the following symptoms or reactions tend to occur when someone experiences posttraumatic stress disorder?
    a. hyperarousal
    b. emotional numbing
    c. intrusive thoughts
    d. all of the above
    e. a and c

TEST ITEMS FOR CHAPTER 6
LOVE

26. According to the Coreys, our need for love includes
    a. the need to be loved by nearly everyone we meet.
    b. the need to be unconditionally loved by those we love.
    c. the guarantee that those we love will never hurt us.
    d. the need to know that our existence makes a difference in at least one person's life.

27. All of the following are myths or misconceptions about love *except*
    a. Love implies constant closeness
    b. We fall in and out of love
    c. Love is complex and the intensity of it may change as you change
    d. True love is selfless

28. Jane is a selfless mother who never lets her children know that she needs anything from them, yet she confides to her friends that she is very hurt that they do not seem to appreciate her. Jane harbors the myth that
    a. love means letting go of fear.
    b. if they really loved her, they would know what she needed without her having to ask for it.
    c. genuine love implies that we take from as well as give to those we love.
    d. love and anger are incompatible.

29. There are common fears of risking in love, and most of them are related to
    a. rejection, loss, the failure of love to be reciprocated, and uneasiness with intensity.
    b. the fear of losing one's identity within an inauthentic relationship.
    c. being egocentric and self-indulgent in our relationships.
    d. narcissistic self-love.

30. When we are in love and vulnerable in the relationship,
    a. we can experience hurt, rejection, and loss.
    b. we need to put up barriers so we will not feel the pain of possible rejection.
    c. we are secure in feeling that our love will endure forever.
    d. it implies that our relationship is based on perpetual happiness.

TEST ITEMS FOR CHAPTER 7
RELATIONSHIPS

31. If there is not enough togetherness in a relationship, the people in it will typically
    a. feel isolated and not share feelings and experiences.
    b. give up a sense of their own identity and control.
    c. devote much effort to becoming what the other person expects.
    d. feel lost and empty when they are not together.

32. Today most therapists practice_____, helping individuals _____their sexual identity.
    a. gay-affirmative therapy; accept
    b. client-centered therapy; affirm
    c. cognitive behavioral therapy; challenge irrational beliefs about
    d. gender-centered behavioral therapy; modify

33. The Coreys give the following suggestion to college students who encounter difficulties in keeping their relationships alive:
    a. Try to live up to the expectations of others.
    b. Devote time to nourishing and revitalizing your relationships.
    c. Know the other person well enough to assume what they are thinking and feeling without having to check it out.
    d. Encourage each other to fully self-disclose thoughts and feelings.

34. According to Carl Rogers, the main block to effective communication is
    a. our tendency to evaluate and judge the statements of others.
    b. the willingness to put ourselves in the other's frame of reference.
    c. challenging ourselves to go beyond what we are hearing.
    d. using active listening skills.

35. John and his wife have a difference of opinion on whether or not they should buy a new home. John says "I look at this matter very differently from the way you do, but I understand that you have your own opinion." He is
    a. being mysterious, expecting his wife to decode his message.
    b. showing respect for his wife's opinion rather than pressuring her to accept his point of view.
    c. being indirect and condescending with his response.
    d. trying to manipulate her with his passive/aggressive response.

TEST ITEMS FOR CHAPTER 8
BECOMING THE WOMAN OR MAN YOU WANT TO BE
36. Mark denies his fears and is apt to be aggressive when confronted. He is competitive and in order to achieve the success he strives for, he feels that he must never be vulnerable in his relationships with other men. Mark's characteristics are an example of
    a. a traditional, masculine gender-role stereotype.
    b. androgyny.
    c. the "new male."
    d. gender schema.

37. Men who suffer from "gender-role strain" often
   a. express hostility in interpersonal relationships.
   b. experience anxiety and depression.
   c. have poor self-esteem.
   d. all of the above.

38. A major effect of gender stereotyping is that
   a. it guides people to behave in a manner that is socially acceptable at no cost to the individual.
   b. it leads to a variety of positive outcomes with respect to one's self-concept, psychological well-being, and physical health.
   c. people tend to adapt their behavior to fit gender-role expectations even if it is detrimental to themselves.
   d. both men and women know what to expect in order to adjust comfortably in this society.

39. According to the literature on dual-career families, one of the most dramatic social changes in the U.S. is
   a. the increase in the number of women who are working outside the home, particularly with children still at home.
   b. the increase in the number of men who are retiring before age 55 and relying on their spouse's income for their primary means of support.
   c. the increase in the number of couples who are choosing not to have children in order to advance both individual's careers.
   d. the reversal of power and status among middle-income men and women across most geographical regions in the nation.

40. Androgynous individual are *not*
   a. able to adjust their behavior to what the situation requires in integrated and flexible ways.
   b. bound by rigid, stereotyped behavior.
   c. comfortable engaging in a wide range of activities.
   d. likely to exhibit multidimensional aspects of their personalities.

TEST ITEMS FOR CHAPTER 9
SEXUALITY

41. HIV cannot be transmitted by
   a. unprotected sexual intercourse with a person infected with the virus.
   b. sharing needles with an infected person during intravenous drug use.
   c. eating food prepared by someone who is HIV infected
   d. women infected with HIV who become pregnant or breast-feed their baby, because the baby builds up an immunity to the virus.

42. What is the correct term for the awareness that each partner in a relationship cares for the other and knows that this care is reciprocated?
   a. compassion
   b. mutual empathy
   c. vulnerability
   d. reciprocal attending

43. Sexual responsibility means learning about
    a.   your body
    b.   your partner's body
    c.   your sexual development and preferences
    d.   health risks associated with sexual activity
    e.   all of the above

44. Erectile dysfunction may be due to
    a.   the side effects of prescription drugs
    b.   low self-esteem
    c.   fear of pregnancy
    d.   all of the above
    e.   a and b

45. The Coreys find all of the following to be misconceptions about sex *except*
    a.   Women are not as sexually desirable when they initiate sex.
    b.   Acting without guilt or restrictions is what is meant by being sexually free.
    c.   The more physically attractive a person is, the more sexually exciting he or she is.
    d.   none of the above

TEST ITEMS FOR CHAPTER 10
WORK AND RECREATION

46. Schlossberg (2004) identified five retirement paths. Which of the following is *not* one of the paths?
    a.   continuers
    b.   adventurers
    c.   slackers
    d.   retreaters

47. Vocational choice is best considered as
    a.   choosing one occupation that will last a lifetime.
    b.   a process that spans a considerable period of time rather than a single event.
    c.   analyzing our abilities and matching them to available jobs.
    d.   an event rather than a process.

48. Jake has a low tolerance for ambiguity and tends to think in terms of absolutes. He is shy and has a difficult time expressing his feelings. He is working as a mechanic and enjoys outdoor activities such as playing softball and camping. According to Holland, Jake has the following type of personality:
    a.   realistic type.
    b.   enterprising type.
    c.   investigative type.
    d.   industrious type.

49. Joe would make an excellent researcher. He is naturally curious and inquisitive, with a need to understand, explain, and predict in a scholarly and scientific manner. Although he has confidence in his intellectual abilities, he tends to feel inadequate in social situations. According to Holland, Joe has the following type of personality:
    a. enterprising type.
    b. investigative type.
    c. realistic type.
    d. conventional type.

50. Ruth is an enterprising type of personality. She is outgoing, self-confident, persuasive, and optimistic. She likes to organize, direct, manage, and control the activities of groups towards reaching either personal or organizational goals. Ruth tends to dislike
    a. activities requiring scientific abilities and systematic and theoretical thinking.
    b. associating with well-known and influential people at social gatherings.
    c. traveling first-class.
    d. expensive hobbies.

TEST ITEMS FOR CHAPTER 11
LONELINESS AND SOLITUDE

51. Loneliness is best considered as
    a. something we actively choose for ourselves.
    b. something that happens to us as a result of certain events in our life.
    c. a disease that should be cured.
    d. feelings of extreme self-pity.

52. Brian tends to be inhibited and uncomfortable in social situations. He is hesitant in expressing himself because he is oversensitive to how others are perceiving and reacting to what he says and how he looks. In fact, Brian tends to get embarrassed easily and will blush when meeting someone new. These characteristics are an indication that Brian is
    a. attempting to avoid life.
    b. shy.
    c. needing solitude.
    d. narcissistic.

53. Melinda recently broke up with her boyfriend after one year of dating and feels lonely. Her loneliness could best be described as
    a. transient loneliness
    b. chronic loneliness
    c. everyday loneliness
    d. existential loneliness

54. How we come to terms with our aloneness during young adulthood can have significant effects on the choices we make. For instance, if we haven't learned to depend on our own inner resources, we are most likely to
    a. reject the pressure to choose a relationship or a career before we're really prepared to do so.
    b. look to our projects or partners for the sense of identity we can find only in ourselves.
    c. feel lonely and establish patterns that will overcome our sense of loneliness.
    d. take responsibility for our own loneliness and create new choices for ourselves.

55. Loneliness is an experience that is common in
    a. childhood.
    b. adolescence.
    c. adulthood.
    d. old age.
    e. all of the above.

TEST ITEMS FOR CHAPTER 12
DEATH AND LOSS

56. From an existential perspective, your awareness of death
    a. enables you to give meaning to your life.
    b. makes life less meaningful.
    c. leads to feelings of hopelessness and despair.
    d. creates an existential vacuum.

57. At first Bill did not believe that he was going to die, but when he finally understood that his time was limited, he came to Kübler-Ross's second stage of dying, which is
    a. anger.
    b. depression.
    c. acceptance.
    d. disillusionment.

58. All of the following services are provided by hospices *except* services that
    a. help dying patients experience a sense of self-worth and dignity.
    b. protect the dying person from facing their grief prematurely.
    c. allow those who are losing a significant person to feel the full range of emotions during the bereavement process.
    d. provide support for the family members so they can prepare for the eventual separation.

59. Most writers on the subject of death and dying agree with the premise that
    a. grief is merely a guilt reaction for not having done enough for the loved one before it was too late.
    b. grieving is a form of self-pity, which tends to make "letting go" even more difficult.
    c. grieving is necessary to recover from a significant loss.
    d. grief is an unhealthy and unnecessary emotional reaction to loss.

60. Although a divorce looks imminent, Janet hopes a separation will give her and her spouse the distance they need to reevaluate things and that they will soon get back together again. She is experiencing the
    a. negotiating stage.
    b. mediation stage.
    c. bargaining stage.
    d. fantasy stage.

TEST ITEMS FOR CHAPTER 13
MEANING AND VALUES

61. When we make no attempt to get to know people different from ourselves, we are likely to
    a. become more open-minded.
    b. retain our prejudicial attitudes.
    c. develop a deep appreciation for other cultures.
    d. modify our beliefs.
    e. a and c

62. When a young man can walk into a store and not be viewed as a suspect because he is White or be mistaken for a bus boy because of his race, one can say that he has

    _____.

    a. White privilege
    b. good luck
    c. been blessed
    d. earned it.

63. Research indicates that meaning in life would *not* be found through
    a. reconstituting our social world, which involves a transformation of consciousness.
    b. meaningful interpersonal relationships with others.
    c. exclusive and narrow pursuit of self-realization.
    d. striving to make a difference in the world.

64. According to the Coreys, the process of finding our values implies
    a. that there is one right set of values.
    b. that a personal search for values gives meaning to our lives.
    c. that the world is without any meaning.
    d. the necessity of allowing religious institutions to define our values.

65. According to the Coreys,
    a. we can do nothing about bettering humanity, since it is an overwhelming task.
    b. the news media is always exaggerating the degree to which violence is prevalent in our society.
    c. it is easier to blame others for the ills of the world than to accept that we might be contributing to those ills.
    d. there is little hope for humanity since we are moving toward a loveless society.

TEST ITEMS FOR CHAPTER 14
PATHWAYS TO PERSONAL GROWTH

66. You might consider seeking counseling when you
    a. feel out of control of your life.
    b. feel stuck in terms of making constructive choices.
    c. are under chronic stress or have stress-related ailments.
    d. are experiencing chronic depression.
    e. all of the above.

67. Joe is feeling overwhelmed by his feelings of loss after his long-term relationship ended. He sought counseling with a good professional counselor, who worked towards
    a. solving his problems.
    b. confronting his irrational feelings.
    c. giving him advice about his situation.
    d. helping him identify specific beliefs that may be getting in the way of living effectively.

68. The Coreys encourage you and their other readers to do all of the following *except*
    a. make plans that will help you achieve your new goals.
    b. avoid overwhelming yourself.
    c. do not expect change to happen easily and quickly.
    d. apply what you've learned from the text and your self-exploration process all at once and with urgency.

69. Dreams can be helpful in:
    a. bringing closure to painful life situations.
    b. working through loss and grief.
    c. resolving anger.
    d. all of the above.

70. From the Coreys' perspective, dreams are:
    a. an avenue to learning more about yourself.
    b. a source of knowledge to help you make better choices and to live your life more fully.
    c. the link between your inner and outer life.
    d. all of the above.

ANSWER KEY FOR ON-LINE QUIZ ITEMS

CHAPTER 1: INVITATION TO PERSONAL LEARNING AND GROWTH

1. b   p. 18
2. b   p. 10
3. d   p. 29
4. b   p. 30
5. a   p. 23

CHAPTER 2: REVIEWING YOUR CHILDHOOD AND ADOLESCENCE

6. a   p. 44
7. b   p. 44
8. b   p. 44
9. a   p. 59
10. a   p. 61

CHAPTER 3: ADULTHOOD AND AUTONOMY

11. d   p. 73
12. c   p. 75
13. b   p. 78
14. c   p. 81
15. d   p. 85

CHAPTER 4: YOUR BODY AND WELLNESS

16. b   p. 108-109
17. a   p. 108
18. e   p. 108-109
19. a   p. 112
20. d   p. 115

CHAPTER 5: MANAGING STRESS

21. a   p. 135
22. b   p. 137
23. d   p. 137
24. b   p. 149
25. d   p. 145

CHAPTER 6: LOVE

26. d   p. 172
27. c   p. 181-182
28. b   p. 182
29. a   p. 186
30. a   p. 177

CHAPTER 7: RELATIONSHIPS

31. a p. 197
32. a p. 212
33. b p. 200
34. a p. 208
35. b p. 209

CHAPTER 8: BECOMING THE WOMAN OR MAN YOU WANT TO BE

36. a p. 232-234
37. d p. 231
38. c p. 236
39. a p. 246
40. b p. 251-252

CHAPTER 9: SEXUALITY

41. c p. 272
42. b p. 258
43. a p. 261
44. d p. 267
45. d p. 263

CHAPTER 10: WORK AND RECREATION

46. c p. 305
47. b p. 285
48. a p. 288
49. b p. 289
50. a p. 289-291

CHAPTER 11: LONELINESS AND SOLITUDE

51. b p. 316
52. b p. 321
53. a p. 318
54. b p. 330
55. e p. 335-336

CHAPTER 12: DEATH AND LOSS

56. a p. 343
57. a p. 357
58. b p. 355-356
59. c p. 361
60. c p. 357

CHAPTER 13: MEANING AND VALUES

61. b p. 389
62. a p. 393-394
63. c p. 379
64. b p. 386-388
65. c p. 397

CHAPTER 14: PATHWAYS TO PERSONAL GROWTH

66. e p. 411
67. d p. 412
68. d p. 416
69. d p. 413
70. d p. 415

PART 10
Website Resources

Chapter 1: Invitation to Personal Learning and Growth

Wadsworth, Cenage Learning, The Complete Psychology Publisher

www.academic.cengage.com/psychology

Recommended Search Words: "Cengage Psychology"

This is a website for both students and faculty alike that provides numerous resources in the field of psychology. It offers a continuously updated professional association conference calendar, links to current research through journal sites and professional associations, and a Faculty Lounge (password required) with resources for instructors.

The Rogers Indicator of Multiple Intelligences (RIMI)

www.personal.psu.edu/bxb11/MI/MIQuiz.htm

Recommended Search Words: "The Rogers Indicator of Multiple Intelligences"

The Rogers Indicator of Multiple Intelligences (RIMI) is a self-inventory created by Dr. Keith Rogers, a professor at Brigham Young University. By taking this inventory, students can pinpoint their dominate intelligences. It takes approximately 15 minutes to complete this inventory. After completing this inventory it can be scored and interpreted online.

Mental Health Net

http://www.mentalhelp.net/

Recommended Search Words: "mental help net"

Mental Health Net is an excellent site that explores all aspects of mental health. It "has become the most comprehensive source of online mental health information, news, and resources available today." This site offers items such as HealthScout which offers daily-updated news articles, online support forums, books, etc. There are links to more than 8,000 resources, so whatever you're looking for about mental health, it's probably here.

American Self-Help Group Clearinghouse Source Book

www.selfhelpgroups.org

Recommended Search Words: "American self-help group clearing house"

This site provides contact information for more than 800 self-help groups and organizations across the United States.

American Counseling Association (ACA)

http://www.counseling.org

Recommended Search Words: "American counseling association"

ACA is a major organization of counselors that puts out a resource catalog that provides information on the various aspects of the counseling profession. The site provides information about membership, journals, books, home-study programs, videotapes, and audiotapes.

American Psychological Association (APA)

http://www.apa.org/

Recommended Search Words: "American psychological association"

This is the major professional organization of psychologists. This resource gives leads for current research and literature on many of the topics in this book.

Chapter 2: Reviewing Your Childhood and Adolescence

Adolescent Directory Online

http://site.educ.indiana.edu

Recommended Search Words: "adolescent directory online"

This Indiana University, Bloomington site offers resources about adolescents that cover a range of health, mental health, and parenting issues.

American Academy of Child and Adolescent Psychiatry (AACAP): Facts for Families

www.aacap.org

Recommended Search Words: "American academy of child and adolescent psychiatry"

The materials available from this site deal with a range of psychological concerns of children and adolescents.

Chapter 3: Adulthood and Autonomy

Erikson Tutorial Home Page

http://web.cortland.edu/andersmd/ERIK/welcome.HTML

This site provides handy information about Erik Erikson's 8 Stages of Psychosocial Development including a summary chart of key facts for each stage, an introduction to each stage and other links to information on Erikson and Psychosocial Development.

SeniorNet

http://www.seniornet.com/

SeniorNet seeks to provide access and education about computer technology and the internet to those who are 50+ years old. The site offers links, information and discussion groups on a wide variety of topics of interest to seniors. If you are interested in learning about computers and the internet you can look up their Learning Centers online here or call them at 415-495-4990 for the location nearest you.

Adult Development and Aging: APA Division 20

http://apadiv20.phhp.ufl.edu/

Recommended Search Words: "apa division 20"

Division 20 of the American Psychological Association is devoted to the study of the psychology of adult development and aging. Here you will find information on instructional resources for teachers, resources for students, links for publications, conferences and to other related Web sites.

Chapter 4: Your Body and Wellness

Go Ask Alice!

http://www.goaskalice.columbia.edu/

Columbia University's Health Education Program has created a widely used web site designed for undergraduate students. Alice! offers answers to questions about relationships, sexuality, sexual health, emotional health, fitness and nutrition, alcohol, nicotine and other drugs, and general health. If you can't find an answer to what you are looking for, you can "Ask Alice!" yourself.
Centers for Disease Control and Prevention

The Centers for Disease Control and Prevention

http://www.cdc.gov/

The Centers for Disease Control and Prevention (CDC) offers news, fact sheets on disease information and health information, articles, statistics, and links regarding health and illness in the United States (also offered in Spanish).

Mayo Clinic Health Oasis

http://www.mayohealth.org/mayo/common/htm/index.htm

This site offers "reliable information for a healthier life" and provides news items, highlights, and specific health category Centers for information and resources on various diseases, medications and general health.

Eating Disorders Shared Awareness

http://www.eating-disorder.com/

This is a site dedicated to helping others through awareness, education, support and friendship. This site provides links to other sites such as Mirror-Mirror (Canada) and Something Fishy (New York) which provide a multitude of links and information on a wide variety of topics related to eating disorders.

National Association for Health and Fitness

www.physicalfitness.org

Recommended Search Words: "national association for health and fitness"

This is a network of state and governors' councils that promotes physical fitness for persons of all ages and abilities.

Food Pyramid

www.mypyramid.gov

Recommended Search Words: "mypyramid"

This website stresses that optimal diets differ for different people and recommends personalized eating plans.

National Center on Physical Activity and Disability

www.ncpad.org

Recommended Search Words: "national center on physical activity and disability"

This site promotes the "substantial health benefits that can be gained from participating in regular physical activity" and "provides information and resources that can enable people with disabilities to become as physically active as they choose to be."

Shape Up America!

www.shapup.org

Recommended Search Words: "shape up America"

Shape Up America is a nonprofit organization dedicated to helping you achieve a healthy weight for life.

Chapter 5: Managing Stress

Stress and You

http://www.chronicfatigue.org/History.html

This site is the realization of a long held dream of Dr. Gerald E. Poesnecker. It is a part of the Chronic Fatigue Unmasked Web site and describes the biological effects of stress including the General Adaptation Syndrome, hypoadrenalism, and chronic fatigue. It discusses the signs of chronic fatigue and makes suggestions about getting help for it.

National Institute on Alcohol Abuse and Alcoholism (NIAAA)

http://www.niaaa.nih.gov/

The NIAAA is a part of the National Institute of Health and provides this site which includes resources and references about alcohol abuse and alcoholism. Included are links to publications and databases such as the National Library of Medicine Databases and Electronic Sources, press releases, conferences, and research programs.

Web of Addictions

http://www.well.com/user/woa/

This site by Andrew L. Homer Ph.D. and Dick Dillon is dedicated to providing accurate information about alcohol and other drug addictions serving as a resource for teachers and student who "need factual information on abused drugs." It provides a collection of fact sheets arranged by drug, link to other resources, contact information for a variety of groups, meetings/conferences related to addictions, in-depth information on special topics, and places to get help with addictions.

Mind Tools (tm)

http://www.mindtools.com/index.html

Mind Tools is dedicated to "helping you to think your way to an excellent life." This site provides shareware and practical suggestions for problem solving, memory improvement, increasing creativity, mastering stress, time management, goal setting links to stress/time management book stores and much more.

Job Stress Network

www.workhealth.org

Recommended Search Words: "job stress network"

This site offers information on job strain, projects, risk factors, and outcomes.

APA Helpcenter: Psychology at Work

http://apahelpcenter.org

Recommended Search Words: "APA health center"

The American Psychological Association provides this resource describing various aspects of work including the myths of stress, the different kinds of stress, and the "Road to Burnout."

The Anxiety-Panic Internet Resource: Relaxation

www.algy.com/anxiety

Recommended Search Words: "anxiety panic internet resource"

This is a great site that deals with anxiety, coping with panic, and stress. Many stress reduction techniques are given. They are currently working on publishing an "encyclopedia/compendium of anxiety and self-help information."

Stress Assess: National Wellness Institute

www.nationalwellness.org

Recommended Search Words: "national wellness institute"

This site offers an evaluation in the areas of stress sources, distress symptoms, and stress balancing strategies.

American Institute of Stress

www.stress.org

Recommended Search Words: "American institute of stress"

This site provides a wealth of information and statistics on stress.

Rape Abuse and Incest National Network

www.rainn.org

Recommended Search Words: "RAINN"

This site offers news, hotlines, a list of local crisis centers, and statistics on the incidence of rape and incest.

National Center for PTSD

www.ncptsd.va.gov/ncmain/index.jsp

Recommended Search Words: "national center for ptsd"

This site, devoted to the understanding and treatment of posttraumatic stress disorders, has well-organized materials for both professionals and the public.

Websites Dealing with Styles of Yoga

http://ezinearticles.com/?cat=Health-and-Fitness:Yoga

http://yoga.about.com

Recommended Search Words: "ezine articles yoga;" "about yoga;" "types of yoga"

Chapter 6: Love

Love Page

http://www.tc.umn.edu/nlhome/g296/parkx032/LVindex.html

James Park, an existential philosopher and advocate of freedom and authenticity in relationships created the Love Page. This site offers many articles that challenge more traditional notions of romantic love and includes a 60-page preview of his book "New Ways of Loving". There are also bibliographies on a wide variety of topics dealing with love and relationships.

Chapter 7: Relationships

Relationships: The Counseling Center, University at Buffalo

http://ub-counseling.buffalo.edu/relationship.shtml

Recommended Search Words: "relationships university of buffalo"

The counseling center at the University at Buffalo offers information on topics such as starting and ending relationships, communication, rape and surviving, and about men and women and lesbian, gay, bisexual, and transgendered people.

WholeFamily

http://www.wholefamily.com/

Recommended Search Words: "whole family"

This site offers extensive information and resources on family life including the Marriage Center, the Parent Center, the Teen Center, the WholeFamily Room (where the family meets to get each other's points of view), the Senior Center, weekly dilemmas, publications, articles on mothering, etc.

Divorce Central

http://www.divorcecentral.com/

Recommended Search Words: "divorce central"

Divorce Central is an excellent site that provides information and advice on legal, emotional, and financial issues for individuals who are considering or going through a divorce. You can use all of their services and can become a member of their online community for free. Links to other divorce-related sites are also available here.

Partners Task Force for Gay and Lesbian Couples

http://www.buddybuddy.com/index.html

Recommended Search Words: "buddybuddy"

"Partners Task Force for Gay & Lesbian Couples is a national resource for same-sex couples, supporting the diverse community of committed gay and lesbian partners through a variety of media. The constantly updated Web site contains more than 200 essays, surveys, legal articles, and resources on legal marriage, ceremonies, domestic partner benefits, relationship tips, parenting, and immigration."

Sexual Orientation: Science, Education, and Policy

http://psychology.ucdavis.edu/rainbow/html/facts_mental_health.html

Recommended Search Words: "psychology UC Davis rainbow"

This site builds on the work of Dr. Gregory Herek, focusing on sexual orientation, antigay violence, homophobia, and other concerns of gay, lesbian, and bisexual individuals.

Human Rights Campaign

www.hrc.org

Recommended Search Words: "human rights campaign"

This organization focuses on securing equal rights for lesbians and gay men. The site provides news updates on legislation related to gay rights and descriptions of public education programs.

Chapter 8: Becoming the Woman or Man You Want to Be

Women's Studies Database

http://www.mith2.umd.edu/WomensStudies/

The Women's Studies Database by the University of Maryland is a resource for links to many different areas of interest such as conferences, computing, employment, government and history, film reviews, program support, publications and other Web sites.

Feminist Majority Foundation Online

http://www.feminist.org/

This site offers many links to a variety of feminist issues including news and events, the National Center for Women and Policing, global feminism and a feminist online store.

Gender Talk

www.gendertalk.com

Recommended Search Words: "gender talk"

This site provides explanations and challenges to conventional attitudes about gender issues and gender identity.

Society for the Psychological Study of Men and Masculinity (SPSMM)

www.apa.org/about/division/div51.html

Recommended Search Words: "APA division 51"

A division of the American Psychological Association, SPSMM promotes the "critical study of how gender shapes and constricts men's lives" and is "committed to the enhancement of men's capacity to experience their full human potential." This site presents contemporary psychological approaches to masculinity and includes extensive links to other related resources.

Gender and Race in the Media

www.uiowa.edu/~commstud/resources/GenderMedia

Recommended Search Words: "University of Iowa gender and race resources"

The University of Iowa's Communication Studies program presents a number of articles and links about the ways in which gender and racial differences are expressed in various media, including advertising, cyberspace, feminist media, print media, television and film, and mixed media.

The Wellesley Centers for Women

www.wcwonline.org

Recommended Search Words: "Wellesley centers for women"

The Wellesley Centers for Women works with the Center for Research on Women and the Stone Center for Developmental Services and Studies by "facilitating the development of new research, increasing efficiency, and expanding the Centers' outreach." It shares with them "a joint mission to educate, inform and expand the ways we think about women in the world." Resources for research and publications for purchase are offered.

Chapter 9: Sexuality

Sexual Health Network

http://www.sexualhealth.com/

Recommended Search Words: "sexual health network"

This site is "dedicated to providing easy access to sexuality information, education, counseling, therapy, medical attention, and other sexuality resources", especially for people with disability, illness, or other health related problems.

SIECUS (Sexuality Information and Education Council of the United States)

http://www.siecus.org/

Recommended Search Words: "SIECUS"

This organization is devoted to providing information on a range of topics pertaining to sexuality.

Queer Resources Directory (QRD)

http://www.qrd.org/QRD/

Recommended Search Words: "queer resources directory"

The QRD (Queer Resources Directory) is about issues relating to sexual minorities -- "groups which have traditionally been labeled as 'queer' and systematically discriminated against." This site is "an electronic library with news clippings, political contact information, newsletters, essays, images, hyperlinks, and every other kind of information resource of interest to the gay, lesbian, and bisexual community."

HIV/AIDS AEGIS

http://www.aegis.com/

Recommended Search Words: "AIDS aegis"

The HIV/AIDS AEGIS is the largest and one of the most important Internet resources dealing with HIV and AIDS. This site provides an extensive collection of related links, documents and news articles.

National Center for HIV, STD, and TB Prevention

www.cdc.gov/hiv

Recommended Search Words: "CDC HIV"

The Centers for Disease Control and Prevention (CDC) offers current information, fact sheets, conferences, publications, and information on the prevention and treatment of HIV/AIDS.

Chapter 10: Work and Recreation

The Occupational Outlook Handbook

http://www.bls.gov/oco/

Recommended Search Words: "occupational outlook handbook"

The Occupational Outlook Handbook is a "nationally recognized source of career information, designed to provide valuable assistance to individuals making decisions about their future work lives" and it "describes what workers do on the job, working conditions, the training and education needed, earnings, and expected job prospects in a wide range of occupations." Users can download pages on the careers of their choice.

The Self-Directed Search

www.self-directed-search.com

Recommended Search Words: "self directed search"

This is a widely used career interest test, which is a very useful resource in matching your skills and interests to specific jobs and careers.

The Catapult on JOB WEB

http://www.jobweb.org/

Recommended Search Words: "jobweb"

The National Association of Colleges and Employers have created a comprehensive set of resources for job seekers and job offerings. The site includes searching employment listings, resources for career practitioners, career library resources, and professional development resources.

U. S. Department of Labor

http://www.dol.gov/

Recommended Search Words "department of labor"

This online site serves as a way to explore topics such as wages, worker productivity, unsafe working conditions, and the legal rights of workers, including protection from sexual harassment.

APA HelpCenter: Psychology at Work

http://apahelpcenter.org

Recommended Search Words: "apa help center"

The American Psychological Association publishes this resource describing various aspects of work including doing more with less, down sizing survivors, working moms, and a focus on stress.

Careers.wsj.com

http://online.wsj.com/careers

Recommended Search Words: "career journal wsj"

This site contains daily updates of employment issues and more than 1,000 job-seeking articles.

Elderhostel

www.elderhostel.org

Recommended Search Words: "elder hostel"

This site provides "adventures in lifelong learning" for adults ages 55 and older. It is a not-for-profit organization with a catalog of high-quality, affordable, educational programs lasting 1 to 4 weeks year round and throughout the world.

Chapter 11: Loneliness and Solitude

The Shyness Home Page

http://www.shyness.com/

The Shyness Institute offers this web site as "a gathering of network resources for people seeking information and services for shyness." It is an index of links to articles, associations and agencies that work with shyness.

The Indiana University Southeast Shyness Research Institute

http://homepages.ius.edu/Special/Shyness

Recommended Search Words: "Indiana University shyness research institute"

The Shyness Research Institute (SRI) is devoted to helping shy individuals understand the nature and underlying dynamics of shyness. It offers a variety of strategies to help shy people to become "successfully shy"—learning to control their shyness, instead of their shyness controlling them.

Chapter 12: Death and Loss

Suicide... Read This First

http://www.metanoia.org/suicide/

Recommended Search Words: "metanoia suicide"

This site is for those who are dealing with suicidal issues in themselves or others. This site speaks straight to the issue and guides the reader through a thoughtful series of steps to resolve their issues. Suicide and suicidal feelings are dealt with including helpful resources and links for more information.

End of Life, Exploring Death in America

www.npr.org/programs/death

Recommended Search Words: "NPR end of life"

National Public Radio (NPR) has aired programs about death and dying in American culture. This website offers both printed and audio transcripts of the programs and many bibliographical and organizational resources as well.

Chapter 13: Meaning and Values

Web of Culture

http://www.globalbusinessleadership.com/

Recommended Search Words: "web of culture geoleadership"

Although this site is intended for businesses it includes a wide range of issues and approaches to increase cross-cultural understanding. It features extensive worldwide information on subjects such as capitals, currency, gestures, headlines, and languages.

Global Climate-Change Resources

www.aaas.org/news/press_room/climate_change

Recommended Search Words: "AAAS climate"

The American Association for the Advancement of Science is an excellent resource to consult for information about global climate change. This site offers leads on what you can do to stop global warming, reports on the impact of global climate change, publications, and trends.

Stop Global Warming Virtual March

www.stopglobalwarming.org

Recommended Search Words: "stop global warming"

This is a nonpartisan effort to unite people who are concerned about global warming. You can add your voice to the hundreds of thousands of other people who are calling for action on this issue.

Spirituality and Practice

www.spiritualityandpractice.com

Recommended Search Words: "spirituality and practice"

This site provides resources for spiritual journeys. The site's founders state: "The site's name reflects a basic understanding: *spirituality* and *practice* are the two places where all the world's religions and spiritual paths come together. With respect for the differences among them, we celebrate what they have in common."

Chapter 14: Pathways to Personal Growth

American Association of Marriage and Family Therapy (AAMFT)

http://www.aamft.org/

Recommended Search Words: "AAMFT"

The American Association of Marriage and Family Therapy (AAMFT) maintains this site. It explains how professional therapy can help couples and families experiencing difficulty. The site also offers links to important family and marriage-related resources including their "Find a Therapist" service.

Mental Health Net

http://www.mentalhelp.net/

Recommended Search Words: "mental help net"

This is an excellent site that explores all aspects of mental health. Many psychological disorders and treatment are discussed along with professional issues. There are links to more than 8,000 mental health resources.

The Student Counseling Virtual Pamphlet Collection

http://counseling.uchicago.edu/resources/virtualpamphlets

Recommended Search Words: "student counseling virtual pamphlet collection"

This resource provides links to useful online information for a range of personal concerns of college students, many of which are discussed in this book.

How to Find Help with Life's Problems (APA Brochure)

www.apa.org/publications/brochures.html

Recommended Search Words: "APA brochures"

This site, designed by the American Psychological Association, gives suggestions about seeking out different types of therapy for different types of problems. The site also answers questions about therapy, insurance, confidentiality, finding a therapist, and choosing one who is right for you.

Dr. Ivan's Depression Central

www.psycom.net/depression.central.html

Recommended Search Words: "Dr. Ivan's depression central"

This site by psychiatrist Ivan K. Goldberg, MD, provides very extensive coverage of mood disorders and treatments and has links to other sites on mood and other disorders.

The Albert Ellis Institute

http://www.rebt.org/

Recommended Search Words: "Albert Ellis institute"

This site shows Dr. Albert Ellis's approach --- Rational Emotive Behavior Therapy (REBT) --- to disputing irrational beliefs. The site also offers: facts about the Institute, questions and answers about REBT, a forum for asking Dr. Ellis questions directly, resources for self-help, therapist referrals, workshop schedules, professional services and products, and a complete selection of all of the Institute's publications and products.

PART 11
List of PowerPoint Slides

CONTENTS

NOTE: We are simply listing the PowerPoint slides that are available for I Never Knew I Had a Choice, Ninth Edition, which you can download from http://cengage.com/counseling/corey.